"This is one audacious book. In fact, Miller makes the case that education is in such crisis that the only appropriate response is to swing for the fences. Somehow it is personal, global, nuanced, outrageous, and perfectly logical. It is a book for the ages, and it presents the first way out of our current circumstances that makes so much sense. It's a must-read."

—**Steve Peifer**, recipient of the 2007 CNN Hero Award,
the 2007 Yale Counseling Award, the 2010 Excellence in
Education Award from the National Association for College Admissions
Counseling, and the 2013 NACCAP Guidance Professional of the Year

"Read this book carefully, for as goes K–12, so goes the nation. Each quarter, I ask my college students if they enjoy their classes. They look at me as if it's a trick question. Truthfully, no, they tell me; most of them do not. They find most classes stifling, rigid, instructor-centric, and dull. Then I ask them if they love learning new things. Yes, they do! This book helps us understand how schools fell off the exciting, engaging, transformative path of teaching and learning new things and how we can change that. Read it carefully—learn new things."

—**Colleen Carmean**, PhD, Assistant Chancellor, University of
Washington Tacoma

"Rex Miller has the rare capacity to go deeply into systems, mine for the wisdom, creativity, and innovation, and then translate his findings for the rest of us to be inspired and welcoming of change. This book is an important part of a larger sea change that has the capacity to reinvigorate education by putting relationships, well-being, and learning back at the center."

—**Michelle Kinder**, executive director of the Momentous Institute,
Oak Cliff, Texas

"For his latest book, Rex Miller has marshaled a distinguished group of professionals to join him in examining successful models of educational innovation around the country. The result? *Humanizing the Education Machine* offers a remarkable and readable wealth of actionable insight. It is a veritable road map to a potential future golden age in education. That future is not inevitable, but this book certainly places it within our grasp."

—**Eric Hamilton**, professor of education, Pepperdine University

"This is not the usual techno-utopian vision of new technology and innovative corporations stepping in to fix the education system. Rex Miller and his MindShift team start from a deep and profoundly human vision of learning as a rich and messy organic process of growth and discovery that no single and simple technology can provide. But new technologies should not be ignored either. Rex Miller and his team have spent the past two years investigating the shining examples that can give us a glimpse of a better, more human future for learning. Their futuristic visions may not be the future we will live, but the subtlety and richness of these visions allow us all to imagine great questions we have never asked before, and great questions is where learning begins."

—**Michael Wesch**, professor of digital ethnography, Kansas State
University

"The research and road map you will find in *Humanizing the Education Machine* will help any school, district, or educational leader leave their traditional mindset and rediscover true learning through a growth mindset."

—**Dr. Nido Qubein**, president, High Point University

humanizing
—— THE ——
EDUCATION
MACHINE

humanizing

—— THE ——

EDUCATION
MACHINE

HOW TO CREATE SCHOOLS THAT TURN
DISENGAGED KIDS INTO
INSPIRED LEARNERS

REX MILLER

BILL LATHAM · BRIAN CAHILL

WILEY

CONTENTS

FOREWORD

People don't care how much you know until they know how much you care.

—Theodore Roosevelt

I dare you to . . .

Buck the System. I chair the nonprofit Center for College & Career Readiness, working with hundreds of districts and thousands of schools across America and around the world. Every day, my team and I hear tales of these teachers—committed and caring professionals *who buck the system to save a child*. These brave souls often work against the systems that employ them in order to do their jobs—to meet the needs of real kids, in real classrooms.

Bridge the Gap. The Education Machine can see only a few "standard models," but great teachers care for the kids as if they were their own family members. The Education Machine believes scientific application of generic teaching principals will "engage" students to "learn rigorous content." You and I know that all of us are motivated by our imaginations, interests, and passions. Learning is human. The modern Education Machine is not. And we must bridge that gap—now!

This book raises a clarion call to a revolution of the heart and mind. Furthermore, Rex Miller and his intrepid team of educators, parents, and experts provide a vision of education with real children at its heart.

Embrace a New World. Grounded in the real trials and success stories of teachers and kids from around the country, Miller and his colleagues challenge us to set aside notions from the obsolete world of the textbook. In their place they call us to embrace a new world—a new culture—of dynamic learning and collaborative investigation. Miller shines a light on those educators who are challenging the system and lifting up the imaginations and passions of children—kids who live in a world of endless possibility constrained by schools with mindless rules and never-ending assessments.

Turn Insight into Action. Researchers collapse human experience into statistics and findings. But we do not need another research project as much as we need to act! We must—as human beings—do something to equip and empower our kids and the teachers who care about their dreams, their fears, and their futures.

Use This Map. We all need—and you now hold—a map that will lead you from the Industrial Age model of education to a culture of creative collaboration. More importantly, that map will get you and many others to the place where we can all join in uplifting the hearts and minds of teachers and students.

That is why, upon its publication, *Humanizing the Education Machine* will become required reading in my graduate courses for school leaders.

—Kevin E. Baird,
chairman and national supervising faculty,
the nonprofit Center for College & Career Readiness

FOREWORD

We all know that excellent schools are the glittering diamonds of outstanding communities. They not only educate the young, but also help to build the symmetrical beauty of a community's physical and emotional safety, employment opportunity, rich cultural treasury, responsible governance, civic involvement, and more.

Unfortunately, we have too few outstanding schools, that is, schools in which teachers and learners are actively engaged in the exchange and mastery of knowledge. Yet we continue to support an educational system built on a failing business model.

An education system built around Industrial-Revolution-era ideas about conformity, interchangeable parts, hierarchy, strategy, centralization, and economies of scale no longer works in our time. We've all read the axiom, "Every system is perfectly designed to produce the results it achieves." And our education business model is perfectly designed to produce nineteenth- and twentieth-century results.

But, of course, education should mirror twenty-first-century business realities! In other words they should reflect a wellness culture, intrinsic versus extrinsic values, fulfilling needs instead of creating wants, open communication platforms, Lean structures, niche markets, responsible sustainability, and rapid iterations of our products, services, and even ourselves.

Over two years ago, Paragon Furniture, Inc., was invited to participate in an extraordinary cohort of education stakeholders. The K–12 MindShift served as the locus for changing the way in which Paragon began thinking about our purpose. We now see that our company creates furniture that assists in the transformation of culture, helps to ignite student curiosity, facilitates positive teacher influence, and contributes to the health of the whole person.

Humanizing the Education Machine is like a perfectly built and tuned amplifier. It pumps out a pure, rich, and powerful message. However, our educational system is tone deaf to the music. But, with our front row seats on the concert of collaborative research and synthesis behind this book, we were blown away by the power of the book's signal transmission and broad range frequency.

Rex has created a high-fidelity story that everybody in any community should know and share. In that way, we can all help to create a relevant and rich learning culture. And remember, however great the costs of change may be, it is far more expensive not to change.

—Ricky Kassanoff, CEO,

and

Mark Hubbard,
President, Paragon Furniture, Inc.

FOREWORD

Data from our K–12 schools in the United States sadly reminds us that, despite decades of well-intentioned education reform efforts, student achievement remains stagnant in America. Over 30 percent of our nation's youth fail to graduate from high school and approximately half of African American and Hispanic students fail to earn a high school diploma. Data also shows that students who do graduate are largely unprepared to enter the work force.

How is it possible that the greatest and most powerful nation in the history of the world built an education system that is now so ineffective, especially when compared to other developed nations?

As the CEO of one of the largest architectural practices in the United States that specializes in educational facility design, I've spent the past 35 years working with educators and students to create environments that facilitate all the activities associated with knowledge transfer. In twenty-first-century terms, what are those activities? How do children learn best in today's world? Is there a new knowledge-transfer paradigm that will lead us out of the doldrums of mediocrity? As a long-time admirer, I was thrilled when I learned that Rex Miller, one of the most successful and compelling research based futurists in the nation, would be exploring the very basic but very complex issue of education and knowledge transfer.

As evidenced by his previous books and now in *Humanizing the Education Machine*, Rex has an uncanny ability to assemble and lead the right people in the right manner and shed light on some of the most important and complicated issues of our time.

To tackle K–12 education, Rex assembled some of the nation's best educators, teachers, government representatives, architects, contractors and furnishing and environmental specialists. The result of two years of work is this wonderful expose of some of the most amazing education success stories you've ever read.

Humanizing the Education Machine is a lively read that immediately grabs our attention and doesn't let go. The stories are fun and the message provides a fresh way of thinking about education. The book gives a road map of the paths to personal learning experiences that engage our students and inspire them to learn.

After decades of propping up an outdated model, isn't it time for our schools to do better? Shouldn't they reflect the human principles we hold most dear—the ability to be an individual in every sense, including the way we learn? Isn't it our real goal to create a student body in this country that consists of self-motivated and enthusiastic lifelong learners who follow a path that is most appropriate and fulfilling for each individual?

This book is amazingly powerful in its ability to help us achieve that goal.

—Dan Boggio, CEO,
PBK Architects, Inc.

FOREWORD

Like so many others, I grew up struggling in traditional classroom environments. Having been diagnosed with ADD as an adult, I finally understood some of my challenges with traditional education in a small-town public school. Physically, classrooms represented a tense place for students like me. Unfortunately, they continue to be the same for many students today.

Classrooms of multiple rows of desks and chairs all facing a single plain chalkboard give energetic children no physical outlets for their natural energy. That layout increases distractions and disengagement. In that built environment, the students who live and work at the behavioral extremes are often underserved, their talent unrecognized and their possibilities undeveloped. Our genuine efforts to leave no child behind leaves a sad wake of unrealized talent and unfulfilled dreams because we fail to engage our kids.

Fortunately, Lorraine Moore, my mother, passed on her passion for education to me. She always reminded me that we had both an opportunity and a responsibility to make a difference for the children of this country. That idea and her drive gave me the opportunity and confidence to turn my experience into doing that—I have found great satisfaction working to make a difference by giving all students the right spaces, tools, and advocates.

MooreCo was invited to join MindShift so that we could lend our industry experience to this wide-ranging assembly of education (and other) professionals. We have all worked to understand the past, current, and future of education. And I am proud of how our eye-opening experiences are so well reflected in *Humanizing the Education Machine*. The book gives a compelling contrast to the current and outdated education model. Readers will clearly see a better path to how we train and equip our kids for the future.

—Gregory Moore, CEO,
MooreCO, Inc.

FOREWORD

We've all heard the sobering data documenting our schools' failure to meet the needs of today's students and employers. We at Bretford see that the real issue behind that failure is a design problem: Our schools continue to function very much as they did a century ago.

But, of course, the challenge facing educators has changed dramatically over that period. The skills that will define students' future success have changed. And students themselves have changed: They're simply and verifiably wired differently from previous generations.

According to the National Association of Colleges and Employers, working well as a team is what today's companies seek and value most in their workforces. But students won't have a chance to learn to collaborate until we see dramatic changes in the design of our K–12 classrooms and teaching practices.

In leading a company that manufactures furniture to support more active, engaging, and collaborative learning environments, I've seen firsthand how the design of learning spaces transforms the activities and outcomes that occur there. And I'm deeply encouraged that futurist Rex Miller has chosen to explore this topic in his new book.

Humanizing the Education Machine provides stories and strategies that give inspiring alternatives to the status quo. This book reveals the approaches that are working for *all* students, enabling us to see what's possible if we have the courage to chart a new course for K–12 education.

The changes presented in these changes are desperately needed. I commend Rex for taking on this subject. We at Bretford are committed to supporting K–12 leaders and students in this critical journey.

—Chris Petrick, CEO,
Bretford

PREFACE

As you read the pages ahead, you will see that *change* is the backdrop issue in this book. Of course, change is the real issue in so much of life. That's why wise people learn to relate to change in intelligent and appropriate ways.

My friend Dan Boggio, is the founder and CEO of PBK Architects, Inc., the largest architectural firm for educational facilities in the United States. Dan also served on the MindShift K–12 project that drove this book.

After 40 years of working with various levels of government, school boards, and other bureaucracies, Dan understands the dynamics of change. When he recently told me his view of why school districts continue to build facilities that are a half-century behind the times, he exposed the true face of change.

"Because school districts are bureaucracies, they are always subject to the political pressures that shape any city. Elected officials always strive to make sure that everyone feels treated equally. So to approve a new, progressive, learning-friendly environment is to invite opposition."

Secondly, Dan told me, "Most senior administrators—the decision makers—are in the final phase of their careers. So they are not inclined to be trailblazers. Retirement is coming up fast. Playing it safe and avoiding controversy are very important in that time of life. They all know that the 'cutting edge' is also the 'bleeding edge.'"

And, third, as Dan said, "Most senior administrators are generally from a generation that was trained in the old 'factory model' school environment. They do not understand or trust the new thinking."

However, the good news is that change is coming faster than some think. Dan reports that, even though most of PBK's work still supports the factory model, ". . . about 20 percent of our work is what I consider progressive." Dan also sees that, as younger people (including digital natives) move into the senior executive roles, they are turning the tide toward learning-friendly design.

We're all joining a battle that has raged a very long time. So it's helpful to hear from a seasoned veteran who has been out on the front lines of change. The past always fights with bloody tenacity to remain. We all have to see it, understand it, and deal with it as we work for change.

But, Dan's view also delivers good news for change agents. New blood has already entered into the cultural veins. For example, digital natives are already bringing renewal, renovation, and a bright future. The past views them as a threat. And rightly so; after all, they are forerunners of a new day.

CHAPTER 1

Numbers Don't Lie

You never change things by fighting the existing reality.
To change something, build a new model that makes the existing model
obsolete.

— R. Buckminster Fuller

Did you know that 70 percent of teachers have mentally checked out of teaching? How is that possible? These are not bad people. They all started out inspired, hopeful, courageous, and even playful. Some of our best novels and films—such as *Dangerous Minds, Stand and Deliver, Lean on Me, Up the Down Staircase,* and *Goodbye, Mr. Chips*—have featured these noble, exciting, and often daring figures.

But after a while, the Education Machine just rolled over too many teachers, mashing the life juices right out of their pores.

I'll tell you something else—by the time they graduate 60 percent of students will have also flown the coop. This is not some abstract number: these are the kids on your block, next door, and maybe in your upstairs bedrooms.

We all know that we live in perilous times. But, more than that, we live in the crumbling ruins of obsolete forms. An age is passing away (as ages always do). Don Berwick famously said, "Every system is perfectly designed to get the results it gets." The prevalent model of public education does what it was designed to do. And in a previous era,

Public education does what it was designed to do. And in a previous era, that served America very well. With the passing of that era the model has become obsolete.

that served America very well. With the passing of that era the model has become obsolete.

For that reason, the Education Machine is in genuine and panoramic crisis; it is in personal, social, economic, and national turmoil. Numbers don't lie. But that crisis is because of its obsolescence, not its malice.

Here are a few other features of its rot.

- The Education Machine does not have the capacity to care. And learning requires people who care.
- The Machine's continual cry of "reform" results in kicking the can down the road for future administrators and teachers to solve. This response only makes matters worse and costs a hell of a lot of money.
- We can't wait. We cannot let the Education Machine move another kid down its aged and rusty assembly line until they are broken or left behind. *Now* is already late.

So, how did we end up with an education system that has not only failed in its mission but has also inflicted so much psychological, emotional, and intellectual damage on so many people that it touches? But, far more important, what can we do about it now?

Now, let's pause and consider some other realities that our work on this book revealed:

- Yes, education has become a Machine. But schools, administrators, and teachers can create a kid-centered, human-enriching, and high-achieving learning experience.
- It takes stepping into only one classroom of engaged kids to see the difference between the Machine and the deeply human experience of learning.
- The challenge of education sounds formidable. But it can be brought down to a human scale and transformed through people who care.

Cynicism says we can't change what must be changed. That is not true; we *can* do something about it. This is not an impossible task. That is what this book is about. When you finish reading, you will know the time and money invested in this book was well worth the price. We can change the way we teach and train our younger members. Do not forget that.

I know what I'm talking about. Over the past two years, my associates and I have traveled thousands of miles and talked to hundreds of students, teachers, administrators, parents, suppliers, authors, and community leaders. We heard their stories of life in

Cynicism says we can't change what must be changed. That is not true; we can change the way we teach and train our younger members. Do not forget that.

the Education Machine. Their time in education was, for too many, a soul-sucking, time-wasting, and stress-producing waste of effort. Not only that, it was a brutally demotivating and damaging experience.

But we also saw transformation. One of the most surprising features of our work was the discovery of fully absorbed, completely riveted students located clear across the K–12 spectrum; we met them in great cities and in small towns, in both "underserved" and resource-rich districts, and scattered across all the data points.

To Humanize the Education Machine

Most people know that the earth's surface is composed of tectonic plates—"a dozen or so big crustal slabs that float on a sea of melted rock. . . . The colliding plates grind past one another about as fast as fingernails grow. . . ."[1] As the plates grow, they break off, creating convulsions of new geologic features. Despite its deadly earthquakes and tsunamis, that process, that revolution, is quite natural and essential to the continuation of life on planet earth.

But isn't it also true that the ideas, values, and structures that form civilizations are in perpetual, grinding revolution? That's how they exchange old and dying forms for new life. The life cycles of the planet exist in continuous, and sometimes quite literal, uprisings. The convulsions of history continually heave old forms over the side, where they slip into oblivion. Of course, individuals, groups, and nations work very hard to find ways to take credit for the upheavals.

This book is a manifesto for a secret, but emerging, revolution.

That revolution is challenging public education's grip over the future and well-being of our kids. We all see the relatively small, but very visible, part of that conflict among policy makers, educators, unions, parents, politicians, and a voracious educational industrial complex. They are all pounding their fists, demanding change, pointing fingers, expanding control, pleading for more funding, and continually changing the rules with no measurable improvement. That war has raged for the past 60 years. Most have fought with good intent; many were and are mercenaries; and some have tried to leverage the dysfunction to gain more power and profit. It doesn't matter; they are all caught in a conflict of irrelevance. It is all part of an era that is passing away.

Today, we all stand before a window of opportunity that recalls Apple's "1984" Super Bowl Ad. That landmark "manifesto" proclaimed the end of Big Brother computing and the dawn of a human-centered experience. As it was then, our highly centralized industrial education system is increasingly arthritic and exhausted. Worse, its death grip is killing creativity—in our kids and in our nation. The mission of this book is to spread hope and methods to parents, educators, administrators, and communities so they may become full partners in the human-centered learning revolution.

Everyone knows the current system is failing to graduate students who are prepared for the demands of the twenty-first century. The United States ranks last among industrialized nations for college graduation levels. Other countries with similar education models are experiencing the same fall out in student engagement and performance. Germany, England, China, Singapore, South Korea, France, Australia, Canada, Japan, and other countries are stepping back and asking the same questions we asked about the effects of their education machines.

Today's oracles, such as Sir Ken Robinson, Tony Wagner, Douglas Thomas, John Seely Brown, and others are painting vividly clear pictures of a harsh system that is killing creativity at the very time in history that most demands creativity and innovation! They are *the* most important survival skills in a postindustrial world.

The book explains how the "Gutenberg to Google" revolution has generated a perfect storm of discontent, dysfunction, and disengagement in our traditional system of education.

While the policy debates and shifting priorities continue to keep schools off-balance and parents in the dark we have a crisis that won't wait.

This book announces that we stand at a true "Oh, my God" moment in history. The numbers tell a story that can no longer be ignored. In addition to the disengagement numbers already cited, half of all students are considered "at risk." More than 25 percent of students live in poverty. 1.36 million students are homeless. None of this is a secret. Yet the system cannot or will not budge.

That's why we need a manifesto, not another proposal. After 60 years of studies, we don't have time for

After 60 years of studies, we don't have time for more research, reform measures, or debate. The revolution has already started. It is even now overthrowing an obsolete industrial regime, structure, and set of values.

more research, reform measures, or debate. The revolution has already started. It is *now* overthrowing an obsolete industrial regime, structure, and set of values. That insurgency will reclaim learning as a fundamentally human experience. Gutenberg enabled the first learning revolution more than 500 years ago. Google now symbolizes the new one. Digital technology is disrupting traditional power centers by distributing knowledge to anyone who choses to join this historical opportunity.

This Book: A Road Map

Before tsunamis bring death and destruction to coastlines, wild and domestic animals sense the coming devastation and escape to higher ground.

Maybe people are catching up. Today's early warning systems are enabling human populations to flee destruction from natural forces. Our purpose for the book is not to build a case for change. That change is *here*; perceptive people plainly see it. At this point of history, a road map to the high ground would be of more benefit to the students, parents, communities, educators, and others who face destruction.

That is why this book is different from any other. Knowing that this subject carries great urgency and demands great scope and depth, we assembled about 60 career educators, a wide variety of specialists, NFP organizations, and business and community leaders who have been successfully working to rehumanize learning (see Figure 1.1). Many of these contributors have been in the trenches of education for decades.

We convened six summits, between June 2014 and January 2016, around the country in order to study very innovative schools that achieved and maintained excellence (often against great odds). Many books document the failures of our public education system. Others provide a vision for twenty-first-century schools. But there are no road

Figure 1.1 Columbus, Indiana, MindShift Meeting

maps for transforming and rehumanizing local schools or districts. Our book gives a very compelling *why* and, more important, clear maps for the new and uncharted territory.

Who Should Read This Book?

In researching and writing this book, our team focus was always on parents, teachers, administrators, and community leaders. This book is for them. It is for those who do not have the time or resources to sift through the many books or conferences or websites in order to gather the knowledge essential to taking action. We wrote this for those who are not willing to wait for local, regional, or national regulations to trickle down or be parachuted in.

That is also why we wrote a manifesto and not a typical market-driven volume. The tsunami is racing toward our shoreline. We are announcing a road to higher ground. In short, we want to save lives and join with others in building a safe future.

How One Family Escaped the Great Machine

It may help you to know the short story of one family who lived through the crumbling of the K–12 system and saw the seeding of new possibilities. That family is mine.

Back in the 1990s we moved to one of the best school districts in the state, not because we were snobs, but because we cared. We wanted our three kids to have fine educational experiences, rolling right through K–12. All three of them are, well, exceptional. By that I mean that they are true individuals. Everyone who knows them would agree. They did not come from an assembly line or central casting. Lisa and I did not know it at the time, but in looking back, we can see that our kids were like canaries in the coal mines. Their experiences (and those of thousands of other students) exposed the toxins in K–12 education.

This book is for those who do not have the time or resources to sift through the many books or conferences or websites in order to gather the knowledge essential to taking action . . . those who are not willing to wait for local, regional, or national regulations to trickle down or be parachuted in.

And, I admit that our three children carried some surprising baggage.

Part of what makes Emily, our 24-year-old bold and beautiful daughter, so exceptional is Asperger syndrome. Her challenges have always caused this lovely and brilliant woman to express very unique social skills, perspectives, and boundaries.

I describe our second child, Daniel, as "a merry prankster." He, the opposite of Emily when it came to social skills and boundaries, did extremely well in elementary school. But later he began to exhibit some discomfort with school rules and expectations. He was eventually diagnosed with ADHD.

Right out of the chute, our third child, Caleb, loved school. But very quickly (and for a whole different set of reasons) he, too, began disengaging in middle school. He started coming home and giving Lisa a hard time.

With all three of our children, we increasingly realized that we were not dealing with an organization of rational, knowledgeable, and empathetic teachers and administrators; we were coping with a machine. For a while, we tried to work with the Machine. We tried to change its speed, update its "software," find a sense of compassion somewhere within its steel-toothed gears, help our kids to adapt to the

We realized that we were not dealing with an organization of rational, knowledgeable, and empathetic teachers and administrators; we were coping with a machine.

Machine, help the Machine to adapt to them . . . but in the long run, there we were, caught between our love for our children and our ingrained respect for the education process.

In all three cases the Machine just kept moving our, and many other, students down the conveyor belt, delaying decisions, ordering tests, and pushing them into ill-fitting boxes. No one seemed to *care*. For example, none of Emily's teachers had training for working with students with Asperger's, or even had a working knowledge of the syndrome. Some of them did not believe she had it. After all, she had an outgoing personality and "looked normal."

One of Daniel's teachers did not believe in ADHD. As that teacher chewed gum and gazed out at us from his "bunker" (beneath his U.S. Marines buzz cut and over his folded arms), you could see that he had already diagnosed Daniel. He could see clearly that Daniel was a skateboarder and he knew *that* was "trouble in River City." In fact, he once said (while Daniel was in the room), "Kids who skateboard are always trouble."

It Takes a Village

According to an oft-quoted African proverb "It takes a village to raise a child." In other words, all the people, values, institutions, and other cultural components of a village should cooperate harmoniously around the nurture, protection, and preparation of each child.

But what happens when the village does *not* contribute to the safe and orderly maturation of a child? The 2015 "Best Picture" Academy Award went to *Spotlight*, a movie about the sex abuse scandal in the Roman Catholic Archdiocese of Boston. After quoting "It takes a village to raise a child," one of the main characters in the film observes that it also takes a village to *abuse* one.

I agree.

After the Machine damaged Emily, Lisa and I felt wounded, angry, and drained. Naturally, we wondered at what point we had missed an opportunity to support our child. We strained to see what we might have done differently. I thought, "Hell, if my background as an executive, my work as an author and futurist, my understanding of negotiating and

Here's the point: two educated, responsible, caring, and hardworking parents could not make the Machine care for, or even protect, those who were entrusted to it.

championing causes can't budge the Machine for one little girl with a clear need and a clear right—does *anyone* have a chance?"

In addition to all that, we hired doctors and experts to help them. In doing so, we reached out to "the village" as clearly and forcefully as we could. We pushed every button and pulled every lever we could find. I'm sure we made mistakes. But, here's the point: two educated, responsible, caring, and hard-working parents could not make the Machine care for, or even protect, those who were entrusted to it. We felt, whether accurately or not, that the village—*our village*—had participated in the abuse of our kids.

When Caleb began to show similar reactions to the Machine, we moved more quickly and boldly. First, I gave him the new Gallup student assessment tool, "Strengths Explorer" (it was not available when Emily and Daniel were in school). It revealed that Caleb would do best in a small, safe learning environment that allowed him to explore his creativity. From our experiences with Emily and Daniel, we knew that would never happen in public school.

One day, Lisa called me while I was on a business trip. "Let's homeschool Caleb."

Of course, I was already very busy in my career. So I began expressing my reservations. But within 10 minutes I changed from feeling defensive about to being skeptical of to expressing full support of the idea. Lisa showed me how home schooling was not only the perfect fit for Caleb but it would also draw upon both our unique gifts and interests.

When we asked Caleb to pick a musical instrument as part of his education, he started playing around on our 15-year-old keyboard. With initial instruction from Lisa, he soon fell in love with music, films, and film score composition.

Over time, Lisa and I watched Caleb step into what author Dan Pink describes as the three elements of total motivation: autonomy, purpose, and mastery. In short, we saw the astounding difference in his experience and engagement level compared to Emily and Daniel. When we moved into the more advanced course work in high school, the Internet became a third teacher in our house. It all worked.

Engaging in education that supported autonomy, purpose, and mastery gave Caleb—and his parents!—a whole new grip on learning. After completing his K–12 education in full engagement mode, he was recently accepted to the Berklee College of Music in Boston.

Furthermore, Emily and Daniel are also doing well. At last, the Miller family escaped the great machine.

What grips me now as I review our experiences is the realization that Lisa and I were mature, resourceful, serious about our children, and determined to do and get the right things for them. *And we could not do it.*

That is because "it takes a village." Let me explain.

The Machine broke Daniel during his senior year. Ironically he also achieved his Eagle Scout Award the same year. The same as with his schooling, we struggled long and hard with his focus and follow-through in Boy Scouts. Every mile and every moment of his journey was hard. And in the end it was high drama: Daniel completed his final requirement and was qualified as an Eagle Scout only three hours before his eighteenth birthday—the deadline! Kevin Christ, Daniel's Scout leader, was in our kitchen quizzing him while I paced like an expectant father in the living room. Then they emerged from the kitchen smiling and the leader extended his hand to me.

"Congratulations, Mr. Miller, your son is an Eagle Scout!"

He shook his head, sipped coffee, and laughed, "I've never had one get down to the wire like this. But I've never lost a boy who told me he wanted to become an Eagle." I was exhausted and grateful. And, like most fathers, I played no part in the delivery.

Schools that were failing 56 years ago are still failing. Our business model makes no sense. And we have run out of time!
—Geoffrey Canada

So, what was the difference? Education had become a soul-crushing Machine, but the Boy Scouts was like a family. Daniel's troop was a community of caring parents and Scout leaders; we were all in it together. I was part of this community; I camped, hiked, and provided merit badge counseling and mentoring to a number of kids. We were a village. We took every child seriously and personally.

Today, I so often think about those who live in "underserved" communities. What hope do they have? How can they conquer the Machine? No wonder that educator Geoffrey Canada says (of his own K–12 path), "Schools that were failing 56 years ago are still failing. Our business model makes no sense. And we have run out of time!" Underserved communities now represent, not years or even decades, but *generations* of K–12 failure and abuse.

No matter who you are or where you live, this thing is personal. This story is about every city, community, parent, student, teacher, administrator, and citizen.

After two years of research and work with more than 60 educators and others with a stake in seeing our schools work and our kids succeed, I and many others are convinced that it just doesn't have to be this way.

But—and this is very important—the solutions will not come from the usual sources. We cannot wait for reform efforts to make any difference. Reform has been the Machine's solution for change since at least 1955—that's right, more than 60 years! But reform is often just a reshuffling of the special interests that feed at the "education cafeteria." Furthermore, reform creates sandcastles and mirages. Sandcastles don't survive the first wave that crashes on the beach and mirages aren't real.

Our work on this book verified that *education* is often a cold, organized, and dehumanizing mass of rules, concepts, and metrics. But, as you will also see throughout this book, *learning* is a profoundly human, organic, and ennobling pursuit of personal dreams and progress.

The Collaborative Hum

Our collection of 60 educators, scholars, designers, futurists, and other specialists saw Education Machines all across the country that had been humbled and humanized. What these efforts produced were not sandcastle or mirages, but oases in otherwise arid wastelands. We've seen thousands of kids as engaged in these schools as Caleb was in our home, empowered by autonomy, purpose, and mastery.

We digested more than 100 books and more than 400 articles, reports, and white papers. We watched countless TED-Ed videos and sat through often-boring White House Education Summit videos that ran eight hours straight with no editing. We attended a variety of conferences. We had pizza night during our San Diego summit in the Junior Achievement Business Park (for kids) and watched the movie *Most Likely to Succeed*.

We saw what *engaged student learning* can look like for kids at a troubled middle school in Florida.

"The collaborative hum" is the vibrating atmosphere of discovery, laughter, honest questions, staccato beeps and clicks of tech tools, and choruses of "wow," "cool," and "awesome!"

We visited classes in a South Texas elementary school that had been reconstituted and again witnessed high engagement. How can a school ranked at the bottom 2 percent in Texas so dramatically shift its culture from custodial to one of high engagement—of both teachers and students?

David Vroonland, Superintendent for the Mesquite (Texas) ISD, described what we saw and would continue to see as "the collaborative hum." This is how he describes the vibrating atmosphere of discovery, laughter, honest questions, staccato beeps and clicks of tech tools, and choruses of "wow," "cool," and "awesome!"

I think this also describes the journey that begins with the next chapter. Come join us. The K–12 MindShift project has invested leadership, research, and resources in imagining new models for a new era in educating our children. We are genuinely passionate about demonstrating what we have learned to those who are caught in whirlpool of diminishing returns on education. We will explain how to lead change at a local level as a parent, administrator, teacher, business leader, and community leader.

The stories we tell are gripping and authentic. Portraying real people caught in real crises, they could give you glimpses of what could work in your neighborhood and school.

Let's get started. Chapter 2 tells the story of how we first heard the clear and compelling call to go around the Education Machine and begin the work of building new models.

CHAPTER 2

Two Guys from Gainesville

We're on a mission from God.
                    —Jake and Elwood, The Blues Brothers[1]

For some reason, I accepted the meeting.

On October 23, 2013, my colleague Michael Lagocki and I sat across the table from two guys who owned a school furniture dealership in Gainesville, Florida. *Oh, God. Another meeting. Another agenda. Another pitch.* But, as they talked, I began wondering *Who are these guys?* My curiosity came fully alive.

John Crawford, in full beard, was warm and relaxed. At a first impression, he might remind you of a favorite high school science teacher or maybe your minister. But, as I increasingly learned over the coming months, he was also an immovable rock. Bill Latham was intense, fierce, and maybe dangerous. His eyes glowed. As these two fellows talked, I began to realize that they were not John and Bill—they were really Jake and Elwood, "The Blues Brothers," on a mission from God.

Their mission? To transform education in America.

Seriously? Two furniture dealer guys from Gainesville?

They had read my book about the dismal state of workplace engagement and what some of the best companies in the world are doing about it.[2]

So they thought I was the guy to lead the charge into the dark valley of an obsolete and contaminated education system.

"But, guys, I know nothing about the education system."

"Yes, but you have a process for tackling monster challenges. We think it will work with education."

"I don't have a network to recruit from."

"We do."

Let's be real. That education monster had already killed and eaten far better and smarter people than the four of us at Table 7.

"My calendar is full and the process is long, involved, and expensive."

"How expensive?

I threw out a number intended to blow their boots off.

"We think we can come up with the funding."

These guys just kept coming. My carefully constructed roadblocks were bouncing right off the road as they plowed into them. So, yes, they were gaining my attention. But, let's be real, the problems in education had formed a monster, a roaring, multitentacled *thing*. It corrupted and controlled relationships, power centers, money, community spirit, and that very human reach for a better life. And it had already killed and eaten far better and smarter people than the four of us at Table 7.

But two furniture dealer guys from Florida had decided that I was their man, that I would lead this venture. "O-kayyy," I muttered, scratching my head and trying to think of something. I bought time by suggesting we identify a list of stakeholders, underwriters, and important voices that might want to contribute. Once we crossed that threshold I outlined a "kick-the-tires" summit to see who would come and how committed they might be to "transforming education."

After lunch, I pulled Michael aside and asked if these guys were for real. He grinned. "If this summit comes together, your job is to manage Bill. Just keep him at a safe distance."

I didn't hear much from John or Bill for the next six months. Then in mid-August of 2014 I answered my phone. It was Bill.

"We're ready to launch this thing! What's next?"

They named the companies and experts they had enlisted. I knew only a few. Worse, I still didn't have any indices for measuring their strengths or their commitment to the journey. My previous two book projects had each required about 30 percent of my focus over a two-year stretch. And that was with people who were battle-tested; we had shared foxholes. Now here I was charging into battle with people I did not know, carrying weapons I did not understand, and facing a giant that had devoured whole communities.

I rubbed my eyes, took a deep breath, and laid out the road map for the next steps in a process I called "MindShift."[3]

"Okay, guys, we first want to invite key underwriters and experts for a day to present the vision, lay out the timeline and process, practice our action learning workshop approach and tackle some of the issues. At the end of the day we'll take the pulse of everyone's seriousness.

That meeting convened in Tampa, Florida, on October 1–3, 2014 (see Figures 2.1 and 2.2). The participants included architects, furniture manufacturers, school superintendents, and several education experts. I also seeded the room with some of my own invited attendees, people who knew the MindShift process and those who had a link to education. My group included a futurist from Disney, leaders from Balfour Beatty (the third largest school builder in the nation), a Pepperdine professor of education, and a few other trusted companions from my past works.

The opening energy was high and positive. But, it still took me a while to get past feeling overwhelmed with the byzantine insanity and the sheer impossibility of public education in America. From my years of experience at every level of business, I could see that we were dealing

Figure 2.1 Tampa, Florida, Kickoff Meeting

Figure 2.2   Michael Lagocki Scribing for Rex Miller

From my years of experience at every level of business, I could see that we were dealing with one of the most fragmented, siloed, contentious, compartmentalized, and toxic institutional hairballs on the planet.

with one of the most fragmented, siloed, contentious, compartmentalized, and toxic institutional hairballs on the planet.

I also knew that all interest groups behave tribally, shouting at one another in different languages on behalf of disconnected and incoherent constituencies. So naturally I was afraid that we might fall into gridlock, speaking at each other through our different professional languages and dialects.

At the same time, it was strangely clear to me that none of those factors would prevent us from going forward. Part of my confidence was in seeing that John and Bill had such a strong and impressive circle of like-minded relationships ready to go. The goodwill in that room brought focus to the mission and not even a nibble on the hairball. I would later learn that *how* that goodwill was created was the secret to toppling silos.[4]

The diversity of the stakeholders in Tampa, their strong and unique voices, and their deep levels of expertise were all very encouraging. As the facilitator, I had to listen, defer, and watch closely for the places and moments when the energy in the room coalesced. I leaned into the pools of enthusiasm or friction. I stirred each pot a bit and then watched it simmer. To my surprise, this group of leaders aligned more quickly than any group I had yet facilitated.

But something else was going on. That meeting was one of those times when truth slowly dawns. I saw, and I think that others saw, that the needs, agendas, possibilities, and problems that called (or justified) this meeting were not the real reasons we were together. We were invaded by something larger than us. Because we were, for the most part, married, parents, and people who cared about community, public education was infinitely more than an issue. We could not talk about it and remain at a cerebral place. That plow sank deep into our personal and family experiences.

And so it was that we settled into conversation that was deeply human; we talked about education as an experience (rather than a policy issue, governmental department, or budget item) and connecting with students as kids. We shared about our favorite teachers, or the other adults—coaches, cops, uncles, wardens, or drill sergeants—who made a difference in our past. Some began to open up about their battle scars from life in the trenches of K–12 education. Others talked about their own kids and their school-based injuries. But through it all, we were all reaching for that thing, that elemental *thing* in the center of our yearning. What was it? Then I saw that our conversational roads kept looping back to . . . the kids.

> *Then I saw that our conversation kept looping back to. .. the kids. Everyone in the room knew that the students are the whole point of education! Yet, it seems that the current state of K–12 education is about anything and everything but the kids.*

Everyone in the room instinctively knew that *the students* are the whole point of education! Yet, it seems that the current state of K–12 education is about anything and everything *but* the kids. The great reform of the educational-industrial complex had centered on only *testing*. Rituals. Standards. Curricula. Government. Politics. Funding . . . and turf! We heard one story about a teacher who tried to change the layout of the classroom in order to create more interaction. But then, the janitorial staff piled all of the desks into a corner. On the pile was taped a message: "The desks will stay lined up, so we can clean the classroom quickly and get in and out. The next time you may not be able to find your desks."

It all seems to come down to a question: Who the hell is education for? Why have we lost that vision? *How* did we lose it? How can we get it back?

Simply experiencing agreement around the real issue generated a soul-satisfying aha moment. To say out loud that "kids have been kicked from the center of education" was a revelation for me. As a parent, I had known it intuitively, but had not been able to articulate it. My wife Lisa and I had dared not think it through or speak about it. But that enormous and monstrous reality did not seem to surprise anyone else in the room.

And it was somewhere around this point when my concerns about Bill dissolved. And it came from seeing him in his element with other educators. If he was dangerous, it was because Bill was a true believer. He was, in a biblical allusion, a man with fire shut up in his bones. He and the others were veterans of the wars for the kids. They knew the story very well. No wonder some eyes reddened and others swallowed hard when they talked.

And, in that meeting, I realized I was not an alien. I was passing through a rite of initiation into what was an emerging personal mission. I was being baptized into the groaning hope and concern of every child, every parent, and most teachers and administrators. Everyone in that room gave a damn. That certainly included one 50-something-year-old man who had spent his life in the corporate world. I felt as though I were coming home to a place I'd never seen.

"There are no silver bullets! Complex problems are never solved but can only be navigated or reframed."

One of the words that kept popping to the surface of our conversation was *obsolescence*. We seemed to find agreement that "the system is broken." That phrase certainly reflected our collective frustration, but at the same time it seemed to assume there was *a* solution waiting to be discovered. We agreed upfront to be suspicious of easy answers. I reminded everyone, "There are no silver bullets! *Complex problems are never solved but can only be navigated or reframed.*"

As we talked, the notion of "obsolete" education began to steer us into a different conversation and tone. We seemed to sail past consternation, recrimination, agitation, and seething frustration. From the circular debates we found a new rhythm in the form of a "from–to" stanza. The conversation took on an improvisational flow generating a clear cascade of insights.

- From Gutenberg to Google
- From tests to mastery
- From content to context
- From memorization to application
- From mind to mindfulness
- From activity checklist to activities with purpose
- From answers to inquiry
- From custodial to engaged
- From taking directions to taking initiative
- From competition to collaboration
- From individual to team player
- From achievement to character
- Extrinsic motivation to intrinsic motivation
- From college-ready to life-ready
- From lagging indicators to leading indicators
- From fail-safe to safe-fail
- From compliance to agency
- From batched learning to tailored learning

This flow of ideas led us into a variety of paths for deeper exploration. Like explorers in all generations, we let go of the past and scanned the valley for the best trails leading to new frontiers. And we found the new path in a new conversation.

- What kind of learning experiences and environments enable kids to thrive?
- What will prepare kids for the world of 2040?
- Can we leave a road map that will enable others to follow?
- Is that road map also a blueprint for community?

At the end of two days we had moved from a "cohort of the willing" to a "company of the committed."

We soon began to see common patterns emerge. Kids were at the center, small groups created magic, silos were torn down, social capital unlocked resources, physical movement and breaks added capacity, creating together transformed learning, engagement drove design, and transparency led to innovation.

My apprehensions about tackling the beast began to recede as I watched these diverse leaders align so quickly. Their stories of what was working where they lived painted new pictures for us to consider.

Those stories also called us to meet in other rooms on other campuses in other places. And, as we traveled around the country together, one transforming effort spilled into another and another. It was as if a large tornado began pulling us away from the dull and dehumanizing tones of public education.

And we soon began to see common patterns emerge. Kids were at the center, small groups created magic, silos were torn down, social capital unlocked resources, physical movement and breaks added capacity, creating together transformed learning, engagement drove design, and transparency led to innovation.

In the story you are about to read, you will see that public education is like the Emerald City of Oz, a walled city ruled over by an intimidating, but deceptive, wizard. Somewhere in that story, we all began to realize that it took only one student—not a bureaucracy, not a think tank, not a U.S. Department of Education—to pull aside the curtain and reveal the truth. It slowly dawned on all of us that we were caught up in a student-led revolution.

You might want to keep reading. Trust me; you haven't read this story before.

CHAPTER 3

MindShift

We Didn't Seek Permission

Never doubt that a small group of thoughtful committed citizens can change the world. Indeed it is the only thing that ever has.
> —Margaret Mead

The MindShift model is a twenty-first-century form of barn raising. It is a volunteer cohort of stakeholders and thought leaders who come together to collaborate on solving large and complex problems. A MindShift group no longer believes that business as usual, including the usual calls for "change," is effective or sufficient.

Like a lot of breakthroughs, we simply stumbled into the idea. This happened a decade ago, when I facilitated a meeting of architectural firms, construction companies, corporate realtors, and others who were tackling a huge problem in that industry. As we worked together, I saw that everyone was addressing the problem from his or her unique perspective. Everyone was locked into his or her viewpoint. But then, in an almost magical moment, one man began to speak. Candidly. Very candidly. He almost groaned his despair with the typical patterns in his industry. And we all saw how the system was designed to create distrust.

From that moment, we began asking brand-new questions, like:

- What would a trust-based system look like?
- Is anyone doing that?

The beauty of new questions is that they change the framework of our thinking; they also take everyone beyond their own wheelhouses. And that tends to make people less rigid, more respectful, and more cooperative.

That was the birth of the MindShift process. We knew we were onto something when that first effort (captured in our book *The Commercial Real Estate Revolution*) won the 2009 CoreNet Global Innovator of the Year Award.

The K–12 MindShift Project

This book represents the third MindShift project.

For this one, we built a cohort of about 60 highly respected and very diverse leaders. And we made sure that they would be able to play together well! Then we spent time together, going to several three-day summits at essential sites around the country; we did this for 18 months. In the process, we become collaborators and friends. And we found that sometimes our best times, our most insightful times, occurred when we were "off duty," such as around a table in a restaurant.

We all saw that our current national path of education reform is both futile and destructive to our kids and nation's future. As a group, we were white-paper-weary, policy-summit-cynical, brainstorm-fatigued, and sick of conferences and workshops. We were also tired of trends, best-selling solutions, new studies, scandals, and politics. However, when these same leaders saw a classroom of kids really engaged with learning, the resulting positive energy and joy invigorated our discussions for days.

What started as a loose and extremely diverse gathering soon transformed into a team compelled to change one piece of the world. That transformation, however, was not because MindShift offered a grand plan or magical process. It just seeped in as each person learned another person's story and discovered a kindred spirit beneath the battle scars. We found concert about the hearts and minds of our kids. The human connection restored hope like the old stump in the ancient proverb.

You are here because you are the best at what you do and you care about the future of our kids. Now that we've established that you are among the best there is no need to prove it over the next few days. We're going to ask that you hang up your superhero capes while we're together!

Though its roots grow old in the ground and its stump dies in the dry soil. At the scent of water it will flourish and put forth sprigs like a plant.

The four criteria for receiving an invitation to join a MindShift are expertise, a diverse viewpoint, a commitment to the journey and the ability to play well with others. Michael Lagocki, our summit designer, facilitator, and live scribe, established our first protocol at the very beginning.

"You are all here because you are among the best at what you do and you care about the future of our kids. Now that we've established that you are among the best there is no need to prove it over the next few days. We're going to ask that you hang up your superhero capes while we're together!"

The Pancake Roundtable Incubator

For more than 15 years I've met once a month with five other business owners at the Original Pancake House on Midway in Dallas. I have referenced this group in each of my books because they played a role in each of them.

The Pancake House Roundtable reflects the soul and values of a MindShift: deep respect, open trust, strong debate, a drive to learn, and no superhero capes. We don't promote our agendas or ourselves; we have learned to focus on helping one another.

Over the years our menu orders have shifted from eggs, bacon, and pancakes to oatmeal and egg-white omelets. And the decades of personal and business achievements, losses, struggles, successes, and the dynamics of aging have all seemed to strip theory and pride away and make us more aware that life doesn't follow our chosen patterns or preferences. We no longer have easy answers. We don't play games.

But there is something stabilizing about a monthly ritual of a meal with friends and colleagues. Like standing around a campfire on a cold night, those breakfasts seem to take us away from the noise, the glitter, and the stress of modern life. In that place we all find a clearer signal for hearing what's coming down the road.

Robert has been our waiter throughout the years. He is worthy of mention because he always served us relationally, never as a transaction.

We've not met anyone quite like Robert. He will ask, "Do you want your usual or do you want to swap the grits for the tomatoes like you did last month?" Then he itemizes your order just to confirm it is right. After 15 years Robert was moved to a new location on MacArthur. Guess where we'll be for our next roundtable.

I presented the idea of my last two books at the Roundtable. It seemed natural since both books addressed issues and industries familiar to them. I didn't expect any response from them about education, except for perhaps a few stories about their kids.

But after Bill and John pitched the idea of a K–12 MindShift, I took it to the Roundtable. I needed to hear their unique input. Besides, I thought, one of them may confirm that the project was as crazy at it struck me in the beginning. But, to my surprise, Greg Wilkinson told me about the Momentous Institute. And he knew a lot about it. He introduced me to Michelle Kinder, Executive Director. He also introduced me to Rosemary Perlmeter, who founded Uplift Education, an association of 34 charter schools serving over 14,000 students.

They both—Michelle and Rosemary—became tour guides into worlds I would have never discovered on my own. They helped me clearly see some of the challenges that confront education. So right out of the chute a Roundtable friend gave me two pivotal relationships, and ones that had nothing to do with his industry. It was all a pure gift that came through relationship. There was nothing transactional about it.

You Can Do This, Too

In his book *Where Good Ideas Come From,* Steve Johnson says that idea incubators (like my Pancake Roundtable) play a central role in change ventures. If you are a parent, educator, or concerned citizen and want to see change, consider creating your own version of a Pancake Roundtable Incubator. It may be your mastermind circle, Wednesday Bible Study group, golfing buddies, neighbors, or another gathering of friends. The forum and regular gathering provides a place to think out loud, listen to

The K–12 MindShift project never sought permission. We just walked in like we owned the place and knew what we were doing.

people who respect and care about what you think, and a forum for processing thoughts, testing assumptions, and arriving at an action plan. Oh, I almost forgot—Johnson also says that great ideas sometimes take 10 or more years of formation before they spring into action.

This is my third MindShift effort. The first one baked for almost seven years before I had the clarity and confidence to take a risk and test my idea with the owner of a large office manufacturer. I was very surprised when he liked the idea and asked for a proposal. I should not have been surprised. After all, I had been thinking about it for years and refining my ideas through discussions with my friends at the Pancake Roundtable. Have you been considering that a similar venue might help move you to action?

I want each of you to understand; the K–12 MindShift project never sought permission. We just walked in like we owned the place and knew what we were doing. John and Bill were not looking for authorization to change the education landscape when they approached me. And yet, if someone asked you to pick a team for leading such a mission, you would not have picked John and Bill or me. You probably wouldn't pick yourself. That is because there seems to be an unspoken rule: "Large-scale, complex problems are reserved for an authorized body of credentialed experts."

That mindset is a myth.

We should never forget that a child was the first one who saw that the emperor had no clothes.

CHAPTER 4

The Learning Manifesto

Human history becomes more and more a race between education and catastrophe.

—H. G. Wells

In Chapter 1, I write that this book is a manifesto for a secret, but emerging, revolution. I also explain, "After 60 years of studies, we don't have time for more research, reform measures, or debate. The revolution has already started. It is *even now* overthrowing an obsolete industrial regime, structure, and set of values. That insurgency will reclaim learning as a fundamentally human experience."

Manifest is, of course, the root word for manifesto. So a manifesto is a statement that is "easy to perceive or recognize . . . a statement in which someone makes his or her intentions or views easy for people to ascertain."[1] It is an articulation that is so *manifestly* true that virtually anyone can see it. It is not a proposal or an argument; it states what people already know but may have forgotten.

As the MindShift team worked on this book, we saw the need to drive a stake into the ground, to mark a spot, to recognize that we have passed through an historic sea change. In other words, *right here* is where we stand *right now*. We don't have to fight old battles or exhume the cadavers of earlier eras. The world has changed. And we wanted to say it with sufficient clarity that it would be manifestly true.

Figure 4.1   The Columbus Manifesto Exercise

A Stake in the Ground

When tools and processes are borrowed from an external source—such as a book, a model that worked sometime somewhere, or an outside agency—they will usually remain separated and isolated from the original ethos. When that happens, those tools and processes lose their human pliability and become a machine (like the Great American Machine of Education). Jack Hess describes this as transactional work instead of relationship building. Projects that are transactional bring everyone together to get "it" done. But, when "it" is finished, the relationships will end.

Process is simply a proxy for the ethos behind it. However, that ethos must be examined over and over in order to keep our tools and processes in alignment with it.

Our stake in the ground, our manifesto, declares our guiding principles, our starting point, and a call to action. If we don't plant a stake in the ground, we have no foundation for advancing; we don't know where we are or where we are going.

At some point (early on and often throughout the project) we have to express or declare the founding ethos and our common interest (see Figure 4.1). That is our stake in the ground, our manifesto. It declares our guiding principles, our starting point, and a call to action. If we don't plant a stake in the ground, we have no foundation for advancing; we don't know where we are or where we are going. The lack of a common starting point explains a lot about our political gridlock, contentious debates, high-pressure tactics, slander, and a continuing focus on what divides us. We can build what we think is a "great" new school or implement a new model of learning, but if it is accomplished through strife, then strife becomes the ethos and that will be the product. Disagreement and conflict will be baked into the whole project. And it will fail.

Balfour Beatty, the third largest contractor of schools in the United States, is one of the leading companies in this effort. Chief Information Officer Mark Konchar shared a valuable insight from research that examined several years of successful and problematic projects: "One hundred percent of projects that start off badly end poorly!"

In full disclosure, we did not set out to write a manifesto. Our research, interviews, and continuing conversations among ourselves and nationally prominent voices simply brought us to a clear recognition of self-evident realities. We've also written this as a manifesto in order to shape and guide our process, not to impose our view on others.

For the sake of stakeholder alignment, we have tried to identify and embrace what we all have in common and what we want to accomplish together. That is so clearly missing in so much of our national, regional, and local debates. At some point we have to ask are we all trying to solve the same problem?

That may sound obvious and simple on paper but it is an art, a delicate and deep art. Like many leaders, I know that art, but it often eludes me.

Finding a core beginning point often seems like trying to land an F–18 on an aircraft carrier at night in a stormy sea.

Getting Beyond Whack-a-Mole

Much of the conflict around school reform is plagued by a lack of a center, a common starting point. So it has become a game of whack-a-mole. You know, problems pop up all around us and we take a whack at them: Common core—whack. Vouchers—whack. Teacher unions—whack. Charter schools—whack. Poverty—whack. Special needs—whack. Funding—whack. Testing—whack. There is no end because there is no center.

The movie *Moneyball* contains a great scene in which Billy Beane, the General Manager for the Oakland A's, played by Brad Pitt, lands his scouts on that "aircraft carrier" of finding the core beginning point, the agreement about the real problem.

The A's were a low-budget secondary-market baseball team that somehow consistently outperformed other teams, despite the other teams' much higher payrolls. But then it all unraveled. After the 1992 season, when the A's fell one game short of reaching the World Series, other teams took their three best players through free agency. That represented a sea change for the A's; they were simply unable to compete financially with the other teams. During the off-season, Beane and his scouts huddled in their offices to figure out how to rebuild and pull off another miracle of fielding another winning team.

Beane was fed up with the futility of trying to pull a rabbit out of the hat every year and then losing his best players to free agency at the end of the season. His scouts, however, were still playing whack-a-mole and trying to solve the problem the same way they had for years. They were stuck (as school reform is) defining the problem the same way as every other team. They saw symptoms, not root causes.

The turning point came when Beane kept asking his scouts, "What's the problem?" They kept answering (with increasing frustration) with old and exhausted reasoning. Finally, Beane declared what I call the Beane Manifesto:

> *The problem we're trying to solve is that there are rich teams and there are poor teams. Then there's 50 feet of crap, and then there's us. It's an*

unfair game. And now we've been gutted. We're like organ donors for the rich. Boston's taken our kidneys, Yankees have taken our heart. And you guys just sit around talking the same old "good body" nonsense like we're selling jeans . . . We've got to think differently. We are the last dog at the bowl. You see what happens to the runt of the litter? He dies.[2]

Suddenly, all the lights came on. Beane and his scouts found the starting point, the real problem. As a result they stopped playing whack-a-mole.

K–12: "What's the Problem?"

When our MindShift team had been working on the K–12 project for six months, we went to Columbus, Indiana (see Figure 4.2). I wanted the group to touch the uniqueness of that place and its ethos. On our second day, I wanted to hear what every person in the group saw. After six months, I needed to know if we were in agreement about the true problem. Had we struck a common chord or were we still in the whack-a-mole phase?

Figure 4.2 Manifesto Exercise Millennial Team

To my surprise, the group voiced common and harmonic chords about education as a *kid-centered learning experience*. That turned out to be a major pillar of our collective view. Public education can so easily become about anything and anyone *except* the kids! We build programs and structures and we choose curricula and hire teachers and build great bureaucracies, but, dammit, we forgot those at the very core of the venture.

The MindShift group saw learning in the context of a community, not an isolated place called "school." In the following summits we built upon our experience in Columbus; we finally were able to craft a preamble that could set the stage for a conversation about education in a Post-Gutenberg era.

Preamble: A Case for Change

Our free public education system, a revolution of innovation in the mid-1800s, propelled our nation to heights never before imagined, and did so for the next 100 years. That system has been an integral pillar of that American promise: *Our kids will all have an equal opportunity to grow beyond their parents and make the world better.*

However, the success of the past now threatens our future. Education as an institution is attempting to compete in a race that is moving at the speed of thought. And we are driving a 575-year-old Gutenberg-powered buggy. Adding horses, improving the wheels, changing drivers, making stricter inspections, ejecting passengers who slow down the buggy, and brutally beating the horses only disguises the fact that the buggy is obsolete.

Attempting to run a Google race in a Gutenberg buggy is a futile strategy. We won't be able to spend enough, test enough, train enough, hire enough, or hype enough. We can no longer keep our promise to the kids, for whom we ostensibly built the system. This generation and future generations have been scammed.

Google (and a vast constellation of virtual "tribes and nations") now power our travel and reach. These new forces have eclipsed the Gutenberg realm with new rules and tools. It is painfully clear that attempting to run a Google race in a Gutenberg buggy is a futile strategy. We won't be able to spend enough, test enough, train enough, hire enough or hype enough. We can no longer keep our promise to the kids, for whom we ostensibly built the system. This generation and future generations have been scammed.

That's why 60 percent of kids have checked out and don't care by graduation. Their school experience is killing their creativity and crushing their hope. This "Oh, my God" level of disengagement, the rising achievement gap, dramatically low test performance, 60 percent college graduation rate, mounting debt, and other pathologies reveal a system beyond reform.

The conditions are so bad that in April 1983 (almost 35 years ago) a presidential commission report, "A Nation at Risk," stated:

> *If an unfriendly foreign power had attempted to impose on America the mediocre educational performance that exists today, we might well have viewed it as an act of war. As it stands, we have allowed this to happen to ourselves.*[3]

What was true then is worse today and rapidly declining. But now, the level of the crisis, the burning platform, means that it's time to declare the model and system obsolete, not simply broken. Unless we let go of the Gutenberg-powered Education Machine, its thinking, structures and culture, in order to embrace an open, distributed, collaborative, tailored, on-demand platform then we will simply continue to whack the most visible, urgent, or frightening mole. We will tackle one isolated symptom after another and never address the truth about the Great Machine.

Of course, we need a revolution, a transformation that is only capable at a local level through local stakeholders. And it has already started.

Self-Evident Truths

> *It is, in fact, nothing short of a miracle that the modern methods of instruction have not yet entirely strangled the holy curiosity of inquiry; for this delicate little plant, aside from stimulation, stands mainly in need of freedom; without this it goes to wrack and ruin without fail.*
> —Albert Einstein

Certain turning points in history have signaled breaks from the prevailing insanity. At those points, certain individuals or groups have

If an unfriendly foreign power had attempted to impose on America the mediocre educational performance that exists today, we might well have viewed it as an act of war. As it stands, we have allowed this to happen to ourselves.

issued manifestos or declarations announcing, "We've had enough! Here is what we believe to be true and what we are committed to do."

On October 31, 1517, when Martin Luther nailed his 95 theses to the cathedral door, he captured what so many people instinctively knew, but had forgotten, about religious abuses. Coming approximately 75 years after Gutenberg converted a winepress into a printing press, Luther's manifesto has long been credited with launching the Protestant Reformation. But the ramifications of the theses spilled far beyond religion. They sparked a time of disruption, war, and (150 years later) a new form of governance called the nation-state was born.

Throughout history, others (like Abraham Lincoln, Martin Luther King, Rachel Carson, Steve Jobs, and Henry Ford) have also announced the end of one era and set a vision for a new one.

But, in 1999, four Internet pioneers and visionaries, Rick Levine, Chris Locke, Doc Searls, and David Weinberger posted their "95 theses" on a website and later published them in a book (*The Cluetrain Manifesto: The End of Business as Usual,* Basic Books, 2001).

Although *Cluetrain* was less monumental and stately than other historical examples, it was a stunning cultural barometer; it detected an historic storm bearing down on the old ways. Much of what we see in the Education Machine versus learning revolution was signaled in *Cluetrain.* For example, it rejected the contrived corporate rhetoric that beeps and burps from the official versions. And it issued a clarion call for authenticity and humanness. As such, it spoke for millions of people; they all felt like the authors had wiretapped their brains—these guys were saying what so many had said or thought privately. For example, they saw:

1. Markets as conversations.
2. Organizations can no longer hide behind walls.
3. They must speak individually and with a human voice.
4. Their customers want conversations, not messages.
5. Speaking in a human voice is not some gimmick.

6. Companies that speak in "the pitch, or the dog-and-pony show, are no longer speaking to anyone"
7. Companies and other organizations must belong to a real community.
8. "Command-and-control management styles both derive from and reinforce bureaucracy, power tripping, and an overall culture of paranoia."
9. If companies want their customers to pay, then the company must pay attention!
10. "We have real power and we know it. If you don't quite see the light, some other outfit will come along that's more attentive, more interesting, more fun to play with."[4]

These were radical ideas in 1999, but they also spoke truths that had been emerging for a long time. The four understood the cataclysmic nature of the sea change in their time. Foreseeing the disruptive force unleashed by the Internet on traditional hierarchical organizations, they predicted a new order.

In our work on K–12 education, we could clearly see that virtually everything in *The Cluetrain Manifesto* applies to public education. Artifice is dead; authenticity is essential.

We have done our best to capture the sea change in education and learning, and we have attempted to state it as simply and clearly as possible. We have no illusions that our efforts compare to the great historical examples (or even to *Cluetrain*). We are just trying to build on what others saw in order to find common ground and commitment in our journey to unlock the joy of learning and true engagement.

Our stake in the ground or starting point revolves around a particular set of presuppositions. We don't claim these are the only ones or even the right ones. These simply came out of our deeper conversations during our summits around the country. They have served to align us around a common set of beliefs about the current state of the Education Machine and our understanding of the human nature of learning. Here is our manifesto. We have organized our beliefs into specific and coherent themes.

> *In our work on K–12 education, we could clearly see that virtually everything in* The Cluetrain Manifesto *applies to public education. Artifice is dead; authenticity is essential.*

The Learning Manifesto

The Heart of Learning
1. Learning is a uniquely human experience.
2. Individuals are unique and learning engages that uniqueness.
3. Curiosity is the gyroscope of learning and creativity.
4. Life application is far more valuable than memorization and testing.
5. The seed of learning requires care and hope.
6. Learning is naturally valuable and intrinsically rewarding.
7. Personal initiative supersedes compliance.

The Education Machine
8. Prefers and prioritizes achievement over character.
9. When institutions exceed human scale they drive toward efficiency.
10. The obsession with high stakes testing often denies students the safety to fail.
11. Efficiency removes agency and common sense.
12. Efficient systems can deliver good service but can no longer care.
13. Every system has a perverse logic. When it exceeds human scale it begins to create the opposite of what it was originally designed for.
14. Public education is a monopoly and no monopoly has ever reformed itself.

The Fallout
15. Well-schooled does not equal well-educated.
16. Fifty percent of kids are at risk. That is a crushing indictment.
17. Zip code outweighs funding and programs in predicting success.
18. Teacher and student disengagement is the product of the Education Machine.
19. Kids know the difference between care and detachment. If both students and teachers are disengaged, then what's the point of maintaining business as usual?

The New World of Learning
20. We have departed from high content and are now in a high concept and context volatile, uncertain, complex, and ambiguous (VUCA)[5] world. That new world requires new skills of critical thinking, communication, creativity, and collaboration.

21. We believe that inquiry—teams, projects, and life relevance—define the context for learning.
22. We should restore character and virtue by weaving it into the context of our learning, not viewing them as isolated subjects.
23. We believe that learning will have to begin at the cradle to extend to competency in order to reflect world realities and deliver social justice.
24. Technology, as it continues to lower costs and expand access, will continue to shift learning from the teacher at the front of the class to collaborative student-centered patterns.

The "What Works" Revolution

25. Holistic and locally led initiatives will resolve our program-rich and system-poor approaches to reform.
26. The answers to providing enriched learning reside in the community and among its stakeholders.
27. Creating social capital is the least expensive and most powerful lever for transformation.
28. Millions spent in early education saves billions in later intervention.

Nathan Siebenga, Principal at Hamilton District Christian High, succinctly summarizes what we have to leave and embrace to fulfill the manifesto:

To Thingify: Students + numbers/metrics + degrees + titles = school today.
To Humanize: Students + character development + societal integration + competency + inspired hope = the schools we desire.

Exposing Hidden Things

There was once an entire hidden universe, a shadow banking system, just below the visible and official banking system. It comprised an entire new language and had created (and concealed) strange financial instruments with acronyms like CDOs, CDSs, and SIVs. They fell outside of banking because insurance companies and hedge funds created them. The experts called them *derivatives*, but no one had a clue what that meant.

Fast-forward to August of 2007 when tremors of a major financial earthquake sent economists into a frenzy. When the Federal Reserve held its annual Economic Policy Symposium Proceedings in Jackson Hole, Wyoming, an odd economist and former managing director for PIMCO by the name of Paul McCulley, made a comment during the second day that detailed the looming and inevitable threat.

"The real issue," according to McCulley, "going on right now is a run on [the] shadow banking system . . . It is the shadow banking system which is about $1.3 trillion in assets. . . ." Until then, most economist and policy makers had never pondered what lay outside the "known" world of banks or hedge funds.

Conversations among human beings sound human. They are conducted in a human voice . . . In just a few more years, the current homogenized "voice" of business—the sound of mission statements and brochures—will seem as contrived and artificial as the language of the 18th-century French court . . .

It would turn out that the $1.3 trillion exposure was only the tip of the iceberg (the full size of the iceberg was about $27 trillion, double the U.S. GDP).[6]

That story revealed a profound reality: *names serve to expose hidden things.*

One of the challenges we faced tackling the Education Machine was that very few of us had any knowledge of the special language spoken within the catacombs of public education. Like the banking system, the Great Education Machine uses state assessments, ACT and SAT scores, grade point averages, AP classes, and college acceptance rates as measures for health. But that also built a very elite and esoteric language that outsiders cannot understand with acronyms like NCLB, ESSA, STEM, STEAM, ABA, AHEAD, IEP, LRE, and more than a hundred others I gleaned from just one website.[7]

The *Cluetrain Manifesto* identified that con game back in the 1990s: "Conversations among human beings *sound* human. They are conducted in a human voice . . . In just a few more years, the current homogenized "voice" of business—the sound of mission statements and brochures—will seem as contrived and artificial as the language of the 18th-century French court . . ."[8]

To insist on clear language—especially about learning—seems like a critical starting point. As Confucius is quoted as saying, "The beginning of wisdom is to call things by their proper name."

The following categories provide a different lens for classifying schools. We asked, "What are kids actually walking away with at the end of their K-12 experience?" When we looked at schools through this lens we discovered a clear ladder and a new sense of urgency for the mission ahead. But classifying schools by test scores, rankings, or grading systems strips them away from the context. We wanted a system that would better paint a picture of what life and learning looked like in different schools. These are not tested or meant as universal metrics. We did share them with administrators for several large districts and found that they opened up entirely new insights and conversations. You might find them helpful for comparing the landscape of schools in your community.

Future-Ready Schools

Our kids will graduate into a world where, according to some estimates, 65 percent of jobs have yet to be invented.[9] This is a major issue. We are just beginning to grasp the skills and competencies needed for the world of the twenty-first century. Furthermore, we estimate that less than 10 percent of schools qualify as future-ready. Here is a quick-reference guide to those schools:

1. *Learning communities:* The engaged public, private partnership relationship with continual learning as a community mission.
   Examples: East Lake Meadows, the Purpose-Built Communities, Columbus, Indiana, and KIPP Connect
2. *Engaged schools:* The active learning models in the form of inquiry, teams, projects, and teacher-facilitator roles.
   Examples: PBL schools, Expeditionary Learning, Entrepreneurship, Design Thinking modeled learning, High-Tech Highs, NuTech, Code Academies
3. *Blended schools:* Schools that provide strategic use of technology to enable as much independent learning as possible and allowing teacher to provide more coaching and facilitation.
   Examples: Achievement First, Big Picture, Actin, Alt.school, High Tech High, Kent Innovation High[10]
4. *Career and technology education:* These are the new generation of what used to be vocational and technical schools. Many are state-of-the-art facilities offering forensic science, culinary arts, film and production,

robotics, aerospace, computer network engineering, coding, and the list goes on. Many offer employment level certifications and college credits. Many students graduate and chose to go to college.

Examples: Birdville Center of Technology and Advanced Learning, IBM's P-Tech, and Mercy Vocational High

Well-Schooled but Poorly Educated

These schools may best be described as "college-ready factories." These schools fall in the crosshairs of Ken Robinson, John Gatto, Tony Wagner, Diane Ravitch, Yong Zhao, and a wide list of educators who criticize testing, the stress of high-stakes everything, and a hypercompetitive pursuit of grade points for college. The underlying questions for these schools are:

"What's the point of these narrow pursuits?"
"Are kids learning what they need for life success and happiness?"
"Are we really just teaching our students how to game the system?"
"Can the system accommodate the "one-off" kid, the one with ADHD, Asperger's, OCD, dyslexia, depression, anxiety, and so forth?"

We estimate that about 40 percent of our kids are stuck in this model of Education Machine.

5. *Enhanced traditional schools:* Traditional teaching models of content and comprehension with a focus on advanced subjects and enriched extracurricular activities
   Examples: AP, STEM, Baccalaureate, and so forth
6. *Traditional schools:* Our common image of the classroom experience with a teacher at the front of the class, lecturing or reading out of a textbook with the objective to prepare kids for taking the next test.
7. *Ladder-up schools:* Schools that give at-risk and underserved kids the resources, time, talent, and structure to compensate for the race they were never meant to compete in. They enhance any of the learning models with extended hours, higher expectations, parent-student-teacher partnerships, strict discipline, and extracurricular activities.
   Examples: KIPP, One Goal, Private School (especially Parochial), AVID, Momentous Institute, The Shelton School

Left Behind

The "left behind" category of students is the one that should keep us up at night. According to the U.S. Census Bureau, the (inflation-adjusted) median income for a household in America is $52,000 (2014).[11] The "left behind" kids come from homes that live on half and less than half of that figure. Some estimate that about 50 percent of our kids fall into the pit. About 10 percent beat the odds and climb out to succeed.

A few years ago, I witnessed the aftermath of a shooting at the LAX airport. I had a vantage point in the administration tower to see all of the activity unfold. The emergency team placed three large, brightly colored tarps—green, yellow, and red—on the road just outside one of the terminals. Mike Feldman, then Deputy Executive Director, explained: "These are triage tarps. Those alive and who will live get taken to the green. Those wounded and who need immediate care get taken to the yellow. Those who are either dead or will likely die are placed on the red. During an emergency there is confusion, limited personnel, and time is precious. This system guides those available to where to go first. Those on the red tarp get checked first."

So, the following is our attempt at describing a triage system for the Education Machine.

8. *Green: Community and vocational colleges:* These schools offer hope (but too often that is an illusory bridge to careers or college) for those who graduate out of a *left behind* school. The hard reality is that 86 percent of these kids were told that they were ready for college. Yet, over 60 percent need remedial classes before they can start. Sixty percent think it will take two years to get through community and vocational college, but after six years only 38 percent finish their two-year program.[12]

9. *Yellow: Custodial schools:* The schools most common in underserved communities have a high percentage of students on free and reduced lunch programs. The primary goal of these schools is to provide basic education and move kids forward as best as possible.

10. *Red: Survival schools:* They are exactly what the description means. Teachers and students try to survive a school in impoverished and often violent neighborhoods. Because the kids live with poverty and danger, they come to school stressed and far behind everyone else.

Examples: Normandy High in Ferguson, Missouri, Detroit, the South Side of Chicago, Baltimore, and so on. These schools are often depicted in shows like *The Wired* and movies like *Dangerous Minds.*

The Tale of Two Communities

The early 1970s became a watershed period for our economy, culture, and schools. The next chapter describes how two similar Rust Belt communities responded to their dramatic reversal in fortune. For Clinton, Ohio, economic prosperity determined its social capital and vulnerability, and led to declining schools. For Columbus, Indiana, faced with the same economic crisis, social capital led to prosperity and resilience. We were fascinated to learn how schools became the catalyst to a process for maintaining that resilience.

CHAPTER 5

How the Road to Transformation Began in Failure

Education is the transmission of civilization. Civilization is not inherited; it has to be learned again by each new generation.
— David Kearns, former chair of Xerox Corporation

A small town just south of Indianapolis holds a secret. Many small towns do. However, when you hear this one you'll likely sit up and take notice. I sure did.

I discovered Columbus by accident. While working with a client in Indianapolis, at the end of a long day, I pulled out onto the beltway to drive back to my downtown hotel. As the day drained away, I quickly flipped on the local public radio station. It was all background noise until I heard: *Columbus, Indiana: A Midwestern Mecca of Architecture*. But it was the end of the program; I learned almost nothing more.

So how could a small and unknown town in Indiana be called a "Mecca of Architecture"? I called an architect friend. He said, "Oh, yes; every architecture student knows about that town." But he was too busy to tell me more. I would apparently have to dig deeper to find out why architects know about Columbus. The mystery deepened and I was intrigued.

My reason for being in Indianapolis revolved around a research project: our team was searching for a link between culture, engagement, and the architectural environments (or workplaces) companies create to foster that culture. Many skeptics in design and corporate real estate have rejected the possibility of ever finding such a link. And I just happened to hear a reference to "a mecca of architecture" within 50 miles of my location at that moment. So, you can imagine my excitement. I felt a bit like Indiana Jones in *The Last Crusade,* getting closer to the Holy Grail.

I immediately started researching the place. That's when I discovered that very few people know the Columbus story. Even the city's municipal website carries no mention of great architecture. In fact, it reveals very little material about Columbus except for a few photos of its most famous buildings.

But, through my Internet research I learned that the American Institute of Architects ranked Columbus sixth in the nation for architectural innovation and design. The only cities ahead of Columbus are Chicago, Boston, New York, San Francisco, and Washington, DC. That little detail grabbed me and would not let go.

The next morning I called the Columbus Visitors Center. A very nice, amiable, retired woman gave cheerful answers to basic questions. But she did not know the city's backstories or why architecture became so central there. At that point, I knew I had to drive down to Columbus. And I knew I needed a guide.

So I rolled out of Indianapolis, down I-65, across the wide expanses of agricultural fields to Columbus. And, in a stroke of good luck, I found Jack Hess, president (at that time) of the local Chamber of Commerce. Somehow, his title made me expect a grinning, fist-pumping, small-town car dealer in a navy blazer and khaki slacks. But Jack was not that guy! Tall and slender with thick black wavy hair, and dressed in a well-fitted pinstripe suit, Jack was East Coast–polished. He was friendly, but didn't play games. So I quickly learned that Columbus was a different kind of town with a unique philosophy. I could see that Jack was a key leader and steward of that philosophy.

As the guardian of the grail, he told me the story of J. Irwin Miller.

The Path to Quality

J. Irwin Miller was born in Columbus in 1909 and graduated from Yale in 1931. As the great nephew of William Irwin, one of the founders of

Cummins, Miller grew very naturally into the family business. In 1934, he was asked to come home (from another family business venture in California) and lead Cummins Diesel, the family's struggling engine manufacturer that had yet to make a profit.

He was able to turn around the company and by the early 1950s built the manufacturer to $100 million in revenue. That is when Cummins hit a wall. "There simply wasn't enough world-class engineering talent to keep up with demand." He was faced with a business problem and a community problem. Miller quickly understood and stated the real problem: "How can we recruit and attract the best engineers and their families to a town they've never heard of and one that has lousy schools?"

Exacerbating that problem, Columbus was growing so rapidly (from the World War II baby boom) that the Columbus school district would have to build an elementary school every two years in order to keep up with the demographics. Compounding the problem even further was the fact that it had been so long since the last school was built, that the school board had no experience with the building process. Like many school boards in the Baby Boom explosion, they wanted something that could be built quickly and cheaply. So they selected a contractor who proposed a prefabricated solution.

It was a disaster. As Jack told me, "Despite using prefabricated construction the school ran over budget and did not open on time. And, within the first year it ran into severe maintenance problems. It was an embarrassment for the board and the community. This failure, however, was both opportune and timely for Miller to introduce some of his thinking on the value of investing in *quality* and a process for building strong communities."

Miller lived by a cardinal rule: "It is expensive to be mediocre; Quality has always been cost effective."

Incredibly, this corporate CEO, facing a shortage of talent, realized that the real problem was, in fact, a very human one. ". . . if you don't have a healthy community, it's impossible to have a healthy company." It begins with healthy schools. That's because good designers and

> *This failure, however, was both opportune and timely for Miller to introduce some of his thinking on the value of investing in quality and a process for building strong communities. He lived by a cardinal rule: "It is expensive to be mediocre; quality has always been cost effective."*

engineers tend to also be good citizens and loving and responsible parents. They want what is best for their children—just as Lisa and I did back in the 1990s and just as you did, do, or will in your child-rearing years. It is a universal heart cry; our children are our messages to the future. We care about them and the message they bear.

Miller knew that a real community is one in which the people build things together. That's why he believed and preached "stakeholder engagement." In other words, leaders must respect all the stakehold-ers—those with valid interest or concern—in any business venture, crisis, community, or grand quest. Failing to do so is to be guilty of Gandhi's relational insight: "Whatever you do for me but without me, you do against me."

So he took the components of the problem and crafted "The Offer": if the school board would choose an architect from his list of five world-class designers, Cummins would pay the architect's fee.

They accepted his offer.

After interviewing all five, the board chose Harry Weese. He designed the Lillian C. Schmitt Elementary School, which opened in 1957. The school generated incredible attention, not only in Columbus or in Indiana but nationally. It sent a message that Columbus was a community serious about investing in the future and more importantly in their kids! It was a community doing something quite different. And, yes, diesel engineers around the world noticed.

Of course, because of the baby boom, the need for new schools kept growing. Immediately after the first school completed, the board came back to Miller for a second school, Mabel McDowell Elementary. Miller and Cummins did it again. Through the Cummins Foundation Archi-tecture Program they have continued to do so.

Jack told me that the experience and relationship with Miller and Cummins shaped something in the citizenry of Columbus. The magnif-icent school designs and the exposure and interaction with some of the leading thinkers of the twentieth century stirred other leaders to follow. The library, churches, city buildings, park landscaping, fire station, and businesses saw the value of great design. They also motivated the learning and collaboration that great design demands.

Miller always saw architecture as a proxy for culture. Or, as Winston Churchill said (and Miller often quoted), "We shape our buildings and afterwards our buildings shape us." In other words, architecture shapes and reinforces the values, attitudes, behaviors, and habits that provide the glue for a thriving community. So, in Columbus, these projects created a reservoir of social capital[1] that is so vital to a democracy.

One of the lessons found to be common in schools that experienced transformation is that culture *is* the work that creates engaged learning. Culture, not reform, is the primary issue. And this may be why the Education Machine so often fails to change the atmosphere. Reform initiatives come across as direct blunt instruments, like using a bulldozer to cultivate orchids. But a healthy culture will naturally produce engaged schools kids who get very absorbed in learning.

When Achievement Drives Culture

When I interviewed Leo Linbeck, CEO of Aquinas Companies and advisor to the KIPP Academy, I learned that he is passionate about the future of education in America and is a strong advocate for rigorous charter schools.

Linbeck can knock your shoes off with his confident and bold assessments, such as what he said to me when we spoke about the future of education:

"History shows that no monopoly has ever reformed itself." And, "Education used to be a proxy for the character traits needed for individuals to self-govern in a democracy: traits like honesty, hard work, and accomplishment. When education went from being a proxy for good citizenship to an end itself, we essentially taught kids how to cheat in order to succeed."

> *Our schools went from a learning culture to an academic achievement culture, synonymous with testing. Kids aren't asked to learn the material; they are asked to pass a test. We are teaching kids techniques for taking tests and how to answer questions.*
> —Leo Linbeck

Those two heavy pronouncements were a lot to absorb in the fifteen seconds Leo stated them. I asked him to expand on the second one.

He answered, "Our schools went from a learning culture to an academic achievement culture, synonymous with testing. Kids aren't asked to learn the material; they are asked to pass a test. We are teaching kids techniques for taking tests and how to answer questions."

In other words, school has become a proxy, not for the character qualities of citizenry, but for learning how to game the system. As Linbeck spoke, I felt like I was getting an eye exam. I left the conversation wearing a new pair of glasses that brought the world into new focus and clarity.

Sometime later, I wore those "glasses" when I interviewed Candi Dearing, principle for Sarasota Middle School. Candi cut to the real issue very quickly by telling me a story about her grandson, Elisha.

"Elisha was home working on an assignment. Dad was helping. They were memorizing the states and their capitals. So I looked up the benchmark (teacher guidelines for what successful achievement looks like) for this assignment and it said, 'Locate and identify the states, their capitals, and territories of the U.S. on a map.'

"I asked Elisha, 'What is a capital and why do you need to know it?'

"'So I can pass the test.'"

Candi continued, "We're demanding memorization, not comprehension. We're not taking that simple step to move kids into the kind of higher level thinking that they will need in this world. In our middle school my teachers and I will routinely crouch down next to a child and ask:

'What are you learning?'

'Why are you learning it?'

'Why is it important?'

'How does this relate to what you've been learning in class?'"

The Lesson of Volkswagen and Teaching to the Test

Is there a connection between a five-year-old memorizing states and capitals in order to pass a test and Volkswagen's cheating on emission testing? Your answer may reveal the glasses you wear.

The drive to become the world's biggest carmaker, while saddled with emission standards that "everyone knew" were unobtainable, led to VW's choice of one very logical course of action: cheat to pass. After all, almost everyone has learned to game the system. You know, cheat in

It seems that no one person sees how any component relates to any other. So we either blame the last person on the assembly line, the one who took the test, or the one who gave the test. Or, we blame the person at the top because, "They should have known!"

order to play on the team, use sexual favors to achieve acceptance to a prestigious college, or slip some cash to the building inspector. Perhaps it is that same gaming the system that led a car manufacturer's need for success to outweigh the moral tension of the moment. Or, did that tension even exist?

We all know it; these corrosive elements begin early and invisibly. But they end up polluting the entire reservoir that is everyone's drinking water. That is why blame is such a futile exercise. Where do you place blame when it is the culture? Do we blame the teacher who gave Elisha the assignment? The curriculum developers who create content to meet the benchmarks? The test creators, the policy makers?

When dealing with the Education Machine, from the inside, it seems that no one person sees how any component relates to any other. So we either blame the last person on the assembly line, the one who took the test, or the one who gave the test. Or, we blame the person at the top because, "They should have known!"

And indeed they should have except for the fact that they are wearing the wrong glasses.

That is why Columbus, Indiana, strikes me as such a rich, and increasingly rare, island of character and integrity. J. Irwin Miller had—and lived—such great insights about the importance of quality and stakeholder engagement. Did Volkswagen consider their stakeholders? Did they demand quality?

You see everyone's values in the way they either build, or destroy, social capital.

We will walk through the Columbus process for building coalitions in detail in the chapter titled "Leading Change at Your School."

When Quality Drives Culture

J. Irwin Miller believed that when people build things together, they reveal their collective quality of spirit, temperament, and character in the quality of the buildings they

When people build things together, they reveal their collective quality of spirit, temperament, and character in the quality of the buildings they construct. He knew that excellence of character would always reveal itself in built things.

What is built and what endures represent the true test of human character.

construct. He knew that excellence of character would always reveal itself in built things.

What is built and what endures represent the true test of human character. What does it say about a town of less than 50,000 citizens who embraced the value of partnering with so many luminaries of twentieth century architecture? While many metropolises hired the same architects to create trophies to elevate their presence on the global stage, Columbus saw an intrinsic worth in the activity of building great structures to serve and uplift its citizens.

It does take vision to create a culture driven by quality. But, it is not the kind of vision reserved for a few or for the privileged. Remember Miller's cardinal rule: "It is expensive to be mediocre in this world. Quality has always been cost effective."

Jack Hess and other city leaders have taken these lessons for building social capital through collective design, and created a framework and organization to steward their legacy. For example, the nonprofit *Institute for Coalition Building* (which Jack leads) now works in partnership with other cities and organizations to share Miller's thinking and the lessons from Columbus's 60-year experiment in participative democracy.[2]

". . . When Business Leaves but the People Stay"

Company towns were common in the years after the war. Many captured a unique snapshot of a past way of life in America. In that time and in those cities, America was predominantly a blend of rich and poor living together and sharing the public commons. They benefited somewhat equally from investments in schools, parks, libraries, and other community initiatives. The kids played on the same sports teams and attended the public school together. They were neighbors, not strangers. All of that began to change when the tide rolled out.

Beginning in the late 1970s the fortunes of the auto, steel, and tire industries, along with unionized labor, began a steep and rapid decline. Emerging from World War II that industrial triad, and their communities and culture, had so profoundly shaped our nation that it represented the face of America and the American dream to the rest of the world. The communities concentrated around the Great Lakes and sprinkled throughout the Midwest slipped into their deepest postwar recession.

After a generation of growth, stability, and a rising and strong middle class, there was no graceful transition.

In his book, *Our Kids: The American Dream in Crisis,* Robert Putnam paints a vivid portrait of the diminishing landscape of opportunity for American kids. He uses his own hometown of Port Clinton, Ohio ("sadly typical of America"), to frame his portrait.

Port Clinton, a suburb of Toledo, benefited from that town's mid-century rise in prosperity. In the 1950s Toledo was the home of seven Fortune 500 companies. Chrysler, Jeep, and GM also had a large manufacturing presence in the town. Putnam begins the story at Port Clinton's peak in 1959 when kids of different socioeconomic status had relatively equal opportunities for success. In tracing its decline, he examines how the fortunes of kids followed two divergent paths based on family income. The future for kids in low-income families would rest primarily on their schools for a ladder up and out of their conditions. LeeAnn, the principle in one of these towns, commented, "What can you do when the business leaves but the people stay?"

When Putnam writes that, in that time, most people had "social airbags," he describes a culture that was once common in factory towns, newly minted suburbs, and ethnic urban neighborhoods. Those airbags seemed to deploy evenly to kids from any part of town.

I know about those airbags: I had many opportunities to take the wrong path in life or check out of school. But the community airbags—neighborhoods, schools, coaches, police, Boy Scouts, and churches—inflated, saving me from disaster. When towns like Port Clinton lost those airbags, the road to success for low-income kids became a harrowing ride down a mountain road that had no guardrails.

Part of the problem with the company towns was their dependence on the automakers in Detroit. The company towns popped up all along the distribution pipe of General Motors, Ford, and Chrysler dollars. But they didn't have a large and locally grown business community. The towns were tied to, and dependent upon, the fortunes of a remote industry. The shift to imported vehicles reduced, sometimes suddenly, the money in the pipeline. Then, because they had an insufficient presence of local businesses, the reduction of income turned the towns into sinkholes.

Responding to Change

In many ways, Columbus fit the profile of the Rust Belt towns, but with one big exception. Columbus was a real, integrated, community of stakeholders. They were neighbors. But the town was also hit by the same economic turbulence of that time. "Between 1989 and the early 1990s, Cummins survived near-bankruptcy and a hostile takeover attempt in a dramatic story of a community coming together."[3]

The company was two weeks from missing payroll when a local bank lent Cummins $30 million to get through to the other side. Because they were neighbors they had a deeper understanding of the risks and the stakes. The state, on the other hand, refused to provide any help to a $6 billion company. How does a small town bank take on such a high level of risk while the state of Indiana looks the other way? Because of the great deposit of social capital, Columbus was (and is) a "neighborly town."

How does a small town bank take on such a high level of risk while the state of Indiana looks the other way? Because of the great deposit of social capital; Columbus was (and is) a "neighborly town."

Unlike Port Clinton, Columbus's community and business leaders rallied and, through private investments of $1.7 billion, absorbed the shock and spurred enough entrepreneurial growth to add 9,000 jobs that other companies shed. While the unemployment rate in the region was 14 percent, it was 2 percent in Columbus.

The town's leaders knew that the ground had shifted. They clearly saw that it was time to re-examine their economic strategy and reinspect the foundation in education that had made Columbus so strong and allowed it to prosper over the previous 30 years.

Becoming Future Ready

Columbus has evolved from a city known for great schools and architecture to a future-ready, integrated learning community. When learning is cultivated and permeates the community, it generates a willingness to come together, talk openly, listen intently, think creatively, and mobilize. This is called social capital; we will circle back to it many times throughout this book. It is an asset that, when built up, is available to be drawn upon in times of crisis. It is often the only asset a community can draw upon when a crisis like the collapse of the Rust Belt strikes.

Columbus drew heavily against that reserve in the 1980s and came out of the crises determined never to take their investment in kids and schools for granted again. Learning is encoded into their DNA. Schools are integral components of community life, not isolated and elite silos.

Social capital is an asset that when built up is available to be drawn upon in times of crisis. It is often the only asset a community can draw upon when a crisis like the collapse of the Rust Belt strikes.

Our MindShift team visited other communities that came to recognize the untapped and uncultivated assets of community and rapidly moved to rebuild and restore their social capital. They worked to tear down the barriers between business, community leaders, parents, and schools; they placed kids and schools back into the center of their growth strategies. They faced the same challenge that J. Irwin Miller faced: How do you attract good families to unfamiliar towns with mediocre schools?

The Columbus story resonates because it is not about heroics. Miller's legacy is often confused with the architectural wonders spread across the town, or the success of Cummins. But those factors actually point to something deeper. Miller often said, "The process is more important than the product." His vision was a process and a framework that transcends individuals and the idiosyncrasies of communities.

The process explains that communities work when they discover what they share in common and when each citizen feels a stake in the community's success. That mindset takes a broad and long view. It takes more time on the front end, but delivers positive outcomes, and delivers them for a long time.

In 1972, Miller's view of stakeholder engagement exploded into public in his rebuttal to Milton Friedman's declaration that "There is one and only one social responsibility of business—to use its resources and engage in activities designed to increase its profits . . ."

Miller countered, "While some still argue that business has no social responsibility, we believe that our survival in the very long run is as dependent upon

Culture is what everyone (in a company, family, school, association, an athletic team, or any other group) does when leadership is not present, watching, or directing.

responsible citizenship in our communities and in the society, as it is on responsible technology, financial, and production performance."

The Columbus archipelago has not only preserved clarity of what it is to be good neighbors, but their near-death experience in the fallout of the Rust Belt gave them a new impetus to capture the cultural and organic treasures of their heritage. From this experience, they have also worked to make it a repeatable and scalable process for others.

Reform versus Culture

Culture is the real issue. It starts there. Culture is what everyone (in a company, family, school, association, an athletic team, or any other group) does when leadership is not present, watching, or directing. It represents, not the rules, but the collective set of "shared basic assumptions." Culture is the "habits of the heart."

Culture is rooted in community; it begins with people who have a common journey into common challenges, and who are focused on a common cause. But culture does not happen by accident and it can't go unattended. For towns like Port Clinton prosperity was the result of a rising tide, not a common cause. When crises hit there were no reserves of social capital to draw upon.

If we understand the real issue, we will also understand the real challenge. Schools reflect the community. Reform does not work when it assumes that schools are standalone places where kids get educated. Columbus understands that schools are both a microcosm of the community and catalysts for community enrichment. The Community School movement is just one sign that the tide is shifting back, "It's about bringing community back to our school systems and bringing schools back to our community," says Norman Browning, leader of the group, Local Schools for Local Children.[4]

The Reform Machine often hits communities with rigid "strategies for success" but soon finds it is no match for the existing culture's deep-rooted habits.

Vision not only means an inspired look into the future, it also means to see the present, clearly and realistically.

Sadly, the Reform Machine is in a hurry. As a result, it has created a low trust and high stakes culture. It operates in an artificial window of about three years before miracles must manifest or heads will roll. It brings us full circle to the dilemma of the Volkswagen syndrome.

Learning rarely happens outside the context of a safe and stable environment where teachers are emotionally connected to, and provide support and hope for, their kids. Columbus has preserved the lessons of civic engagement put into practice in the 1950s and still adapted with the times. It is impossible to navigate the future when our sense of the past is lost. Resilience and insight depend on that perspective. Vision not only means an inspired look into the future it also means to see the present, clearly and realistically. There could be no iPhone without an exiled Steve Jobs, just as there could be no Midwestern Mecca of Architecture without a failed school project.

The Choluteca Bridge of the Information Age

The Choluteca Bridge in Honduras is famous for two reasons. In 1998 it survived Hurricane Mitch in almost perfect condition, withstanding a year's worth of rain during seven days of that severe storm. Mitch also moved the Choluteca River away from the bridge and into a new channel, and erased the roadways on either side of the bridge. The bridge now stands as a curious monument to a powerful hurricane, but goes nowhere.

The next chapter, "Gutenberg to Google," describes a similar disruption considered by many as consequential to the invention of the printing press. Digital media has served as a disruptive innovation that has swept past one historic information-based enterprise after another, with one exception—education. The Education Machine is still a bridge for many but is in danger of becoming a curious monument to an antiquated notion of learning.

CHAPTER 6

Gutenberg to Google

If you run an education system based on standardization and conformity that suppresses individuality, imagination, and creativity, don't be surprised if that's what it does.

—Ken Robinson

The Education Machine is not weird or diabolical. It is just a system that, as Berwick says, is "perfectly designed to get the results that it is getting." It is the child of the Gutenberg revolution, a "continental divide" of history that marked the end of oral culture and established the power and dominance of the printed word. That DNA permeates everything within the Education Machine. The print era created (and still creates) systems designed for standardization and conformity. Clarity and consistency are what the printed word does best. That is not a bad thing. It is a tool, like a hammer. It is only "bad" when you need a screwdriver.

Consider Gutenberg's world. In 1455 Europe was a collection of disparate dialects, fiefdoms, parishes, villages, tribes, religious sects, overlords, and militias. The printed word enabled loose coalitions to "get on the same page." It brought about common language, common understanding, common purpose, and common standards. It enabled a new level of coordination and cooperation never before possible, and it did so marvelously well.

The Education Machine has provided a "perfectly designed" system for preparing people to function and excel in a Gutenberg world. Brian Dassler, Deputy Chancellor of Education Quality for one of the largest

> *We're stuck in a zone your model calls "well-schooled but poorly educated." We are meeting and exceeding requirements for testing, graduation levels, and college prep. But we're not producing twenty-first century–ready kids.*
> —Brian Dassler

school systems in the nation, gave me one of the best descriptions of the dilemma they face.

"We've done a decent job over the past 12 years raising our overall state performance from one of the bottom 10 to one of the top 10. But we're stuck in a zone your model calls 'well-schooled but poorly educated.' We are meeting and exceeding requirements for testing, graduation levels, and college prep. But we're not producing twenty-first-century–ready kids. Our progress has come from using a series of carrots and sticks to improve our accountability. That progress and movement offers a real trap. If the system is a washcloth we've been wringing every drop of water out of it. We are hitting the limits of how far we can go with this strategy and are already beginning to see some of the psychological and social-emotional costs as a result."

He also knew that to produce twenty-first-century kids requires teachers who are comfortable with the culture of learning, not only knowledgeable about the content. That culture meant moving away from carrot-and-stick incentives that used to work to coax kids into memorizing material and preparing for tests. The new skills of collaboration and creative problem solving would require new strategies that tap into intrinsic forms of motivation, what Dan Pink identifies as autonomy, mastery, and purpose.

Ultimately, it is futile to force a system to perform other than the way it is designed. For one thing, the system will punish efforts to change the culture. This dilemma is at the heart of why reform has not worked and will not work.

The Challenge to Google Immigrants

Schools are asking our teachers to prepare kids for a land they have never seen. "Gutenberg" and "Google" are not only technologies apart; they are worlds and mindsets apart. They are foreign lands; naturally they use foreign languages, governance, and rules for success. It's as if we are trying to teach French from a textbook, but with teachers who do not speak the language and have never traveled in France.

Dassler described his experience with teachers who try to function in a Google world: "They are not only uncomfortable with the new technology and technology in general, but suspicious of it. That is not how they learned and their experience is what they fall back on."

As he talked, I thought about my grandmother who immigrated to the United States from Tasmania in the early 1900s. A tall and intimidating woman, she spoke with a Margaret Thatcher accent and bluntness. Her son, my father, who also had an imposing presence, never challenged or tested her. She spoke English, but was not familiar with the American money system. Her solution? She put on a tough front going in and then held her hand out when she paid for something, expecting change and with the body language that said, "You had better not short-change me!"

I Don't Even Speak the Language!

Meredith had a lifelong dream of becoming a diplomat. Shortly after graduation she secured an entry-level job at the State Department. Meredith grew up with a deep appreciation for her parents' home countries and cultures: France and Germany. During college she studied French, German and Russian and excelled in European history. She has traveled the continent many times.

When she reported to work, the State Department immediately placed her in the diplomatic core to prepare for an embassy role. She was a standout with the unusual possibility of an assignment in the first year.

That day arrived, sooner than even Meredith expected. News came down that the Secretary of State had asked to meet with Meredith. She nervously took the elevator to the 10th floor and walked down a long, high-ceilinged, marbled hallway to the Secretary's office. She was greeted, "Please have a seat, Meredith."

"You have excelled in your work and are at the top of your class. Congratulations! We have what we think is a vital assignment for you and our country. In 30 days you'll be sent to . . ."

As the Secretary was speaking, Meredith excitedly imagined any of a number of European countries, even Russia.

". . . Pakistan." Meredith wasn't sure if she had heard correctly.

"It is a current hot spot; we need to rotate out some of the people who have been there for a while. You've adapted rapidly since you arrived. We think your energy and performance makes you the right person for the position."

Stunned, silent, and numb, Meredith cleared her throat and barely managed a whisper, "But Madame Secretary, I don't even speak the language."

Our colleges are among the best in the world. We're simply training them to provide the best nineteenth-century education possible. It's no wonder they are unprepared for a Google world.

We train teachers well. Our colleges are among the best in the world. We're simply training them to provide the best nineteenth-century education possible. It's no wonder they are unprepared for a Google world. Yes, they feel frustrated by a system that handcuffs them; *of course,* in time, they become cynical. The best teachers quit at a rate of 30 percent within six years! Their attrition rate is higher than the rate for police officers.

Digital Immigrants and Natives

Those born into a family (or a town, state, country, idea, etc.) will always view that identity with a natural sense of informality, proficiency, and confidence. That's because they are natives. Immigrants, on the other hand, have relocated to a strange and unknown place. Therefore, they must learn the language, geography, customs, money system, values, and other features of their new home.

Digital natives are generally understood as those born after 1998. They are the first generation in history that understands more about how the new world really works than those of us "in charge." In 10 years the 70 million young people in this cohort will be rewriting the world based on their Google worldview and skills. The rest of us will be left behind.

Think about the immigrants who settled in New York City during the early 1900s. Their kids or grandkids read the newspapers to the adults, translated English into their native tongue, or helped count the money needed and the change returned when they ventured out into the marketplace.

Fast-forward: if you're over 50 years old, you have probably asked a child to set up a smartphone, program the stereo, or simply set the digital clocks on the appliances. The kids, of course, did it quickly and without any need for instructions. In 2002 I bought my first iPod. It was white, had an aluminum frame, was slightly bigger than a deck of cards, and had a circular touch dial on the front. It also had a small gray-tone LED display. Daniel, 10 years old at the time, was fascinated by it. So I let him play with my iPod as a way to get it set up. After a few hours he came bounding down the stairs into my office; I heard excitement and a bit of mischief in his voice.

"Hey dad! I can turn this into a video iPod!" My anxiety rose. I had no clue what this meant at the time and like an immigrant I said, "No way, you might break it and I'm sure that's not covered in the warranty."

Daniel looked confused. I've seen that look many times in the years since that day. It means, *What, you don't get it?* He handed over the iPod and said, "Gee dad, it's just a Linux program, no big deal."

We're really not that different from the immigrants of past generations.

In 2013, I delivered the keynote address to the 49th Annual Associated Schools of Construction International Conference. The audience included over 200 professors and deans. I spoke on "How to Teach When the Students Are Smarter Than You." Of course, it stirred conversation and debate. Many admitted their discomfort and said that they really did not know how best to teach these kids. Some pushed back, thinking that anything less than keeping the role of the expert would compromise their influence and control over the outcomes of the class.

The Gutenberg Revolution

Gutenberg had no idea what effect his printing press, made from a winepress, would have on the rise and future of Western civilization. His first project, ironically, was to print indulgences for the Catholic Church. These were small slips of paper that functioned like coupons; parishioners bought them from the Church as a means of getting their more commonplace sins forgiven.

The historical breakthrough and subsequent cultural revolution occurred when Gutenberg reproduced a full bible, including the ornate illuminated images and calligraphic letters. What once took a monastic scribe two years to reproduce by hand was achieved in two weeks by the printing press—a 98 percent reduction in time and cost.

In fewer than 70 years more than 1,000 printing presses were operating across Europe. We have never in history seen, within a span of 150 years, the simultaneous intensity of innovation in art, science, religion, exploration, commerce education, and that period's crowning achievement—the nation state, a government formed on an idea and constituted by commonly held principles.

Clay Shirky commented in 2009, "1650 was closer in spirit to the time we live in now than it was to 1450. The change was so enormous, but what was also clear is that there was never a moment when everybody said, 'Oh I get it. This is what the printing press is going to do.'"[1]

The Google Revolution

The current Google revolution is having a chaotic, conflictive, and disruptive effect that is similar to Gutenberg's printing press, multiplied across the globe. We've seen six-year-old million-dollar entrepreneurs, the rapid rise and burst of a global financial bubble, governments dethroned, a new kind of warfare that still confounds our best minds, and a 2016 presidential campaign season that is convulsing the political structures. All of these represent the fallout of a Google revolution. Shirky rightly concludes, ". . . the old model breaks faster than the new model gets put in its place, and I think we are in for a lot of that."

On January 9, 2007, Steve Jobs walked onto the stage of MacWorld and announced three new products. "The first one is a wide-screen iPod with touch controls. The second is a revolutionary mobile phone. And the third is a breakthrough Internet communications device."

He then summarized, repeating three times, ". . . an iPod; a phone, an Internet communicator . . ." and after the third refrain he asks, "are you getting it?" Not yet, they had not pieced it together. "These are not three separate devices, this is one device . . . today Apple is going to reinvent the phone . . ." The audience went crazy. That 14-minute presentation by Jobs is certainly worth watching today.

I often ask audiences to list the numerous ways that they use their smartphone. The answers come back: texting; travel directions; flight reservations; music; games; counting calories; alarm clock; banking; hotel reservations; transportation plans; video conferencing; reading; listening to books; taking classes; watching movies, sports, and news . . .

The top uses for mobile phones in order are: texting, Internet browsing, photography, social media, and alarm clock. Oh, and phone calls (in seventh place).[2]

More important, how has this *mobile phone world* changed the way you live? This is an important question; if we grasp and fully understand how it has not only reordered our lives but also reprogramed our habits and rewired our brains, we can better appreciate what kids experience in the classroom and the vast disconnect between their personal world and their school world.

> *Jamie Casap asked, "Who can name the first five presidents of the United States?" Everyone in the room suddenly seemed uncomfortable. Jaime then asked the group, "What if I said I'll give you 30 seconds to look it up? How many of you could get the answer right?" Everyone in the room raised his or her hand!*

Jamie Casap, Global Education Evangelist for Google, asked our EdShift 2016 audience, "Who can name the first five presidents of the United States?" Everyone in the room suddenly seemed uncomfortable. Jaime then asked the group, "What if I said I'll give you 30 seconds to look it up? How many of you could get the answer right?" Everyone in the room raised his or her hand!

The point Jaime was making is that no one would think twice about using a calculator to find the answer to a hard math problem. In the early 1970s, however, that was a contentious educational debate.

After ticking off the many uses of mobile phones, I sometimes ask audiences, "How many of you keep it next to you on your bed stand? How many of you look at it just before going to sleep or check it just as you wake up?" Most hands go up. If it is that central to how we live, just think how much more it is embedded in the lives of our kids. Why would we not only allow mobile phones into classrooms but also integrate them into our kid's learning?

Because we are digital immigrants. It's that simple.

Disrupting a Linear World with Logarithmic Change

How did the iPhone burst onto the world stage, seemingly out of nowhere? Why did the competition not anticipate it? One simple answer: Moore's law.

The pace of chance is increasing exponentially, and students today are learning skills for jobs that do not currently exist. Learning must include the ability to adapt, collaborate, and bounce back in a world of flux.
—Brian Cahill, California Division President for Balfour Beatty

In 1965, Gordon Moore, one of the founders of Intel, observed that the computing power of a microchip was doubling approximately every 18 months at equal or less cost. That observation has become codified as Moore's law.

Moore's law states that when a number repeatedly doubles, it quickly outstrips our ability to calculate the new total and comprehend its size. A logarithm is a mathematical device to calculate and understand the trajectory of that compounded growth.

For example, I often ask kids, "Would you rather have a penny that will double its total value each day over thirty days or a million dollars today?" Most kids will take the million dollars. When I ask the same question of my adult audiences, most know that this is a trick question and pick the penny. However, I then ask why, because at day 27 the million dollars still looks like the better deal. The penny doubled is only $671,000. Day 28 is the "wow," when it doubles to over a million, and then doubles two more times to over $5 million.

When we apply this analogy to business our linear brains grasp improvement and growth for perhaps one, two, and three years into the future. We lack the capacity to accurately imagine 10 to 20 years out. That means we have a natural bias to work on things that show short-term improvements. We can't see the invisible power of compounded growth. If we could, we would have all invested our pennies and become millionaires.

This is exactly what happened to Kodak. In 1975 Steve Sasson, a Kodak engineer, invented the first digital camera with an image resolution of .001 megapixels. Your current smartphone probably has a resolution in the range of 10 megapixels. As you can imagine, his bosses were unimpressed. It was like going to them and saying, "Hey, I've got one-tenth of a penny and if we keep doubling this penny we'll be rich!"

In 1989 Sasson and another Kodak engineer invented the first commercially viable digital camera. This time his bosses were impressed but uninterested because growing digital photography would over-shadow their huge film business.

In the meantime Moore's law was working in the background. The .001 megapixel was doubling in capacity and costs were lowering until 1995: eight iterations of improvement. That is when Casio introduced the first consumer digital camera with a .256 megapixel resolution. That is all that it took! Kodak's fate was sealed when the company stayed with its proven product instead of taking a risk on an innovation that occurred within their own company. This is an important example for any organization that ignores Moore's law.

This now explains why the competition missed the iPhone. Nokia, Motorola, Palm, and Blackberry focused on incremental improvement and were on track up until the imaginary 28th day.

Steve Jobs said they had been working for years on several elements: hard drives, telecommunications, software, user interface, and Internet capabilities. All of these elements were getting smaller, faster, and less expensive at a compounded rate. At some point in the development cycle Apple was able to integrate these into a single revolutionary new category of device and experience.

For this reason, 1,700 CEOs said that the number one thing that keeps them up at night is finding ways to innovate; in other words, they have to fight to stay ahead of Moore's law.[3] In 1960 the average life span of an S&P 500 company was 60 years. In 2015 it was about 13 years with a continued declining curve in the life span. Ten years ago, news of one of these companies folding shocked us. Now we simply take the news in stride. The average life span of a corporate CEO is under four years. There is no forgiveness in business. It must adapt to keep pace with Moore's law or die.

Unfortunately the kind of logarithmic innovation we have been referring to is ignored by education. Every information business on the planet has been leveled by the dramatic decrease in cost of information and the equally dramatic increase in access. Education should be no exception.

It used to cost me up to $60 to take a cab 12 miles to the airport. With Uber it is $22.50 with no tip. Why is it that in 1973 the cost of my in-state tuition at the University of Illinois was $495 a year, and today it is $15,000? In 1973 the average cost for an elementary student was $1,300; in 2015 it is estimated at $12,000.[4]

This chapter focused on the jump from Gutenberg to Google. Despite the historic importance of television, I left it out because the

Education Machine still deeply reflects its Gutenberg roots and heritage. But you will see television along with oral culture provided in the matrix.

The next chapter considers five dominant communication platforms that have shaped history and culture: oral, print, broadcast, digital, and social–mobile.

The matrix of platforms, coupled with categories such as learning, art, education, leadership, and others, should help to provide a good understanding of the profound shift to a digital (Google) platform. That matrix will further explain the disruption of the Gutenberg universe and how and why learning is undergoing a radical transformation.

CHAPTER 7

The Learning Matrix

Mapping the Five Eras of Learning

History becomes an astonishing succession of new media toppling old empires by repatterning perceptions of time and space.[1]
—Michael Schrage

W e all know that communication tools change over time. But we often miss the invisible and profound ways those changes bring to the way we think and how we go about our lives. To illustrate that, I sometimes ask my audiences about their cell phones prior to 2007 (the year before the iPhone was introduced). The answers usually describe the phone itself (gray brick, black flip phone, etc.)

"What did you use your phone for?" Of course, all the answers refer to phone calls.

"Do you remember roaming charges?" They all nod in affirmation and some share stories of learning the hard way the expense of making calls outside their call area.

"Okay, now what about your smartphone? What do you use it for?"

The answers are as numerous and diverse as the people in the room. They call out, "Maps, photos, Facebook, listening to music, texting, web searching, navigation, banking, ordering food, Uber, booking a hotel,

Facetime, listening to audio books, Pandora, tracking fitness, checking my home security . . ." The list of uses seems endless.

In fact, using a smartphone to make phone calls ranks *seventh* behind: alarm clock, social media, photography, Internet browsing, reading (including e-mails), and the number one use, texting.[2]

Here's another question I often ask, "Who have you met or reconnected with through some form of social media?" I am often astonished at the number of stories of new relationships, even marriages. Others located family members and former school friends and acquaintances.

My point here is one profound truth: this new social–mobile media is repatterning our perceptions of time, space, relationships, and abilities. It is already toppling old empires. The visible dramatic ones like the Arab Spring are the least significant. There are deeper shifts taking place inside our inner world. Here is how it works:

- When our communication tools change, our perceptions change.
- Changed perceptions create changes in our understanding.
- Changed understanding changes our psychological makeup.
- Changed psyches change our interaction with the world.
- Changes in our interactions with the world change our relationships to one another.[3]
- Changes in our relationships lead to new forms and ways of collective activity.
- New ways of collective activity lead to new institutions or platforms to facilitate collective efforts.

When the primary means of storing and distributing information changes, everything changes. We can see clear dividing lines in culture, society, commerce, and education/learning when a new media emerges to dominate the communication landscape. The ripple effect marches unevenly with a few institutions anchoring society and adapting. But many are breaking down or being swept away altogether.

When the primary means of storing and distributing information changes, everything changes.

This chapter surveys five eras, each shaped by a dominant means of communication: the spoken word, the mass reproduction of the printed word, the broadcast-image word, the digital-multimedia word, and the emerging social-mobile word.[4] It concludes with a two-page summary grid of the five eras.

Toppling Old Empires

Seventy years after Gutenberg invented moveable type, Martin Luther challenged the old order of ceremonial and royal authority when he posted his 95 Theses. It would take another 130 years of conflict, war, and upheaval for a new order of society to emerge with the Treaty of Westphalia.

It would be another 300 years before television would pose a similar challenge to a print-dominated world. Television grew from 9 percent of homes in 1950 to 90 percent by 1960.[5] In 1960 we saw a political earthquake in the presidential campaign. Richard Nixon, the Republican nominee, had served two terms as vice president, the most influential vice president in history to that point. He also served under one of the most popular presidents in modern history, Dwight Eisenhower. But those credentials were undone in one broadcast.[6] On September 26, 1960, Nixon and John F. Kennedy spoke on television in the first live broadcast presidential debate. Kennedy understood the medium. He looked into the camera, smiled, and provided summary statements. It also helped that he was young and telegenic. Nixon dismissed the power of the medium and told his aids that substance would win over style. We all know the outcome of that presidential campaign.

Over the next 15 years, American society experienced a dramatic restructuring of social and civic values, the failure of respected institutions (such as the military in Vietnam and the presidency with the Watergate scandal), and a profound culture shift.

By 1992, the Internet was available to anyone with a computer and modem. Internet access grew at a similar rate as television and in 2013 reached 90 percent of U.S. households.[7] Barack Obama became the first president in the social media age.[8] His 2008 victory over Hillary Clinton in the Democratic primaries reflected an updated version of the contest between a young, fresh, media-savvy Kennedy and the establishment candidate, Nixon, who played by old rules. Of course, the cultural and civic disruption was no longer only an American experience; it spread globally.

The iPhone issued a challenge to the "old" order just as we are regaining our balance from the overthrow of print and broadcast. When Steve Jobs launched the iPhone 2007, it fundamentally shifted how information would be stored and distributed. It held more computing power than NASA had possessed when it landed a man on the moon in 1969. The growth of cloud computing now frees storage from our phones, computers, and other devices. The continued exponential improvement and miniaturization of processing capabilities makes all these devices more portable and more affordable. In 2013 more than 143 million people in the United States, and 17 percent of the global population, owned smartphones!

Education as an institution has been able to insulate its power structure and preserve its mindset and traditions from a rapidly changing world.

The Pattern of Technological Change

What does all of this have to do with education and learning?

First, education as an institution has been able to insulate its power structure and preserve its mindset and traditions from a rapidly changing world. Many parents have seen that most teachers are uncomfortable using new media in the classroom and that our curriculum and tools are decades behind the experience students have the moment they step outside the school and pull out their smartphone.

Second, just because it feels insulated does not mean that its power, influence, and effectiveness is secure. In fact the battles over reform, testing, choice, and charters going on across the country are simply the first challengers coming through the widening breach of irrelevance.

Third, social–mobile media is a tool. A powerful tool but it follows the same principles as a screwdriver, hammer, and other tools; they work best when used as designed. What seems obvious when using a screwdriver or hammer seems lost when we use digital media tools. For example, using a tablet merely as an electronic book misses the point. Why not use it for its interactive capabilities, its social dimension, its ability to cut, paste, reframe, and to link to information?

Taking a closer look at these media–defined dividing lines (eras) will help us better understand why our Gutenberg-designed education system came under challenge in the 1950s and has been continuously assaulted ever since. It will also help define a strategy for change and a method for adapting to future shifts. Maybe it can also help us redefine what success for the future might look like and how to measure it.

It seems clear that the mindset that created our intelligence testing in the early 1900s, and then academic achievement assessments in the 1920s, was designed to work within a Gutenberg context where mastering content was highly valued and useful. Shifting our sights and preparations so we can compete with the other OECD countries on PISA seems like a distraction from the goal of understanding learning within the context of a social-mobile world. The PISA standards were designed in the 1950s and simply reflect a more rigorous, comprehensive, and globally measured assessment. Even if PISA standards are an improvement over the current U.S. assessments, they were still designed with the same Gutenberg mindset.

Why Would I Send My Kid to Your School?

In 2005 I was asked to speak to one of the departments of a small private college. Tuition at the college that time was $30,000 a year. The dean was concerned because recruiting was showing signs of softening. The college had to provide more and deeper scholarships to keep attendance levels from declining. He felt his department was stuck in the wrong kind of thinking about how to improve the college's offerings. Debate centered on offering "more interesting" topics, opposed by those who felt these would only dilute the quality and reputation of the school. There was no interest in considering that a deeper or larger shift might be taking place.

I presented a similar historical matrix to the one I'll be providing later in the chapter. They all felt it was interesting, compelling, and worthy of consideration. That wasn't the response I was hoping for. I could feel the dean's dilemma. I reached into my backpack and pulled out my fourth-generation Classic model iPod. It was about the size of a deck of cards, with an LCD readout on the upper third and Apple's patented click wheel. I held it up and asked how many owned an iPod. Only one person in the room owned any kind of MP3 player.

"What is this thing I'm holding in my hand?" I got a few answers like "music player" or "a hard drive."

"What does it do?" I got a few more answers like "plays music, plays audio books, creates libraries of content," and "personalizes your listening."

"Why is this significant?" Now the room was almost mute.

So I gave them my finale. "This device is my on–demand content provider. I can listen to what I want, when I want, where I want as often as I want. I can download books, lectures, sermons, podcasts, and music. I can theoretically get the best content in the world on any subject I may be interested in. For the past 40 minutes you've shared with me that your primary value as professors and as a college is the quality of your teaching, your *content*. If I can now get the best content in the world and listen to it on my terms, then why would I pay $30,000 a year to send my child here? What is your value proposition in a content-abundant world?

Remember, this was back in 2005. Those devices were relatively new and for some in the room completely new. I had challenged some sacred assumptions about the purpose of their institution, their value to society and their personal worth. They didn't like it and they expressed that opinion. I told them that the value of learning has irreversibly shifted away from acquiring content to the experience or context.

> *We all—scientists and teachers— seem to be trapped within the silos of our disciplines and the dominant media environment that shaped us.*

This story simply illustrates the challenge we all face in the process of becoming experts within a system of knowledge or practice. Our success is built on mastering the disciplines of that particular domain—and mindset. We're trapped in Einstein's observation that, "No problem can be solved by the same level of consciousness that created it." Thomas Kuhn, the author of *The Structure of Scientific Revolution*, put it this way. "Under normal conditions the research scientist is not an innovator but a solver of puzzles, and the puzzles upon which he concentrates are just those that he believes can be both stated and solved within the existing scientific tradition.[9]" Do you think this statement might apply as much to education as it does to science? We all—scientists and teachers—seem to be trapped within the silos of our disciplines and the dominant media environment that shaped us.

The System's Logic Drives Behavior

Education is currently trying to define twenty-first-century skills. When you look at many of those skills they follow a Google worldview logic. We are almost 20 percent into the century and the Google worldview and logic are already shifting to a new worldview and logic. It is the worldview of a social-mobile culture and is rapidly building to a new inflection point with embedded sensor technology and the Internet of Things.

The value of the Learning Matrix is that it provides a framework for understanding the invisible internal logic that drives organizational, institutional, or even national culture. The movie *The Matrix* carries a parallel message. Neo is a programmer by day, a puzzle master within the system. At night he is a hacker attempting to find answers to deeper doubts and questions about his boring and unfulfilling life. His hacking leads him to Morpheus, the one who may have the answers to his questions. But he is also considered enemy number one by the ruling system. The story is Neo's journey to break out of the system by discovering the hidden logic (the Architect) that runs it. In doing so, Neo exposes the artificial constraints on those who are content to comply. The system attacks and has power as long as Neo's mind remains a part of the system. Neo only breaks out by overcoming a series of these assaults until in the final scene his mind exerts its will over the system by saying "No" to a final attack. He withstands this final barrage and in that moment sees the source code, the internal logic. He is no longer governed by what drives the system but now has mastery over it. Neo restores the proper order, humanizing the machine.

> *The Gutenberg legacy is incapable of advancing the mission to produce twenty-first-century ready kids. The costs are unsustainable in light of what technology can accomplish. We continue to repackage reform and try it again while expecting different results. We are now starting to go backward. We have an increasing number of at-risk kids.*

It's a universal story. The things we create to serve us can become the enslaving monsters that rule and destroy us. The Education Machine has become that enslaving monster because we accept it's internal logic without question and we feed it what it wants. The Learning Matrix puts the monster back into its cage. It is a tool to serve us, not a master to be served.

The Tipping Point for Education

I believe we stand at a tipping point with education. The Gutenberg legacy is incapable of advancing the mission to produce twenty-first-century-ready students. The costs are unsustainable in light of what technology can accomplish. We continue to repackage reform and try it again while expecting different results. We are now starting to go backward. We have an increasing number of at-risk kids.

Candi Dearing, principal at Sarasota Middle School, shared a story of what occurred during her time at Celebration High School in Celebration, Florida. Celebration is a master-planned community originally built by the Disney Development Company. Imagine driving into a small community that looks like the movie set in *The Truman Show*. This small town of under 4,000 attracted affluent families with a median annual income of around $95,000.

The community invested several million dollars and two years investigating what a world-class education might look like. The team had traveled the world to see what was possible in creating the best learning experience possible. In partnership with Disney the school would have access to top chefs, scientists, and designers to teach and provide learning experiences that no other school could offer. The community, including Disney, was excited. But when the proposal was shared with the parents they reacted against it.

Why?

One stand-out comment from a parent went like this, "This is not how I got into Harvard and you are not going to try this experiment on my child!" When you consider the fact that Celebration is a recreation of the ideal Middle American suburb, then you realize that parents did not move to Celebration in order to be different. They moved there to relive and recreate a time and an experience from the past.

Parents often react to new ideas, such as project-based learning. Their first question might be, "Will these help my child get good test scores?" Parents feel great pressure to keep pace with their kids' education. It is comforting for them to see that school doesn't look all that different from the school they attended. It doesn't take much to push them outside their comfort zone.

We created the Learning Matrix to understand how much the world has changed. We also contrast that with how little the school experience has changed. Perhaps, by looking at some of these inflection points, we can let go of our attachment to the familiar and get to work reframing what learning looks like in a world that is driven by complexity, exponential change, and an increasingly interconnected world.

The Oral World

"The magic of oral culture lies in intimate connection. The dividing lines—between art and religion and science and literature—don't exist in the same way they do in our visually mediated rational world."[10] In oral culture, learning was experienced through dialogue, discovery, mentoring, and apprenticeship. Elders held a revered position as repositories of tradition, knowledge, and wisdom. People lived in a three-mile-an-hour world and it typically encompassed the distance they could travel in a day. Life and learning held a close link. Walter Ong wrote that speech (in oral culture) owns a unique quality of immediacy and intimacy. It naturally draws you closer. The tradition of mentoring and apprenticeship that oral culture formed defines the highly relational quality of learning. This kind of life-forming, life-affirming experience that some of us had through an extended relationship with a teacher, coach, or an influential adult was once commonplace. In this respect the message and messenger become unified.

Years ago, I drove past the Anatole Hotel in Dallas with my friend Don, who was a master brick mason. Although he had never seen, and knew nothing about, the Anatole, he identified the project's master mason by the way the bricks were laid. That opened a deeper conversation about exactly what it takes to become a master brick mason. Part of the training through Apprenticeship to Journeyman is to learn the technique of your master mason so completely that a master's eye could not see the difference between your work and the signature technique of the master mason. Once you reach the level of master mason, you build on the tradition, improve it, and over time, create your own signature technique. We more clearly see this in the traditions of art or classical music composers like the lineage of Beethoven, Cherny, and Liszt.

The Printed Word and Individual Learning

"The development of the printing press signaled the world's first step into mass communication, arguably the most profound dividing point in history. The general population stood on the same informational foundation as kings and popes."[11] Print separated the message from the messenger. It shifted learning from its immersion in context and life to content and intellectual thought. Print locks ideas onto a page and freezes time. It offers the ability to reexamine, analyze, break apart, and reconstitute ideas. It captures the past and creates a springboard to build forward. It moves our time awareness away from rhythms and cycles and toward a linear mindset that sees time as progressive. Print standardizes thinking so we can "all sing from the same sheet of music." It shifts the experience from an aural collective intimacy to visual privacy. It birthed the era of the individual, as set apart from his or her kin or tribe.

Walter Ong captured this distinctive shift: "the individual finds it possible to think through a situation more from within his own mind out of his own personal resources and in terms of an objectively analyzed situation, which confronts him. He becomes more original and individual, detribalized."[12]

Victor Hugo's novel *The Hunchback of Notre Dame* was written in 1831. The story took place 400 years earlier, in the time of Gutenberg's invention. Hugo expressed not only how the Catholic clergy felt over print as the new medium toppling its empire, but also how leaders in a previous order felt when their domain is overtaken. "The book will destroy the Edifice. . . . The press will kill the church." Print dramatically changed the world and quickly led to one of the most prolific periods of innovation in human history. The inquiring dialectic mind soon converts to the rational analytical mind. Hugo's epitaphs to the institutions of oral culture remind us that the same fate awaits every institutional era. As Hugo wrote in *The Hunchback of Notre Dame*, "It was the cry of the prophet who already hears emancipated humanity roaring and swarming; who beholds in the future, intelligence sapping faith, opinion dethroning belief, the world shaking off Rome."

The Broadcast Word Brings Edutainment

I was born in 1955 and was part of the first generation that was raised immersed in broadcast. My first media language is broadcast, my second is print (the language of school), and my third language is digital media. "These kids, raised in the language of television but schooled in the language of print, labored each day in the restrictive world of school. Three o'clock brought relief from the rigors of an oppressive print regime. Television, on the other hand, demanded nothing but instead gave a continuous stream of pictures to entertain and open the world. School had their bodies, but television captured their hearts and minds."[13]

The broadcast era does not mark a radical shift in the delivery of education. It does mark the time when kids began to mentally check out of school. I don't think it is education's fault altogether. Broadcast's power comes from two factors: centralized control of the means of production and a message that is crafted for the widest possible audience or the lowest common denominator.

Two shows provide a window into what edutainment might look like in a pure broadcast world. The first is *Sesame Street*, which debuted in 1969 and reached up to 7 million households. The second is *Blues Clues*, which launched in 1996 and after two years was seen in almost 5 million households. *Sesame Street* optimized broadcast's ability to entertain. Each show was a fragmented collage of short vignettes. Characters provided the thematic continuity for the show. The show's humor was often nuanced and adult. It also followed a variety show format. *Sesame Street* made it appealing to adults as well as children. However, it did not have a significant effect on learning until the show shifted away from the fragmented vignette format to a single theme approach in the mid–1990s.

Blues Clues, on the other hand, followed a radically different strategy and proved more effective as a broadcast vehicle for learning. The show had two characters, Blue, the dog, and Steve. It followed a single narrative. The dialogue was slow and demonstrative. But why was it more effective than *Sesame Street?*

The same episode was shown the entire week, five days in a row. Research found that this format for pre-K kids worked better. In the first viewing a child would catch the theme. Another viewing allowed the child to follow the story, a third showing begins to uncover clues and so forth until the child has absorbed and integrated the lesson.

Digital Connected Learning and the Power of Engagement

One great challenge for schools is that kids live in a media–rich world but go to class, for the most part, in an environment of Gutenberg-bound tools and experience. We could bridge this gap if we better understood the underlying ethos of digital media.

"Digital-connected learning" takes us back to the past and simulates the future. It is the first medium combining text, sound, image and data. It is inherently synthesizing. Digital media possess attributes of oral culture's relational and intimate discovery, print's highly rational and abstract power of analysis along with broadcast's light touch of stimulating streaming novelty. It packages these three experiences within a hyperlinked structure of seren-dipitous discovery and social interaction. Digital media is multisensory and multimodal. Oral culture produced a holistic and integrated mind. Digital media allows one to connect data and patterns in ways that simulate system's thinking and the development of arche-typal patterns and language found in oral culture. The general (global) pop-ulation can now read, listen or watch the best minds, talent, or moments either one-on-one or one-to-many. Consider, for a moment, the implica-tions to anyone who understands the social impact and has access to an Inter-net connection.

Digital media opens up the world through search. Search then leads to connecting. When connected communication becomes interconnected, it leads to dialogue and sharing and then to cooperation. Cooperation leads to creating together; that grows into collaboration. Collaboration leads to community.

[Kids] no longer grind out their lessons by rote memorization. They no longer sit passively in front of a television and say, "Huh?" when asked what they learned. Children are absorbed in an interactive-game environment, pursuing treasure hunts of knowledge over the Web.[14]

Digital media opens up the world through search. Search then leads to connecting. When connected communication becomes intercon-nected, it leads to dialogue and sharing and then to cooperation. Cooperation leads to creating together; that grows into collaboration. Collaboration leads to community. Does the experience in most of our classrooms facilitate this progression of learning?

Social-Mobile and Personalized Learning

When I first produced this matrix in 2004, social-mobile learning did not exist. However, the same logic applies. What is inherently different with social-mobile learning is the increasing capability to personalize your experience and become a traceable node within a global network (the quantified self). I share examples in the chapter "What Every Adult Needs to Know About the Future."

But, let me share one story that illustrates what happens when our familiarity with the past causes us to miss the demands of the present.

While sitting at an outdoor table at a street café, I overheard four mothers at a nearby table discuss their frustration over the difficulty of getting their kids to put away their smartphones and do their homework. When I told them I was writing a book about education, they allowed me into their conversation. They explained that their kids would rather text, listen to music, and browse their phones than read and memorize their homework. They all agreed that taking away the smartphones and restricting use to the weekends was the answer. They asked my opinion.

I asked the mothers how much they used their smartphones. Two women were checking messages on their smartphones while they were talking to one another. I asked, "What if your children's phones were integrated into their learning as one of the key tools? What if social interaction was designed into the lesson as a way of collaborating and testing one another?"

My questions represented a bridge too far. Unfortunately it is a bridge too far for most schools, too. I'm not claiming that smartphones are the answer or that there are not some deep and serious issues regarding their addictive use. My first-grade teacher, Mrs. Stavoe, taught us how to hold a pencil, how to form our letters, and how to write sentences. We also worked to recognize and sound out words and then form them into sentences. These were our primary tools for learning. I heard one educator say that from first grade until third grade we learn to read and then going forward we read to learn. I have yet to see a teacher or a classroom consider a smartphone as a tool for learning and meticulously teach students how to use this tool to that end. Yet it is the most ubiquitous device that students and their teachers live with.

The five time frames in the following matrix offer insight into how and why learning has shifted and will continue to shift. I hope it also makes clear case that education needs to break loose of its Gutenberg worldview if it hopes to re-engage kids and create future-ready students.

The Learning Matrix expands on this exploration in a table format to better draw out the contrasts of each period. It is an abbreviated version with short descriptions as an overview. If you're interested in the long-form table you can download it by going to www.humanizethemachine .school. Go to the Resources section and click on The Learning Matrix (the password is MATRIX).

The Learning Matrix

	Oral/Relational Learning BC–AD 1650	Typographic/Structured Learning 1650–1955	Broadcast/Interest Learning 1955–2005	Connected/Active Learning 2005–2015	Mobile/Personalized Learning 2015–
Understanding	Look deep inside: insight	Look deep outside: facts	Trust instincts: compile opinions	Look at context to re-contextualize	Post impressions to get reactions
Truth	Relationally connected	Principle-based	An inner sense validates	Wisdom of the crowd—Wiki	What works for me
Learning	Life learning	Content learning	Experience learning	Collaborative learning	Discovery learning
How We Know	The whole	The parts	The fragments and chaos	The system	The algorithm
Self Knowledge	Tribe	Individual	Audience	Participant	Quantified
Timeframe	Present tense	Past tense	Future tense	Future-perfect tense	Virtual time travel
Mode of Reasoning	Dialectic	Logic	Ideation	Systems thinking	Iteration and prototyping
Worldview	Theocentric	Newtonian	Einsteinian: macrocosm	Bohmian: microcosm	Kurzweilian: singularity
Sense of Progress	Cyclical	Historical	The new: novelty	Logarithmic: inflexion points	Convergent

(continued)

The Learning Matrix (*continued*)

	Oral/Relational Learning BC–AD 1650	Typographic/Structured Learning 1650–1955	Broadcast/Interest Learning 1955–2005	Connected/Active Learning 2005–2015	Mobile/Personalized Learning 2015–
Collective Memory	Bard	Book	Documentary	Database	Facebook
Positions we honor	Elders: repository of history and wisdom	Expert: credentialed and proven	Personality and youth: appeal and novelty	Innovator/Designer: redefining our experiences	Social entrepreneur: integration of meaning
Authority & Leadership	Ordained or rule of might	Credibility or Control	Relevancy or Influence	Resonance or Catalyst	Innovator or world changer
Influence	Position	Credentials	Impression	Empower	By doing
Commitment	Covenant	Contract	Agreement	Reciprocity	Community
Art	Symbolic	Perspective	Conceptual	Interactive	Emersion
Management	Steward	Manager	Leader	Collaborator	Network connector
Wealth Base	Land	Capital	Distribution and debt	Intellectual property	Platform
Work Metaphor	Farm	Factory	Service	High tech	Free agent
What is Valued	Reliability	Productivity	Quality	Creativity	Agility
Exchange Medium	Barter or trade	Currency	Bank credit	Virtual exchange	Bitcoin

CHAPTER 8

The Pandorification of Learning

The Future Is Here

> *Communications tools don't get socially interesting until they get technologically boring. . . . It's when a technology becomes normal, then ubiquitous, and finally so pervasive as to be invisible, that the really profound changes happen.*
>
> —Clay Shirky[1]

M y first impression of Dr. Page Dettmann was that I had met a quiet and reflective academic. But within the first minute I saw her flip a switch and turn into a fast-thinking, checklist-driven, visionary trailblazer on a mission to transform learning.

Our MindShift team met the Sarasota County (Florida) Executive Director of Middle Schools when we arrived in Sarasota for a summit on the future of learning. We heard about the results in Dettmann's seven schools, representing close to 6,000 students. Our 60 educators, futurists, architects, and other specialists knew that the success of her middle schools has become a nationally prominent model. Naturally, we were eager to spend a day with Dr. Dettmann, her team, and her kids to study their progress after three years of a radical shift in teaching and engagement.

Sarasota, with a population of just over 50,000, has a large retirement community; the city is often called "God's waiting room." It is also known as a coastal city, with affordable housing and respected opera, ballet, and other visual arts. *U.S. News* had recently ranked Sarasota as the 14th-most-livable city in America. Tourism, health care, and construction provided the economic base but the community needed to build on emerging industries to make it more attractive to young families. Marine science, Ringling College of Art and Design's digital arts program, health innovations, and performance sports offered a new growth trajectory and a new image. In order to create this new future their schools would have to excel, especially in the STEM (science, technology, engineering, and math) curriculum.

In 2009 community and school leaders looked closely at troubling statistics. Sarasota schools ranked as barely average and students showed little interest in STEM. The leaders knew that middle school was the point where achievement began to fall and kids began to drop out of school. Fifty percent of students in the county received free or reduced lunch (that number ranges between 35 and 85 percent from school to school). Sarasota was like many other communities: great wealth was concentrated in a few gated areas and the majority of the citizens struggled. The leaders could see that good schools—more important, twenty-first-century ready schools—were vital to Sarasota's well-being and future.

Dr. Dettmann, with the partnership of Mark Pritchett and the Gulf Coast Community Foundation, felt that transforming the middle schools provided a linchpin strategy and a place to test new concepts before scaling a program for the district. 2010 became a year of discovery, learning, visiting, strategizing, and prototyping. Mark described it as similar to IDEO's Design Thinking approach. The program they developed is called STEMSmart with an emphasis on math and science.

None of the kids looked up. They were deeply engaged in learning. They seemed oblivious of 35 adults roaming throughout the room, exploring and kneeling down for a closer look at the equipment and activities taking place. One of our team educators observed, "We were the least interesting thing in the room."

Two things immediately stood out when we walked into the first classroom of our tour. First, the furniture was dramatically different from what we were accustomed to seeing in traditional classrooms. Instead of rows of student desks facing the teacher's front and center desk, each classroom was furnished with a half dozen pods (table and chair clusters for four to six students). Each pod gave the students clear visual access to flat-screen monitors. Second, none of the kids looked up. They were deeply engaged in learning. They seemed oblivious of 35 adults roaming throughout the room, exploring and kneeling down for a closer look at the equipment and activities taking place. One of our team educators observed, "We were the least interesting thing in the room."

We saw the goals, the content, the timeline, and the purpose displayed on the front wall in each class. Every student seemed to know what to do as soon as they entered.

After we toured several classrooms our team reassembled in the library to talk with a panel of students from sixth to eighth grade and their teachers. We listened to the kids describe their experience. They had a deep understanding of the new learning strategy and displayed a high level of ownership for their learning and progress. The kids knew the daily routine and did not wait for instructions when they entered class to begin a project or the lesson of the day.

We also learned that the classes included kids from different grade levels. We asked how they liked it. One of the sixth graders told us that she liked having an older student who could help her with some of the material. She knew she had someone who would also look out for her. An eighth-grader said that helping younger students had helped him learn the material better. Furthermore, when he graduates from the middle school to high school, he will already know more than 30 students there, "So it won't feel as intimidating."

The teachers explained how their role had shifted. They felt they were able to invest more time in designing the learning and coaching rather than managing the classroom. Perhaps our biggest insight was about how the culture had changed. Two years earlier, negative behavior and violence were big issues. The environment was stressful. But, at that point, they had no recorded discipline problems for the 2015 school year. When we asked why, one teacher said, "When you're looking at another student's face instead of the back of their head it makes them human." She also said that the kids love their classes and feel engaged in learning. The interest and achievement in STEM has dramatically improved.

And, of course, such a transformation passes through painful stages of growth and adaptation. For example, because the funding to convert a

. . . they had no recorded discipline problems for the 2015 school year. When we asked why, one teacher said, "When you're looking at someone's face instead of the back of their head it makes them human."

single classroom and change the curriculum ran about $50,000, not all of the science and math classrooms had been converted. When a girl who had experienced the STEMSmart model in her sixth grade was assigned to one of the old traditional classrooms along with the traditional curriculum for her seventh grade, Dr. Dettmann received a letter from the girl's father asking if his daughter had done something wrong. His letter, and other similar letters, show how important the new classrooms and curriculum are to students and parents, and confirm the new direction. They also give evidence of the sad futility of remaining in the same old Gutenberg model. Too many schools lack the capacity, the vision, or the leadership to provide every student with what Page Dettmann's kids experience every day.

Later that day, we were offered a different lens on the experience; we met with some of the business leaders supporting the transformation. Several of them joined us for dinner. I sat next to Kristian, one of the founders of a telecommunications firm with more than 300 employees. "So, why are you supporting this change?" I asked him. He replied that, because of his own bad experiences in the Education Machine, he simply didn't want another creative kid to go through the same stultifying process.

In creating a new learning experience, Page and her team studied schools that were successful in breaking out of tradition and rethinking learning. She embraced and followed a form of problem solving called Design Thinking.

Design Thinking evolved at Stanford University in the 1970s to address the challenge engineers faced in designing technology and software for humans. You and I have bought, at some point, a confounding piece of technology and wondered, "Who was this designed for?" To solve the challenges of human-device interface, Design Thinking places the designer in the role of a user (not simply interviewing users, but as a user) and creates a role for users to codesign the solution.

For example, I worked with a hospital that wanted to improve patient care. They hired IDEO, who developed a process called Patient

Journey. Nurses and doctors went through a complete admission process as if they were patients and were passed through the hospitals on gurneys like other patients. The experience radically changed not only many of the processes, but also the facility. One of the insights is just how much

> *". . . Design Thinking is neither art nor science nor religion. It is the capacity, ultimately, for integrative thinking."*
> —Tim Brown, *Change by Design*

time a patient might spend waiting in the hall, flat on their back on a gurney, looking up at the ceiling. One of the nurses who went through this journey was able to count the number of holes in a ceiling tile.

Imagine a process called the Student Journey or Teacher Journey. What is the current day-in-the-life experience and what might the future experience look like?

This is a very effective framework for anyone challenging old forms. It starts by gaining empathy for those you are hoping to serve, putting yourself in their shoes. Before you can help anyone, you must experience life through his or her lens. Our trip to the middle school placed us inside Page's world to experience a day in the life of that school and some of its students.

How Do We Envision the Future?

I am trained as a futurist, so I designed the Sarasota summit to take our MindShift group into that world and way of thinking. Instead of trying to "solve a problem," we considered what the possibilities might look like. Futurists do not predict the future, but rather try to see or imagine it. To do that requires a shift of framework and narrative—creating new language and categories, interpreting leading indicators, designing cartoons and animations, developing or detecting the new rules, and rearranging past structures or contexts into new shapes and sounds.

Timelines are also important to futurists. Projecting 10 years from now seems to free the mind from sinking into "problem solving," but also keeps that projection imaginable. Projecting longer time frames seems to inevitably swerve into fantasy. In other words, everything can be different and more imaginable when you place it in the near and somewhat familiar future.

The future always intrudes into the present. Just as the past is always here, but leaving, the future is always here and still coming. But the future's presence is not always obvious. We need skills and tools in order to find the future. Like an old radio receiver, those skills and tools scan the horizon and pull in the (sometimes weak) signals of things to come. Once these signals are captured, we look for what is common and distinct and begin a process of looking for trend lines.

The clues for the future of learning are usually found outside education and schools. We often find them in outliers or positive deviants, schools that defy conventional wisdom and get superior results.

Jane McGonigal, PhD, best-selling author and Chief Creative Officer for the Institute for the Future in Palo Alto, California, gave a keynote presentation for the 2016 SXSWEdu conference in Austin, Texas. She told the conferees to always ask questions when we see or hear signals from the future:

- What kind of change does this represent, from what to what?
- What is driving this change (the future force behind it)?
- What will the world be like if the signal gets amplified?
- What if it becomes common or even ubiquitous?
- Is this a future we actually want?

During our Sarasota summit we engaged in a futuring exercise to imagine if a company like Facebook, Southwest Airlines, Amazon, Nordstrom's, Uber, Google, Zappos, or another game-changing companies were to run education. For example, we playfully imagined:

"How would daily announcements or class instructions sound if a Southwest Airlines' flight attendant delivered them?"

"What if you could schedule time at a school Genius Bar to get help on a project or assignment?"

"What if school replaced buses with Uber . . . and called it Scoo-uber?

"What if classrooms were spread across the community, the library, park, recreation center, a business, or at city hall? A Scoo-uber can pick students and deliver them to the proper location."

The Pandorification of Learning

Michael Lagocki, a well-known graphic scribe, has become a vital part of our MindShift process. He captures our comments and stories on large white boards—sometimes filling a whole wall—creating a mural that illustrates the evolution of our conversations. When completed we have a wonderful piece of art and, more important, a visual synthesis of our work.

After capturing all of the ideas and listening to the playful applications to learning, we found a nice framework to shape our scenarios. And that framework addressed several challenges that are always present when individuals or groups try to think creatively. The mind needs mental bridges that take it outside its cloistered world. That is why the 2016 SXSWEdu exercise described earlier picked familiar and interesting companies for our consideration.

Pandora, a music-streaming app, is the child of the Music Genome project. The leaders for this project identified 450 essential attributes of songs. From these musical traits, mathematical relationships (algorithms) were used to create a signature for each song. Pandora uses these algorithms to allow listeners to find music that matches personal preferences. It works by first selecting an artist and a song as the seed for a new station. When the song is finished Pandora streams a new song based on the attributes assigned to the first artist and song. The simple binary choice of "thumbs up" or "thumbs down" begins to build a very complex and refined personal radio station.

For example, I like Eric Clapton. In particular I like several of his versions of "Crossroads." So, if I choose that, the next song Pandora selects may be another Eric Clapton song—maybe "Tears in Heaven" from his acoustical unplugged album. I prefer his blues and rock so I tap "thumbs down." The next song is Stevie Ray Vaughn's "Texas Flood." Big thumbs up. In a short time the algorithm translates my selections into a genre of music that becomes my signature. I seldom have to make adjustments.

Now, imagine a learning genome built on a range of key attributes. The genome, a "Pandorification," is made up of subjects, times of day, people type, focus, creativity, effort, energy, personality type, and so forth. The Genome then goes to work with thumbs up and thumbs down directions. It tracks what I enjoy learning, where I learn best, what time of day, my optimum mode of testing, my level of engagement, and other details. It provides a tailored stream of learning that gets continually smarter and continually improves my engagement.

Using this concept, let's look at two stories from the future of learning.

2025: Sarah and the Pandorification of Learning

Sarah is a 14-year-old freshman at FutureNow Academy in San Diego. At the beginning of her academic path[2] Sarah takes a series of assessments—cognitive, academic, personality, and other—to prepare for FutureNow and to program her learning genome. The cognitive strengths assessment helps her to identify her interests, preferences, and what engages her most. Her academic assessment takes her through several different modes of learning, linking each academic subject with the process that will work best for her. It determines she is a social reader but tactile when it comes to learning math and science. She also takes a battery of non-cognitive assessments developed through the University of Pennsylvania, covering areas of emotional intelligence, resiliency, her growth mindset, and level of well-being.[3]

These baseline parameters seed her signature learning style and inform her learning stream. With this, Sarah and her algorithm launch their journey together. Sarah's equipment includes a palm-sized Interactive Intelligent Learning Buddy (IILB, nicknamed IILBe) and an 11- by 7-inch multitouch film screen with a virtual keyboard.

On the first day of classes Sarah awakens early. As she prepares her breakfast, IILBe quickly scans and records her choices for the morning. IILBe also captures her level of excitement and nervousness about her first day.

At the school shuttle stop, Sarah greets some kids she knows and some she doesn't. IILBe observes their interactions and registers familiar versus formal tones as well as the balance between positive and negative dialogue. Sarah's driverless shuttle arrives at school in a smooth sequencing of more than 50 shuttles, all synchronized to arrive and depart in a continuous flow. As Sarah enters the school, IILBe directs her to math, her first class.

Because math is not Sarah's favored subject, she often finds herself daydreaming in middle school math class. So IILBe tries a different strategy for Sarah. During the set-up IILBe learns that lectures or clever videos receive "thumbs down" for engagement. When the teacher partners Sarah with two other students, IILBe records a high level of engagement and interprets this as "thumbs up." But this preference needs to be cross-referenced with Sarah's ability to demonstrate comprehension and mastery. If she does, then IILBe creates a reinforcing feedback loop to return to this partnership approach for future math challenges.

At the end of the class there are no bells. IILBe prompts Sarah to go to the next class. But then IILBE senses a drop in Sarah's energy level and focus. The last class was a positive experience, but it still represented hard work for Sarah; it just did not come naturally to her. Although the engagement with the other kids was positive, it still required some effort because she did not know them before class began. So IILBe decides to help Sarah recharge. Instead of taking a direct path to the next class IILBe guides her through the courtyard, filled with sunshine and a beautiful and fragrant garden. This has an immediate uplifting effect. Sarah has time to sit and enjoy the moment. IILBe guides her through a three-minute mindfulness exercise that Dr. Amit Sood developed at the Mayo Clinic. She remembers three positive people in her life and sends them a virtual thank-you.

Sarah then enters a class in contemporary English literature. When the teacher asks each student to name his or her favorite novel, Sarah chooses *Happy Together*, a science fiction novel set in 2050. It is the story of Anna, a young girl, and her animatronic friend, based on Ray Kurzweil's 2005 book *The Singularity Is Near*. The teacher asks Sarah to read her favorite passage.

Sarah unfolds her screen and immediately finds her favorite section. As Sarah reads the passage she reaches her highest level of engagement and enjoyment for the day. IILBe tracks her emotional response to the passage.

That evening at dinner Sarah's mom and dad scan ILLBe's dashboard to review Sarah's day. In addition to recapping the events, ILLBe allows them to find and explore the inflexion points of Sarah's day.

Sarah and IILBe had a full and fun first day in high school. ILLBe feels very natural to her. She has never before experienced a day that seamlessly flowed from one event and experience to another. In the past she often hit brick walls or mentally checked out. But ILLBe helped her navigate effortlessly through every challenge. Even her teachers seemed more attuned, almost clairvoyant, about when and how to help. As ILLBe prompts her to wind down the day with a mindfulness exercise, Sarah expresses gratitude for ILLBe; she knows they would be happy together. IILBe continues to work, taking in the many terabytes of data from the day and fine-tuning Sarah's learning genome for tomorrow.

2025: The Free-Range Learning Community

Jaime, a 12-year-old sixth grader, lives with his mom, Maria, on the Southside of Chicago. Maria, an immigrant who fled Cuba, doesn't speak English well, but she has picked up enough to follow basic conversations. The welfare check is essential to Maria and Jaime's life. Government attempts at reform, restructuring, and bold programs have left Maria and Jaime's community in worse condition. Everyone knows that something has to change.

More than 6,000 students are spread over eight middle schools. Community leaders, knowing that middle school years are critical years for students, close five of the schools and turn the remaining three into open-plan, project-based, blended learning centers. The revenue from the sale of property and equipment and the reduced operating costs release resources that can be invested in other uses.

The bold program is called the Free-Range Learning Community Co-Op (FRLCC). The program begins by mapping a community's social assets: libraries, parks, museums, recreation centers, embedded local businesses, health-care providers, nonprofits, public services, and so on. The mapping process then invites the identified resources to partner with the schools. The partnerships can include the use of private facilities, supplying part-time teachers or coaches, and providing internships or other support. Once the levels of support are identified, software begins to match the resources with the students' needs.

Most of the learning takes place outside a school building. The schools are primarily used for assessments, coaching, recognition, filling the gaps, and celebrating achievement. The Learning Genome baselines Jaime's academic and non-cognitive skill levels and compares them to his learning and life goals. The school then fits Jaime with his own personal IILBe. Jaime's IILBe has seen signature genomes very similar to Jaime's; it knows how to map a new course for him.

And Jaime has to find a new course—for his life! In the face of gangs and turmoil at home, Maria does her best but doesn't really understand the value of school. She has pulled Jaime out of class several times in order for him to go home and watch his little sister. They moved a few times during the school year, seeking lower-priced housings.

But Jaime has a passion for architecture. Could he follow the education path required to learn architecture it in the new course of his life? Can the new technologies make a difference in low-income families like Jaime's?

On Tuesday morning, IILBe notifies Scoo-uber to pick Jaime up at 9 AM. This allows him to get his sister ready for school. Scoo-uber also picks up two other students before 9:00 AM. Because of new technologies, on that Tuesday morning Jaime and his classmates are able to visit the Robie House designed by Frank Lloyd Wright at the University of Chicago.

Jaime and his classmates got a full tour of the house and its history. In addition, a professor from the William Heck Research Center for Architecture is there to show them some of the hidden design and engineering features of the house. The professor has brought four virtual reality headsets, one for himself and the others for the students. This is their first exposure to augmented reality. The professor guides them through the house; they are stunned at how the headsets allow them to see the mechanical, electrical, and plumbing fixtures behind the walls. He then takes them to the patio so they can scan the landscaped grounds. He sets the program to go back in time and see the area when the house was first built in 1909. Then they watch the changes unfold in 10-year increments.

After the tour the students and the professor return to the Research Center. The professor leads them the long way around so that they can walk through the neighborhood and hear about the architecture of the early 1900s and the history of the area.

Back on the campus of the University of Chicago, they learn that each building has a compelling architectural story of its own. Jaime cannot remember ever experiencing such a happy and engaging school day. IILBe records his emotions and will put this learning to work again.

Scoo-uber picks the kids up at the Research Center at 4:30 PM and drops them all at their homes within an hour.

Jaime's next day is a little rougher. A shooting in the neighborhood has put the community on edge; Maria cradled her daughter, rocking back and forth, all night long. When Scoo-uber arrived Jaime is exhausted and stressed. During the seven-minute trip to the learning campus, IILBe takes Jaime through mindfulness exercises.

When he arrives a school physician escorts Jaime to the campus

Futuring utilizes different dimensions; the feasible, the possible, the plausible and the imaginable.

"Chill Room;" with muted lights, soft furniture, white noise, and appealing food and beverages, to help to restore Jaime's sense of peace and ability to focus on his studies.

The Free Range model takes away the stress and pressure of bells, schedules, and stampedes between classes. In addition, many kids arrive at school with worn or dirty clothes, and some have not bathed. The school stocks jeans and T-shirts in all sizes. It also provides showers and can even wash the students' clothes during the day.

As you can see, the FRLCC represents a complete, holistic, and very human approach to learning. It prioritizes student health and peace, and uses technology to support the unique needs of each student; no one is lost in the robotic regimens of mainlining. The FRLCC discards old concepts about the uniformity of time and place. Learning is viewed as a seamless and continuing part of life, not a silo of elite and bureaucratic instruction.

Threading It Together

Futuring utilizes different dimensions: the feasible, the possible, the plausible, and the imaginable. Each serves a different function. The stories of Sarah and Jaimie fall in the range of the feasible and possible.

> *The question is not what a classroom or school will look like in 30 years. It is whether it will exist at all in its current form.*
> —Brian Cahill

Many of the elements in the story are already here today, but are used outside education. Each of the scenarios is entirely possible. For example, Altamonte Springs, Florida, recently abandoned plans to build a new and technologically advanced bus system. Instead, they partnered with Uber.[4] Clues to the future present themselves everywhere.

Some of the technologies and insights in Sarah and Jaime's stories can be found in the models of Uber, Siri, the iWatch, Oculus Rift, Austin Community College, Birdville Center for Technology and Advanced Learning, the Apple Genius Bar, Pandora, Gallup Strengthsfinder, Atl-School's, School of One, Quest for Learning, Momentous Institute, Delos Well Living Lab, My Fitness Pal, the StessTest app, the NREL Energy Dashboard, Khan Academy, Dragon Dictation App, Rosetta Stone, Institute for Coalition Building's Stakeholder Wheel, and Social Asset Mapping guide.

As William Gibson said in Talk of the Nation on NPR in 1999, "The future is already here, just not evenly distributed."

Will We Improve the Past or Make the Future?

With the iPhone, Apple chose to make the future. Nokia, Motorola, Palm, and BlackBerry pursued improving the past. Instagram represents another example of making the future. It is simply an app. In 2010 the future was imagined to be sharing on social media. Ironically, Instagram's icon is a graphic that resembles the Kodak Instamatic camera. In the same year that Kodak declared bankruptcy, Facebook bought Instagram for $1 billion.

Improving on the past is a bad strategy if your universe intersects with Moore's law (processing power or speed will double every two years).

In his 1970 book, *Future* Shock,[5] Alvin Toffler predicted that living in a world where the new and novel overshadowed the familiar would cause psychic and social breakdown. Since 1955, 88 percent of Fortune 500 companies have disappeared due to what is called "creative destruction."[6]

Glenn C. Wintrich Jr., Dell's Innovation Leader, has said that their past success was based on what he called "fast follow." In other words, wait until an innovator like Apple or Microsoft announces a new product and then quickly follow up with something cheaper and faster. Given that the innovation cycle of 18 months has tightened and there is no longer enough time to get a product to market and monetize it before the next innovation makes it obsolete, Dell is being forced to get into the innovation game.

Let's assume that the Education Machine is a fast follower and pose this question, which challenges both Dell and education: How do you take a culture that pays for and attracts talent that is good at reverse engineering (copying), rewarded for rapid copying at lower cost, trained and managed to engineer and not innovate, and then flip it on its head and expect the same people to become innovators?

What Improving the Past Looks Like in Education

In 2015 I attended a panel SXSWedu with Mary Cullinane, Chief Content Officer for schoolbook publisher Houghton Mifflin Harcourt. Prior to the conference she wrote,

There's no doubt that we need a radical change. But, given the high stakes (who wants to experiment with the education of our kids?), the largely bureaucratic and matrixed environment that is our current K–12 system (adoption process anyone?), and shrinking and shifting budgets (healthy lunch versus interactive whiteboards—you decide), is radical disruption even a realistic goal?[7]

I asked if she had looked outside her building lately to see what the rest of the world was doing, and had she seen the disruption and rapid drop in her own company? I then asked what she thought about Khan Academy. Ms. Cullinane said that Khan Academy couldn't be taken seriously "because they are a bunch of homemade videos on YouTube." I guess she had not seen one lately. Clayton Christensen, renowned scholar, Harvard professor, and author of *The Innovator's Dilemma,* is exactly right when he says that disruptive innovation is invading education. Salman Khan's videos started as homemade, but then Moore's law and Metcalfe's law took over.

According to Metcalfe's law, the value of a network grows exponentially more valuable with each added machine or participant. For example, the first fax machine was, well, worthless. But the second made it useful . . . for two parties. Then, the 3rd, 4th, 5th, 289th, and so forth kept increasing the value. Moore's law also increased the speed, lowered the cost, and improved telecommunications. Finally, as an example reflecting the two laws, fax machines gave way to scanners and now scanners are obsolete because our mobile devices can take and send scanned images.

Three months after my exchange with Ms. Cullinane, the College Board, providers of the SAT, announced they were partnering with the Khan Academy to provide preparatory training for the new SAT assessments—for free. Other partnerships with the Khan Academy are changing the face of learning and offer specialized content: NASA, The Museum of Modern Art, The California Academy of Sciences, and MIT.[8]

What Making the Future Looks Like in Education

Previous SAT prep courses were standardized. But Khan Academy allows personalized training. Khan Academy's content is free and provides one bridge for those on the other side of the achievement gap. The content will expand. The achievement scores can be cross-referenced and data analytics will improve and suggest new content. Can you see where this is going, in view of Moore and Metcalfe's laws? There will be a tipping point where Khan Academy has the best content, flexibly designed, for personalized learning on a global scale.

Max Ventilla is the founder of AltSchool, one of Silicon Valley's billionaire club charter schools. They are creating a *Learning Progression Dashboard*. It assesses a child on the front end (formative assessment) and predicts how he or she will do on a test. It matches the child's results with other kids with similar results and then maps the best learning strategy. It functions a lot like our Pandorification of Learning. Max said, "We are changing the role of educators from someone operating in the dark to someone who can actually guide a student through their optimum personal path." He told his SXSWedu audience that we have to reconsider adding more bodies to teaching as a solution. "It's about a force multiplier, and technology is that lever."

AltSchool has also created an application called a Student Playlist; it is similar in concept to an iTunes playlist. It provides a personalized curriculum for students. With its "parent portal," the platform reduces the cost of flexibility and transparency by providing a newsfeed-like report on how each student is doing in real time.

AltSchool plans to build out this platform and prove its effectiveness with one or two schools. Once complete, they plan to license it to any school or district. Play out this trajectory through Moore and Metcalfe's laws.

Sarasota Middle School, Signature Academy, the Engage2Learn model, High-Tech High, the NuTech schools, Expeditionary Learning, and Quest for Play are each examples of a growing base of *student-led* learning models. This new direction requires a complete mind shift and new culture and skills, but is an accessible strategy for schools to explore.

The final example is the growth of *blended learning*. The Christensen Foundation defines it as a formal education program in which the student is learning partly in class, partly online at home, and the mix and support is tailored to the "modalities along each student's learning path."[9] This approach also changes the role of the teacher from the "sage on the stage" to a coach, mentor, and troubleshooter. The Christensen Foundation is tracking the success of schools using blended learning and developing a rich source of case studies to view. Numerous schools districts across the nation are testing the model.

Each of these examples of the new era of learning is moving up the innovation curve at the speed of Google. The real magic will happen when these schools and their respective paths begin to converge. Apple's 1984 Super Bowl ad announced a new era of personalized computing; Apple's 2007 unveiling of the iPhone fulfilled that promise to humanize technology. Everything points to a similar experience in humanizing learning.

Creating a Future for Everyone

For now, "magic" is only a reality for about half of our kids. A growing income gap means almost half of our kids start and stay behind, creating an even wider digital divide between the haves and the have nots. Jaime's world is a tragic reality for more that 44 percent of kids. That is 32 million of them! The next chapter takes us deeper into that world and asks the question, "Is zip code destiny?"

CHAPTER 9

Changing the Odds

Getting Beyond Zip Code Destiny

It is easier to build strong children than to fix broken men.
　　　　　　　　　　　　　　—Frederick Douglass

I heard that Kostoryz Elementary School in Corpus Christi, Texas, was a turnaround story that our K–12 MindShift team should see. So I flew down to take a look.

When I exited the freeway the area quickly changed from nice restaurants and retail shops to a new landscape of payday loan shops, ethnic restaurants, laundromats, and appliance and furniture rental centers. Large apartment complexes lined both sides of the street as I got near the school.

Kostoryz Elementary is a two-story windowless building, bleached white with jagged rust stains ringing the roofline. The school was built in the 1960s to support a new and growing middle-class community. But two of the pillars supporting Corpus Christi at the time, the petroleum industry and the military, started leaving about 30 years ago. That's why the school is now surrounded by multifamily homes. Two blocks away, the rows of low-income apartments confirmed the shift in that community.

Soon after arriving at the school, I saw buses unloading kids. Later, I saw a new pattern: cars and vans drove up and dropped off some kids. In fact, many kids arrived after school started. Toward the end of the day, we saw the same pattern in reverse. The principal explained the kids arriving and departing in private vehicles: "These kids come from homes where work comes first and family needs come second. School is often seen as a place where their kids will be fed and taken care of for the day."

A year earlier the new superintendent developed a strategy to give each school in the district more flexibility and autonomy to deliver learning according to the different student needs. But, then a new mandate—improve test scores!—changed all that. So, the system tightened up, and compliance and conformity replaced the more flexible approach.

One area principal told me, "We've gone back to the 1960s in the way we are teaching. I've been in this district 30 years and thought I would go another six years to retirement. We're not teaching kids anymore. We're not even offering them a stimulating place to come to. This is my last year."

The more I saw, the more I wondered why so many cannot see the true face of children and their well-being in America. For example, how is it possible that 1.3 million American children are homeless? Or how can 15,540,000 children—21.1 percent of all children—be living in poverty in American in 2014?

By any measurement, that kind of "reform," taking teacher discretion away in order to narrowly focus on test scores, does more harm than good.

As we moved through the K–12 schools in our research, assisted by some real world "tour guides," we began to climb inside a life and culture that is daily reality for almost half of the kids in America.

The more I saw, the more I wondered why so many cannot see the true face of children and their well-being in America. For example, how is it possible that 1.3 million American children are homeless? Or how can 15,540,000 children—21.1 percent of all children—be living in poverty in American in 2014 (see Figure 9.1)?

In that same year, 6.8 million children (9.3 percent of all children) lived in "extreme poverty" (annual income of less than half the poverty level, or $12,115 for a family of four).[1] And, according to the Pew Research Center, only 50.9 percent of low-income kids graduate and go to college, compared to 80.7 percent from middle- and high-income families.[2] Perhaps the real scandal of these numbers is found in the fact that millions of Americans are completely unaware of them.

In his book *Our Kids: The American Dream in Crisis* (Simon & Schuster, 2016) Harvard professor Robert Putnam says that we are precipitously close to becoming a caste society based on socioeconomic status (SES). ". . . SES had become even more important than test scores in predicting which eighth-graders would graduate from college.[3]"

In our visit to Corpus Christi, our team broke up into car- or van-sized groups in order to go out and explore different zip codes throughout the area. We scoured those areas in order to take their pulse. We drove through the zip codes that enjoyed fine schools, upscale grocery stores, well-groomed and watered lawns, new car dealerships, majestic places of worship, parks, and playgrounds.

Figure 9.1 Students from Disadvantaged Families and Communities

At the other end of the social spectrum we also saw barred windows, police officers hovering over handcuffed and prostrate men, mortuaries (death is a growth industry in these zip codes), unemployed men standing at street corners, barren and littered yards, chop shops, and check-cashing and pay-day-loan stores.

Then we also took time to envision and describe a day in the life of various students. How do these very real environments shape the hopes and dreams or fears and desperations of the community's younger members? We wanted to know how life in a particular zip code influences student learning.

Beating the Low Expectations Syndrome

A study revealed that in the 2012–13 school year, for the first time in fifty years, more than half of American public school children lived in low-income families.

—Dale Russakoff, The Prize

After hearing Jaime Casap, Google's Chief Education Evangelist, speak at the 2015 SXSWedu conference in Austin, I flew to Philadelphia for a one-hour conversation with him. That hour was worth every dollar of the trip.

He told me that he was born in 1969 to a single mother who fled the violence and terror in Argentina after the 1966 revolution. Ironically, she arrived in Hell's Kitchen, on the West Side of New York City.

The harsh realities of street violence and living on welfare were simply ambient noise in Jaime's life. The struggle for survival turned personal the first day of class at PS 111.[4] When the teacher called his name, Jaime replied, "Que?" He recalls that as that moment when he realized that he did not fit in. And fitting in was necessary to survive.

During our interview he observed that the atmosphere of violence became more personal as he got older, "I went to more funerals in high school than most people go to in two lifetimes." The conditions of Hell's Kitchen served as motivation to get out. He knew that the best way to do that was through education.

Jaime's journey points to the power and potential of education touching and transforming a life.

> *I went to more funerals in high school than most people go to in two lifetimes.*
> —Jaime Casap

That's why, in July 2015, Jaime was invited by First Lady Michelle Obama to share his story in the White House at the Beat the Odds Summit. He told the audience of 140 students (who also overcame tough challenges and were college bound) the following.

I'll be the first to admit it wasn't always easy. There are distractions and enticements all around you. Those minding the dead-end roads will work hard to lure you with assurances of quick power and riches. You need to have your own distractions.

You also need a pair of very thick and solid "reality distortion glasses." Everything around you shrieks, "You will not make it!" All you see, read, and hear will proclaim, "You are not meant to succeed. You don't belong here."

Those who argue, "Just go to school and keep out of trouble" clearly don't understand what it's like to grow up in our environment. You don't need to look for trouble. Trouble finds a way to get to you. You have to be stronger than most people understand.

Do not, I repeat, do not wait for anyone to believe in you. Believe in yourself, strap on your glasses, and prove them all wrong!

Often we ask our students the wrong question, "What do you want to be when you grow up?" I don't like this question. First, there is a very good chance your "job" doesn't exist yet. Second, I do not expect kids growing up in communities like Hell's Kitchen to tell me that they want to be a microbiologist or a sustainable materials architect.

> *Often we ask our students the wrong question, "What do you want to be when you grow up?" I don't like this question. First, there is a very good chance your "job" doesn't exist yet.*
>
> *Instead, I want to ask you, "What problem do you want to solve?"*
> —Jaime Casap

Instead, I want to ask you, "What problem do you want to solve?"

I want you to think about the knowledge, skills, and abilities you need to solve this problem.

When I ask you to think about what problem you want to solve, I am asking you to take ownership of your learning. I am asking you to begin to create mastery for the most critical skills you will need. I want to give you the opportunity to think about purpose.[5]

A Day in the Life

What is it like to work in a Survival School? Teachers soon learn that kids bring their pain to class. They also realize that nothing in their training prepares them for that pain. I want you to meet some teachers and read their stories.

Alyssa teaches at an alternative school in Baltimore. If a student gets kicked out of his or her assigned school the alternative school is their last resort. Alyssa's school population is 85 percent African American, 10 percent Hispanic, and other ethnic groups make up the rest. The school has one white student. Alyssa, who has 26 students and teaches English, told me, "A lesson plan can take two weeks in this school because I have to address so many different needs. A good day is when the kids follow instructions and pay attention. When they show interest it feels like my work is making a difference."

These days are not the norm.

One of my worst days was the day I tried to show a New York Times *documentary about a maximum-security-prison baseball team. It was a lesson on the power of unity. It is an inspiring story. I was planning to use baseball as a metaphor in their lives. Instead one boy jumped up and turned over his desk. He said, "F—'n no way, I'm not doing this!" He ran out of the classroom.*

I tracked his caseworker down and learned that his brother was just sent to prison. The movie was the last thing he wanted to see. It was a trigger. Steinbeck is so irrelevant here . . .

Many of my better days are simply setting aside the lesson and talking about our lives.

These kids have grown up with a victim mindset. They are told over and over they don't have a chance. The message is, they are less and so we expect them to do less. When they hit even the slightest obstacle there is no reason to rise up and overcome.

—Alyssa

We have paramedics called three or four times a week. A lot of these kids have grown up together so they bring their baggage with them. I had two students whose moms did drugs together and one owed the other money—so they fought about it. One picked up a hole-puncher and threw it in my direction. It shattered the door. It happened so quickly. Nothing is super premeditated.

I was hired on the Monday of new teacher orientation. If I were to do this over I would have liked some training on how these interventions work. There is a method to it. I would have also liked to get bios on my students a few months before school. Who are these kids?

I'm not sure about their futures. I don't have a lot of hope for some of them. They just repeat the cycle, stuck in what they know, experience and are surrounded by. We simply put all of the same kids who think the same way in the same box together. They've never seen anyone who has broken out, beaten the odds.

These kids have grown up with a victim mindset. They are told over and over they don't have a chance. The message is, they are less and so we expect them to do less. When they hit even the slightest obstacle there is no reason to rise up and overcome. They expect failure but not the learning kind. Only two of my 26 kids have a father in their lives.

The big lesson for me is that I had to learn how to do life with my kids. *Jaynie is one of the sweetest students I've had. She's called Big Body and she shines love on people. At the beginning of the year she had multiple drug charges. Her grandma was the dealer. Jaynie's been clean for six months. What turned her around was the threat of 16 months' jail time. I think she's going to make it. It has taken a village. Mom is not in the picture; dad is long gone. Teachers have picked her up when Jaynie couldn't get a ride and taken homework to her. I wish I had more stories like hers.*

The Toll on Good Teachers

Will is an Eagle Scout and a William and Mary graduate. He majored in public policy and trained in early childhood learning. His experience is similar to Alyssa's. Will said that two of the schools where he taught were not high functioning.

The teachers had no voice and dared offer no ideas. Both schools were built on fear and control.

Ninth grade seemed to be a pivotal year. There is a lot of pressure for "social promotion," to keep kids in their age cohort. Even if kids are reading at a second- and third-grade level.

These kids develop incredible coping mechanisms. If you can't read you are going to throw up a lot of blocking and distractions. You will float through and simply focus on fun or getting high. A lot of energy gets channeled into preserving self-image. A kid won't try so you won't know he can't read. It's better to be labeled as bad or a troublemaker than stupid.

Will, who studied specifically to teach in at-risk communities, is leaving after five years. He's burnt out and considering moving to the policy side of the war.

Dwight was part of a 2015 SXSWedu panel titled Transforming Schools Using Brain Science.[6] At the time he was a fifth-grade teacher. Of his 16 students, 5 were functioning at a third-grade level, 4 were in special education, 2 were advanced in math, and 2 were average. "The academic issues were only the beginning. Life was the real issue."

One of his advanced math students was emotionally disturbed from psychological and sexual abuse. He was suspended for urinating in the classroom. Dwight asked him what happened. "I told her that I had to go real bad. She told me if I had to go that bad then use the trash can."

Three of his students were homeless. Two kids had very supportive and active parents and two no support at all; they stayed out all night and ate poorly.

The repercussions of neglect, homelessness and abuse define the daily reality for class. The slightest correction can send kids into crisis. One student exploded, all because he could not understand a math problem. Another student had a bad night because his parents were arguing at each other so he watched *Animal Planet* all night. When he came to class he simply put his head on the desk and took a nap. "You've got to sleep some time."

Survival Mode

Journalist Paul Tough has observed, ". . . children who grow up in stressful environments generally find it harder to concentrate, harder to sit still, harder to rebound from disappointments, and harder to follow directions. And that has a direct effect on their performance in school. When you're overwhelmed by uncontrollable impulses and distracted by negative feelings, it's hard to learn the alphabet."[7]

A missing piece to these discussions is that these kids *can't learn*. It's not that they don't have the

It's not that they don't have the intelligence. Many are bright and eager to learn. It's also not enough to simply say life gets in the way. The obstacle is more fundamental. Their brains are in survival mode—fight or flight.

intelligence. Many are bright and eager to learn. It's also not enough to simply say life gets in the way. The obstacle is more fundamental. Their brains are in survival mode—fight or flight. The neglect, abuse, instability, and chaos these kids live with create perpetual vigilance, an always-on alert condition. That means the adrenal gland secretes that on-edge readiness along with cortisol, which shuts down all nonessential functions like learning. *Learning can't take place.* In fact the stress of trying to focus on something new and challenging can be the spark that sets off a combustible response in one kid; that spark quickly ignites the class.

Is Education Rigged?

According to Stanford professor Sean Reardon, "The achievement gap between children from high- and low-income families is roughly 30 to 40 percent larger among children born in 2001 than among those born twenty-five years earlier. In fact, it appears that the income achievement gap has been growing for at least 50 years. . . . [8]

Education is the mythical starting line in a race for success and happiness. But, what if the race is rigged? What if zip code predetermines winners and losers?

Imagine that your daughter goes out for track and field as a cross-country runner. But she is not allowed to train, must stay up late most nights to study, has never seen what a successful runner looks like, eats junk food as a daily diet, and isn't taught the rules. Furthermore, when she arrives for her first race, she is forced to wear heavy boots and carry a hefty backpack.

Next to your child is a kid whose parents both competed in track at a collegiate level. Her bedroom has posters of her track heroes and she has watched thrilling competitions over and over again. She had a coach when she was five and her parents run with her in the evening. Does your daughter have a chance?

Let's run a similar education race between two kids. One is in the top income quartile, based on the U.S. Census ($75,000 + annual income) and the other in the bottom half ($25,000 and less for a household of four) (see Figure 9.2).

> *Education is the mythical starting line in a race for success and happiness. But, what if the race is rigged? What if zip code predetermines winners and losers?*

Figure 9.2   Income Starting Line Gap

Each child begins with the same amount of school funding. In fact, the low-income child will probably have direct and indirect access to additional federal and state funding. The difference is what happens outside and around school.

"Starting-line disparities hamstring educational mobility. Among first-grade students performing in the top academic quartile, only 28 percent are from lower-income families, while 72 percent are from higher-income families."[9]

Reardon's research reaches an astounding conclusion: Kids at the bottom start the race far behind, and school does little to change that. The narrow gap observed in early years widens simply because learning complexity grows. "At K-1 a child in the bottom half starts one year behind. By elementary school it widens to three years; in high school the gap is insurmountable at six years behind."[10]

Rice University's Glasscock School of Continuing Studies' report, *The Early Catastrophe: The 30 Million Word Gap by Age 3*, concludes, "After four years these differences in parent-child interactions produced significant discrepancies in not only children's knowledge, but also their skills and experiences with children from high-income families being exposed to 30 million more words than children from families on welfare. Follow-up studies showed that these differences in language and interaction experiences have lasting effects on a child's performance later in life.[11] "In low-income neighborhoods there is one book for 300 children. In middle-income communities there are 13 per child!"[12]

Many studies mark third-grade reading as a critical predictor of future success. "In 2011, 82 percent of fourth-graders from low-income families—and 84 percent of low-income students who attend high-poverty schools—failed to reach the 'proficient' level in reading on the National Assessment of Educational Progress (NAEP)."[13] The same challenge of starting and staying behind for low-income kids applies to math.

An even stronger predictor of future success is fifth-grade math skills. "Analyzing data from six long-term studies, they found the strongest predictor of later achievement to be children's school-entry math skills, followed by reading and ability to pay attention. The big surprise was that math skills ranked as the most important predictor of school success."[14] "Sixth graders with . . . a failing grade in math, or a failing grade in English had only a 10 percent chance of graduating within four years of entering high school. . . ."[15]

The Parent Factor

In Reardon's research he found that the gap in the funds that parents dedicate to their kids' education has, over the past three decades, widened dramatically between lower and upper income families. In 1973 lower-income parents spent about $830 per child per year while upper-income parents spent four times that amount. By 2006 low-income families were able to spend $1,300 compared to $9,000 for upper income kids (some of this came as a result of trading mom's time in the workplace for money).

Robert Putnam tells it plainly: "Kids from upper-class backgrounds are once again widening their lead in the race that matters most. Kids from low-income backgrounds . . . are working more or less diligently to improve their prospects in life, but no matter how talented and hardworking they are, at best they are improving their play at checkers, while upper-class kids are widening their lead at three-dimensional chess."[16]

The Education Machine cannot address these kinds of disparities. These are one-off kids. Sure, they come out of conditions that have similar debilitating attributes. But don't miss how each child's mix of neglect, abuse, chaos, trauma, health deficits, and so on calls for attentive cultivation. But instead they get bulldozer treatment.

Any objective review of K–12 education in America would conclude that we have certainly been paying, but not paying attention, for those low-income students who must cope with an education game that is rigged. For many, that reality is the cumulative outcome of multigenerational failure. Their parents, their grandparents, and sometimes their whole community and family network were forced out of the education game. They were not bad or irresponsible people: they just saw that the winners and losers were already designated. So, they did what they could to support themselves and those who depended on them. They found work where they could.

It is time to care, to give an honest damn, about the students who live with insufficient money, health care, home, peace, and practical and multigenerational support for their journey. The Education Machine cannot do that. That is why, throughout the second half of this book, we'll explore *what* can be done and *who* can do it. And that must start with helping those in the bottom of the quintiles and indices of life.

I started this chapter at Kostoryz Elementary in Corpus Christ. That school went from an institution hell-bent on improving test scores to a fully engaged human learning environment. We met two kids there who had previously been "outsourced." They were both diagnosed on the Autism spectrum. When we visited the classes three weeks into the new school year they were both integrated into their classes—happy, engaged, contributing, and learning. Their classmates didn't treat them any differently from anyone else. Because of Lisa's and my experience with our kids, this was a very moving experience for me. I thought, "Here I am in an elementary school ranked 4,041 out of 4,128 in the state, and this is a more humane, connected, and uplifting experience than anything I encountered with my daughter in the number one ranked school in the state."

We circled back to Kostoryz Elementary after year one of the new active learning model. The teachers demonstrated 62 percent growth in the 16 best practices which included small group instruction, formative feedback, future-ready skills, standards-aligned design, differentiation (tailoring instruction to student

Any objective review of K–12 education in America would conclude that we have been paying, but not paying attention, for those low-income students who must cope with an education game that is rigged. For many, that reality is the cumulative outcome of multigenerational failure.

differences), and scaffolding (taking kids progressively up a ladder to mastery). In the same period students experienced a 20 percent gain in math scores from 4th to 5th grade and a 26 percent gain in reading scores from 4th to 5th grade on state standardized assessments.

Healthy Communities = Healthy Schools

Fifty percent of our kids start behind, and stay behind. And that gap is widening. And, incredibly, here in the twenty-first century there does not appear to be anything narrowing the gap. But, back in the middle of the last century, J. Irwin Miller recognized a fundamental truth. In order to have a healthy company, he needed a healthy community. That begins with healthy schools. What was true for Columbus, Indiana, and has proven true for 60 years is true for every community. According to Gallup's Brandon Busteed, "Corporate leaders are desperate to find talent ready for the workplace but only 11 percent of CEO's feel that the students coming out of our institutions are properly prepared."[17]

Will corporate leaders be able to make the same leap that Miller took and reframe their focus from shareholder value to stakeholder engagement? Education as a catalyst and steward of learning provides the basis for a sustainable future.

> *Corporate leaders are desperate to find talent ready for the workplace but only 11 percent of CEO's feel that the students coming out of our institutions are properly prepared.*
> —Brandon Busteed

The teachers and administrators we have seen who have bridged the gap and are raising survival schools out of their death spiral start with early warning systems and human-based interventions. They set a culture of high expectations, work to engage parents and the community, invest in extracurricular activities, place equal emphasis on social and emotional learning for both kids and teachers, and shift the ownership of success to the kids.

The Learning and Life Connection

In November 2015, Barbara Barnes, author of *It's the Kids—Forty Years of Innovation in How We Educate Our Children*, joined the MindShift team for our San Diego summit. She shared the extraordinary story (also told in her book) of *21st Century Prep* in Chattanooga, Tennessee.

It all started in 1989, when Barbara invited futurist Joel Barker to speak at a California educational conference that she designed. One evening after the last session, as Joel interacted informally with some teachers, he presented an educational concept he had developed called "EFG—Ecological, Futures, and Global." Something galvanized the teachers (in fact, they continued to meet informally, and at their own expense, for several years). And Barbara immediately saw the value of Joel's idea; she knew they had to find a school wherein they could build a prototype of the EFG model.

In 1991, the informal teachers group formed an educational conference in England; Joel attended and shared the EFG concept in more detail. One of the conferees was an official with the Chattanooga, Tennessee, City School District. In 1993, that district closed a junior high school that was failing. Then the school buildings and grounds were converted to a K–12 magnet school. All teachers and staff had to apply for positions in the new school. It would be called 21st Century Prep. The Chattanooga official invited Barbara and Joel to use EFG for the school curriculum. They both joined the effort.

Prospective students had to apply if they wanted to attend. Based on the zip code demographics, the school administrators expected an even split between Caucasian and African American students. But when the students began applying, it became clear that African American students would comprise at least 65 percent of the new student body. At that point, white flight began. Before long 21st Century Prep became an all-black school.

The first year was, consistent with one of Joel's signature concepts, a true "paradigm shift." True "mastery" was required in order for a student to be promoted to the next level of learning. Every student had to commit to a long-term novel-writing project. All parents had to provide 18 hours of service to the school each year (and the school was very serious about that; Joel told me that four students were not promoted because their parents did not serve the requisite hours).

At the end of that first school year, the school had a waiting list of *white* families wanting to enroll. Why? Because of their innovative approach: "students, who had failed at other schools, saw the connection between school and the rest of their lives. . . . This school demonstrated that investigative, applied learning motivated students, significantly improved learning *and* increased test scores."[18]

Now, that is a story we should see on our theater or TV screens: the students of an all–black K–12 school created such a great story of achievement and academic excellence that the white parents began lining up for the chance of getting their kids enrolled at 21st Century Prep! In so doing, they confirmed once again that most humans—regardless of their zip code—love, honor, protect, and reach for the same things.

Humanizing the System

At–risk kids are the most vulnerable students inside a system that tries to deliver efficient service by taking away the elements of learning that make it human. It is no longer just our underserved communities who feel the oppressive nature of the Education Machine. Leo Linbeck is right when he says, "We are all at risk." It is not just our kids, but our nation." The next chapter explains how the education system has taken on a life of its own. Without constant vigilance to constrain its appetite for efficiency and control it will continue to remove what makes learning human.

CHAPTER 10

Humanizing the Great Education Machine

Whatever you do for me but without me, you do against me.
—Gandhi

Alyssa's big aha moment in her first year of teaching came when she realized that she had to shift from doing good work with students to "doing life together." She had to move from being an expert to living a real life as a human, and from a one-size-fits-all lesson plan to authentic teaching moments. Alyssa, who was bright, perceptive, and empathetic, did not learn that in college. Her mission to make a true difference came from a different place, and it certainly superseded institutional assumptions and expectations.

The secret behind Alyssa's revelation throws a light on the grand failures of institutional initiatives. It also explains why human action, pursued with quiet persistence and a mission focus will help us succeed.

Institution-led crusades require experts, authorizations, lots of money, and control. Human-led efforts require none of this. That is why they work.

Newark—*The Prize*

In the early 1970s, Newark, New Jersey, fell into a rapid decline. Industries closed or relocated to safer and more dynamic places. Then, as the social fabric ripped apart, Newark became a war zone.

Ultimately, in 1995, the state government stepped in to take control of the schools.

Dale Russakoff, in her book, *The Prize,* told the story that began in 2010 when Cory Booker, then mayor, Chris Christie, governor, and Facebook's Mark Zuckerberg partnered to turn Newark schools around. The effort, called One Newark, invested $200 million and installed an "A team" of leaders. According to Russakoff, "What Booker, Christie, and Zuckerberg set out to achieve in Newark had not been accomplished in modern times—turning a failing urban school district into one of universally high achievement."[1]

> *Here is the inconvenient truth: Education, including education reform, is part of the problem. We have not made a dent in the problem, and in some cases we've made it worse.*
> —Cami Anderson

Their general on the ground was a young, aggressive, hard-nosed Teach for America zealot, Cami Anderson. She came in with "an insular and uncompromising management style."[2]

Sadly, the project unraveled, all the money got spent with little effect, and the community was left wounded and cynical. In fact, as has so often been recorded in the history of military occupations, the whole project created a deeply resentful insurgency.

Anderson herself summarized the story very succinctly and candidly: "Here is the inconvenient truth: Education, including education reform, is part of the problem. We have not made a dent in the problem, and in some cases we've made it worse."[3]

What Institutions Can and Cannot Do

> Few things help an individual more than to place responsibility upon him and let him know that you trust him.
> —*Booker T. Washington*

By design, institutions can deliver services, but they cannot care. It seems that care is always expressed more purely in more intimate relationships—marriage, family, and friendship. But those small societies cannot do everything. The need for efficiency and collective strength pushes certain activities and dynamics "up" into larger, corporate, even governmental structures. Individuals within those institutions—like doctors, nurses, and teachers—can certainly demonstrate care for those they serve. But the need for efficiency and accountability necessarily constrains the caring impulses. Those same doctors and nurses and teachers are always under pressure to serve greater numbers, manage a larger caseload, complete more paperwork, and master ever-changing procedures and policies. At some point, everything and everyone in the institution gets forced into bureaucratic behavior.

> *The machine trains you and the shadow culture conditions you to "manage" your caseload, your patients, or your classroom. But, often before we realize what is happening, our school, hospital, prison, or other institution can quickly become an update of* One Flew Over the Cuckoo's Nest. *And anyone can turn into Nurse Ratched.*

Every institution contains a "shadow culture." That culture grows naturally as reinforcement of what the institution was designed to deliver. It keeps people in line. There will always be the unique and delightful Patch Adamses of the world, or Sally, your pharmacist who seems to care that you get the right meds.

The machine trains you and the shadow culture conditions you to "manage" your caseload, your patients, or your classroom. But, often before we realize what is happening, our school, hospital, prison, or other institutions can quickly become an update of *One Flew Over the Cuckoo's Nest*. And anyone can turn into Nurse Ratched. The shadow culture can train perfectly nice people into using their positions to manipulate and humiliate the inmates into models of obedience and order.

You remember Jack Nicholson, as Randle McMurphy, in the film version of Ken Kesey's *One Flew Over the Cuckoo's Nest*? He was a criminal, but he was not crazy. So when he had to take a psychological evaluation for his crime, he gamed the evaluation. He assumed that time in the mental institution would be easier than prison. But he quickly learned that the system was designed to remove his soul. His resistance ultimately ended in the system judging him crazy and dangerous. The system won.

One of Ken Robinson's chief complaints is that our schools are reverting to diagnosing and medicating any active, precocious kid with ADHD. He says, "Our children are living in the most intensely stimulating period in the history of the earth. They're being besieged with information and calls for their attention from every platform—from computers, from iPhones, from advertising hoardings, from hundreds of television channels and we're penalizing them now for getting distracted. From what? Boring stuff at school, for the most part."[4]

Robinson sees a correlation between the rise of standardized tests and the rise of ADHD.

Of course, medications have helped many kids focus and manage their behavior. But I also know from experience and from many parents with kids diagnosed with ADHD that many children feel as though the medication takes away their soul; they don't feel like themselves and they don't like it. The kids who resist and try to hold onto their own identity are judged as being troublesome. The spirit of Nurse Ratched is the shadow inside many institutions.

Iatrogenic Medicine

In the 1970s an increase in medically related deaths launched several investigations. A shocking discovery emerged: at some tipping point in size and complexity a system develops a perverse logic and begins to produce the opposite of its intended mission. "As our means dramatically improve, the number of patients who die or become worse is skyrocketing—so much that the condition has its own term, *iatrogenic*, meaning an illness that the doctor (*iatros*) induces (*genic*). New laws enacted to correct the problem actually exacerbate it, solving a problem in one area creates five more in other places, and new innovations (inserted instead of integrated) bring with them a whole list of side effects."[5]

> *Humanizing the Education Machine and taming the shadow beast of reform must begin by recognizing that learning is fundamentally human and humans are unique.*

That process is the third leading cause of death.[6] Imagine a 747 crashing every day; that's the number of iatrogenic deaths! In 2013, the number of "doctor-caused" deaths was estimated at 143,000 a year. One of our friends, a nurse, told us about "death by decimal." That is when a nurse gives a 1-millimeter dose when it should have been a .1-millimeter dose. She also said that when a nurse needs to be hospitalized, she or he will recruit a small team of nurse-friends to help out.

The Greek word for school is "schole." So should we call school-induced maladies "scholegenic?"

Figure 10.1   Conformity is Soul Killing

Humanizing the Education Machine and taming the shadow beast of reform must begin by recognizing that learning is fundamentally human and humans are unique. Institutions become beasts when they grow beyond human scale and human comprehension (see Figure 10.1). Our job throughout the remaining chapters of this book is to show you how to tame the beast and humanize the machine.

Ferguson and Jennings: Four Miles and a World Apart

Jennings, Missouri, lays nine miles northwest of St. Louis and four miles southeast of the now infamous Ferguson. Jennings' median household income is less than $29,000 a year. The town's politics are

The most powerful weapon in her arsenal is social capital. Anderson knows that building social capital must be at the center of any community transformation.

tumultuous; the mayor and the city council can't seem to get along. In late 2015, the mayor tried to issue an executive order to investigate two council members; at the same time there was a petition to impeach the mayor.

However, a disruptive force in this little universe is creating a groundswell of hope and opportunity for the kids in this city. Education is working! In December 2015 Jennings became the first unaccredited school district in Missouri to regain full accreditation. Tiffany Anderson was the pleasantly tenacious superintendent responsible for that turnaround. Her strategy was aimed at reversing Lower Expectation Syndrome by systematically removing constraints and excuses and engaging the community.

Her formula:

- Build social capital (trust, community engagement and goodwill).
- Raise expectations with kids and parents.
- Hire and develop motivated teachers.

She fights a daily battle for the hearts and minds of the community and her kids. She understands Maslow's pyramid of needs; her kids can't learn if they are hungry, inadequately dressed, and feel unsafe. The most powerful weapon in her arsenal is social capital. Anderson knows that building social capital must be at the center of any community transformation.

Social capital is the tapestry of relationships, values, behavior, and cultural assets that empower the magic of cooperation in any communal group.

Jennings is bordered by the only two remaining unaccredited school districts in Missouri: Calhoun and Ferguson. Michael Brown, the young man killed by the police in Ferguson on August 9, 2014, graduated from Normandy High. You could say that Brown overcame the odds and graduated, just like Jaime Casap. But, when you graduate from a school that has been at the bottom for 13 years, you have escaped more than graduated. The landscape of low expectations is the only view most kids have.

On graduation day Michael Brown put on one of the two gowns the school could afford. The gowns were handed from one student to the next as they graduated.[7]

His graduation was just eight days before he stole a box of Swisher cigars from a convenience store. The officer on call responded to the report of a *robbery in progress* and the incident ended in a tragic shooting and Michael's death. His death erupted into more than a year of protests and national debate over police violence, discrimination, and systemic poverty. The Black Lives Matter movement began in Ferguson and expanded to other cities. On the anniversary of the shooting, a friend of Michael's, Tyrone Harris Jr., graduated from Normandy. When protests broke out he took shots at an unmarked police car. In response police critically wounded him.

The cycle tragically continues. Tyrone's girlfriend, Qunesha Colley, reflected, "He didn't want to be one of those African Americans that's known for going to jail and getting a GED," Coley said. "He made it through, and I salute him so much for that."[8]

A Surge Opportunity for Ferguson

The war in Ferguson spilled into the streets because there was no social capital left to spend. In fact, the town faces a desperately deep deficit. At this point, no amount of money, new policies, or swapping out "bad people" for "good people" will help Ferguson experience what is taking place four miles up the road in Jennings. Those four miles may as well be 4,000 miles.

But, perhaps there is hope for Ferguson. In the spring of 2015, Dr. Joseph Davis was appointed Superintendent of the Ferguson-Florissant school district. His address to the audience announced his ground war for building social capital:

In the spring of 2015, Dr. Joseph Davis, the new superintendent of the Ferguson-Florissant school district, announced his ground war for building social capital:

"For me, it's about building relationships, being in schools and in the community, and letting people see me. . . . What I will do is work on building those relationship so we can work even more so as a team."

"For me, it's about building relationships, being in schools and in the community, and letting people see me. . . . What I will do is work on building those relationship so we can work even more so as a team."[9]

A Human-Scaled Solution Penetrates the Chicago Public Schools

In his book *How Kids Succeed,* Paul Tough gave an in-depth look into the concerted effort of some education superstars to rescue one Chicago school, Fenger Academy. Although Fenger was part of a broader effort, it became the poster child for the mayor and future leaders. This story sounds very similar to Newark, and it should. High profile institutional interventions have often created "scholegenic" conditions for students and their families.

Fenger Academy is on the South Side of Chicago, in the Roseland area. Famed crime fighter and leader of *The Untouchables* Eliot Ness graduated from Fenger. Until the 1960s, that community was a predominately Italian Catholic neighborhood. Today it is 98 percent African American.

The Chicago Public Schools (CPS) were taken over by the city in 1995 (similar to what happened in Newark). Over the next 20 years a string of high profile educators—like Paul Vallas, future Secretary of Education Arne Duncan, and Elizabeth Dozier—tried to turn things around for the CPS. In 1999 Vallas received a $500,000 NASA grant for Fenger, and turned it into a Magnet School. But nothing touched the culture or the neighborhood.

The reality is that at Fenger, we're a neighborhood school, so we're just a reflection of the community. And you can't expect to solve the problems of a school without taking into account what's happening in the community.
—Elizabeth Dozier

Beginning in 2004 The Bill and Melinda Gates Foundation started giving what would eventually total more than $80 million to the CPS.

In 2006 fewer than 6 percent of 400,000 CPS kids could expect to graduate from college.

In 2008 only 4 percent of Fenger kids met standards.

In 2016 the aggregate ACT scores were 14.5.

After six years, in 2015 Elizabeth Dozier resigned. When Paul Tough interviewed her she sounded a lot like the humbled Cami Anderson.

> When I came into this job, I discounted questions like, "what families do kids come from," and "what effect does poverty have on children?"

The reality is that at Fenger, we're a neighborhood school, so we're just a reflection of the community. And you can't expect to solve the problems of a school without taking into account what's happening in the community.[10]

Until 2006 Jeff Nelson was a motivated young teacher inside Chicago's Education Machine, also on the South Side. He believed that many of his kids had a chance to graduate and go to college. He then read a report that said only 6 percent of kids in the Chicago Public Schools would go on to attend college. That meant that in his class of 32 kids, only 2 would beat the odds.

Seeing how well his sixth-graders were doing, he decided to see if he could replicate his approach. So he launched One Goal, with a focused mission: One Goal teaches highly effective teachers to deliver a 40-minute class every day to low-performing kids who seem to have potential. It is an accredited class and runs through a student's junior and senior years of high school. One Goal is also a highly personalized program to help a student develop study skills and life skills. It provides personal coaching, and builds an awareness of what it's like to go to college.

Benito, a high school student in an at-risk zip code in Chicago, was one of those low-performing kids. But he had a teacher who felt he was smart enough to beat the odds, even though no one in Benito's family had ever gone to college, and he didn't even *know* anyone who had gone to college. His world thought college was a fantasy. So, naturally, Benito was a victim of Low Expectation Syndrome. Like so many others, he didn't try to succeed in school, or anywhere else. But one day, a One Goal–trained teacher who believed in Benito asked him if he wanted to go to college. He gave his usual brush-off. But she pressed him further, telling him about One Goal classes.

He signed up. Over his junior and senior year Benito connected with his own education. From that spark started a fire, and Benito became a leader in school. By the time he graduated, he had been accepted into several colleges.[11]

One Goal has now expanded to Houston, Texas, and enrolls more than 2,500 kids per year. The cost is $1,500 per student. The program has an 85 percent college acceptance track record.[12]

Because Jeff took a human-scaled approach to the problem, he hasn't drawn the wrath of the Chicago Teacher's Union. In fact some One Goal

But one day, a One Goal–trained teacher who believed in Benito asked him if he wanted to go to college. He gave his usual brush-off. But she pressed him further, telling him about One Goal classes.

He signed up. Over his junior and senior year Benito connected with his own education. From that spark started a fire, and Benito became a leader in school. By the time he graduated, he had been accepted into several colleges.[11]

teachers belong to the union. They come because they see it works and they see that it protects them from their Union Machine and makes it less likely they will be eliminated.

Two Billionaires—Two Different Outcomes

Facebook's Mark Zuckerberg famously provided the $100 million to launch the One Newark initiative. But I want to tell you about another billionaire that you probably haven't heard of: Atlanta real-estate developer and philanthropist Tom Cousins. Tom is responsible for the transformation of East Lake Meadows, a community that once seemed destined to be another story of failure.

Tom was born in 1931. After military service and graduation from the University of Georgia in 1958, he started building and developing homes with his father. Today, he owns the Atlanta Hawks, Cousins Properties, and other commercial and sporting properties. Tom is widely considered one of the men most responsible for the remaking of Atlanta in the 1970s and 1980s.

A man of strong faith, Tom has always been particularly moved by a Bible passage that captures a conversation between Jesus and his disciples:

"I was in prison, and you visited me."

". . . When did we ever see you sick or in prison and visit you?"

"I tell you the truth, when you did it to one of the least of these my brothers and sisters you were doing it to me!"[13]

In the 1980s, as that biblical passage continued to burn in his heart, Tom began wondering how to help people before they fall into the judicial system. A short time later, Atlanta's Police Chief told Tom that

75 percent of all crimes in Georgia came out of five communities in Atlanta.

Tom pounced: "Which one is the worst?"

"East Lake Meadows; we call it little Vietnam. Believe me, Tom, you don't want to drive through there after sundown!"

But, Tom wondered, what if the most dangerous place in Atlanta could improve, even turn around? That could create strong ripple effects and present new methods in tackling crime. Tom wanted East Lake Meadows!

One additional factor made East Lake Meadows even more attractive. The old Bobby Jones Golf Course was also in that community. It was run down and neglected, but surely represented an untapped (and high profile) asset. The vision started coming together; Tom would buy the golf course, redevelop the public housing, build a new school, and provide the social services that could give the community a new future.

After some pieces fell quickly and easily into place, Tom learned that nothing would move forward without the support of Eva Davis.

Eva was the larger-than-life matriarch and president of the East Lake Tenant Association. East Lake was her kingdom and she was its queen bee, having lived there since 1971. Former President Jimmy Carter, who had his own history with Eva Davis, let Tom know his skepticism of making any progress. "The President told me that in all his negotiations he had never met someone as stubborn and difficult as Eva Davis. She was tougher than Begin or Sadat."

As it turned out, the drama featured four key players: Eva Davis represented the tenants, Carol Naughton and Renee Glover came from the Atlanta Housing Authority (AHA), and Greg Gironelli spoke for Tom's group, the East Lake Foundation.

Renee Glover, the head of the AHA, vividly described the situation:

The public housing program had become the "devil's bargain." That is, in exchange for a social, financial, and housing arrangement—with

> *Tom pounced: "Which one is the worst?"*
>
> *"East Lake Meadows; we call it little Vietnam. Believe me, Tom, you don't want to drive through there after sundown!"*
>
> *But . . . what if the most dangerous place in Atlanta could improve, even turn around?*

no or low standards and without personal accountability or responsibility—one could live in a compromised, dangerous, and dysfunctional housing development. Because it was the only affordable option available to them, families needing assistance with paying their rent found themselves in environments where, over time, they were exploited and destroyed by the chaos that resulted from concentrated poverty and low expectations and standards.

The unintended but predictable consequence of these environments was that society's criminals and predators were empowered, and the vulnerable, law-abiding, very low-income families who found themselves trapped in these no-win situations were imperiled.[14]

Renee's comments unmask, again, the true logic of a system unconstrained by human volition and conscience.

Renee saw the details of how the status quo had become a "devil's bargain." So, in defiance of HUD's mandate for how the funds were to be used, she eagerly partnered with Tom Cousins and his East Lake Foundation. This was her heroic reach to have a good effect on a crumbling system.

Because of all the confusion, politics, turf battles, and racial suspicions, it took six years for Tom and the other leaders to gain Eva Davis' trust. She even filed a lawsuit to stop the process. Greg and Carol made the trip every Friday over that six-year period to participate in the planning committee meetings. Greg estimated it took over 200 meetings to win trust and begin to gain traction.

The process was unlike any other redevelopment process the players had ever seen. The residents met with their attorneys first for a few hours and then would open to the public, the Housing Authority, and the East Lake Foundation. Most meeting started with Ms. Davis yelling at everyone; her anger and vitriol reflected a hard life. She would call them liars, cheats, thieves, honkies, crackers, and more. Racism and classism were thrown in every direction; the meetings turned into mud fights. Greg and Carol remember several meetings that were so emotionally jarring that they needed the long drive time to decompress on the way home. Their mission and recognizing that their role was simply to serve this community helped them return to the table.

In one meeting, Eva launched a very personal attack on Carol. In doing so, she crossed a line. The meeting ended on a very sour note. But Eva circled back and called to apologize. In that call, she also expressed her genuine appreciation for what Carol and Greg were trying to bring to her world. This opened the door for Carol to get to know some of Eva's story.

Eva was born in a small Georgia town. When she was a child, her parents gave her to the local sheriff as a playmate for his daughter. She slept on a pallet in the girl's bedroom. But she could not eat with the family. Eva's mix of anger and affection toward this family, and her sense of abandonment from her own, created the context for Eva's distrust and vigilant protection for her residents.

Eva faced a new reality at the end of this process. She was caught between wanting a redeveloped community for her residents on one hand, and losing her authority and stature on the other. She would be accused of being an Uncle Tom and a sell-out. The residents were being asked to give up their homes and, not only that, but to give them up to a government that had consistently let them down and abandoned them. They also had to trust that a white billionaire real estate developer would do the right thing.

But, of course, everyone had a story. And everyone had been shaped by his or her own story. All the stories—formed in abuse, neglect, exploitation, distrust, and more—had left wounds. Then, in the reactions, salt was added to wounds. That process became a vicious cycle, destroying hope and possibilities. That has happened over and over in every community development in the country.

But, sometimes, a spark, the breeze from a butterfly's wings, or something miraculous happens that pulls all the disparate parties into some kind of cohesion.

And so it was that East Lake was a partnership between a billionaire and politicians, similar to Newark. There was strong opposition from the community, similar to what occurred in Newark. But, there was a common mission to restore human dignity, and the redevelopment always stayed in its proper position—a means to that end, and not the other way around.

> *However well intentioned, the institutionalized applications of "care" all assume that people are incapable of helping themselves, that people are the problem, and that everyone needs the institution's help. And, of course, that help will be on the institution's terms.*

When they reach a certain scale, grand initiatives and institutions cannot seem to avoid flipping *means* and the *end goal*. As the means become *the goal*, test scores override learning, and "improved schools" come at a cost to communities. Fear and insecurity drive these systems.

However well intentioned, the institutionalized applications of "care" all assume that people are incapable of helping themselves, that people are the problem, and that everyone needs the institution's help. And, of course, that help will be on the institution's terms. The system isn't doing this for people out of a sense kindness. It is, to paraphrase Gandhi, doing it *to you*, not for *you*. The system resents that it has to do anything at all. It is, as Renee said, a "devil's bargain."

One of my lessons from East Lake is how belief in the mission to restore dignity will require that we remain patient when the Eva Davises of the world spew the distrust and betrayal out of their systems. All of that is part of "doing life together." It may not be efficient, but it turns out to be highly effective.

The common thread between Alyssa, Tiffany Anderson, Jeff Nelson, Tom Cousins, Carol Naughton, Greg Gironelli, and Eva Davis is this: They all saw the vital catalyst as "doing life together." They didn't have a short-term or romantic vision. They knew that the very hard work of building community requires time! And time is the one thing that systems based on delivering service efficiently do not like and do not have. When we don't have time then we fall into roles (and roles by themselves are fine and provide frameworks). But when roles have to be protected or feel threatened they produce masks. That is when shadow culture dormant in the system turns to serve itself instead of the mission.

Getting beyond the roles and masks is messy, off-script, unapproved, sometimes vulgar, and unpredictable. When you do unmask the roles and begin doing life with others, then the timelines, processes, and procedures give way to a relational flow and rhythm. Newark was thwarted by an artificial timeline and institutional arrogance. East Lake Meadows took six years and two hundred meetings just to launch. It was anything but efficient.

Social Emotional Literacy

The American Psychological Institute defines socioeconomic status as, ". . . the social standing or class of an individual or group. It is often measured as a combination of education, income, and occupation." Reform attempts to improve the plight of children with low socioeconomic status have exposed a deep chasm in the Gutenberg model. Its focus on the mind and academic learning has overlooked or marginalized noncognitive learning and emotional health.

The next two chapters bridge this chasm. In particular we will explore the central role of social and emotional literacy as vital for at-risk children. It is also key to the kind of internally motivated learning that educators believe is essential to developing twenty-first-century survival skills.

CHAPTER 11

The Healing Power of Social Emotional Literacy

". . . a student's ability to learn is deeply impacted by the quality of his or her attachment to teachers and peers."

—Lou Cozolino

In its pure form, medical care is the point where science, training, equipment, and compassion come together, allowing one human to extend effective care to another. That pristine idea is the root of many stories of selfless doctors, nurses, and other medical care professionals who went to heroic efforts to help others.

So, how does medical care *itself* become the third leading cause of death? In Chapter 10, we considered the parallel between an iatrogenic (illness, injury, or death caused by medical care) impact on patients and the similar effect of education on students.

When a system becomes toxic to its customers, clients, or patients, change is inevitable. Societies have a way of withdrawing authorization from systems that fail in their mission. They finally just get fed up with the explanations, excuses, accusations, promises, and reforms. For example, we know that growing distrust of the medical system is a primary driver of the alternative medicine phenomenon.

The same dynamic is at work in learning. Our team saw the flowering of new forms and platforms for learning all across America—Free Range Learning, School of One, Quest for Learning, Khan Academy, AltSchool, High Tech High, NuTech, home schooling, and so forth. If learning does not thrive in the officially sanctioned and funded institutions of the Education Machine, it will break out in other non-sanctioned ways and places.

And that is why Lisa and I drove down to Deep Ellum, an old and mostly abandoned industrial section on the east side of downtown Dallas. Today it is a hipster community with arts, entertainment, trendy restaurants, and a few coworking (membership-shared work space concept) and digital media firms. We sat in a Deep Ellum venue called DaVerse Lounge, where we heard founder Will Richey open the evening with a poem:

> *When I share my joy,*
> *I multiply my happiness.*
> *When I share my pain,*
> *I divide my sadness.*
> *And when I embrace the two,*
> *I become whole . . .*
> *WE become . . . Whole.*[1]

DaVerse Lounge was showcasing about 30 students from middle through high school in an exhibition of Spoken Word. We arrived early but found the parking lot full; the vehicles included four school buses. When we walked in, we saw over 400 people in the audience and another hundred young kids in the front entry engaged in art projects hosted by Art Love Magic. We didn't know what to expect.

Kids from fifth grade up to college students walked onto the stage to share their artistic expressions. Some presented with dramatic flair, some with choreographed movement, and some simply trembled, holding the microphone and staring at the floor until the audience loved them into being at ease.

I first met Will in a workshop he led at EdShift 2016, where he introduced a room full of teachers to the idea of emotional literacy. Will and his DaVerse Lounge team have reached many kids by creating safe environments in which they can process their life stories. They train them to tell it well and give them the confidence to get up in front of others.

Kids from fifth grade up to college students walked onto the stage to share their artistic expressions. Some presented with dramatic flair, some with choreographed movement, and some simply trembled, holding the microphone and staring at the floor until the audience loved them into being at ease.

Htee Ku Shee, a high school student at Irma Rangel Young Women's Leadership School, shared a poem that cut to the heart of learning (and which gives clear warning to the toxic Education Machine). I include an excerpt with her permission:

> *Dear school system,*
> *Why are you killing our writers?*
> *Our readers, our thinkers, our creators?*
> *You label them as numbers*
> *And deprive them of their colors*
> *Drained of their imaginations*
> *There's no room left for creations*
> *Dear school system,*
> *Each day you gain a robot for society*
> *You lose a Beyoncé, an Edger Allen Poe,*
> *And a person who knows!*
> *Who knows how important art is,*
> *How important words are,*
> *And how important they are.*
> *So save a life today*
> *I beg you please!*
> *You only have to do one thing*
> *Just let them breath.*

When Will and his DaVerse Lounge team presented at a TEDx, held at SMU, Will said this journey began when he had to confront the mask of his public façade. He discovered in his search how to shed that mask and change from a *human doing* to a *human being*.

"In our process and walk together we get to reprocess our life journey.[2] It is not just about poetry; it's about personal connection. It's not only about writing; it's about self-reflection. It is not only about reading off the page; it's about taking pride in the ancestry of your name. It is not only about performing; it's about hearing your voice and its resonance with others."

Social and emotional literacy play vital roles in humanizing the Education Machine. They set the foundation for future-ready kids.

Your Brain on Learning

We are social creatures with brains attuned to those around us. This means that we should seriously consider placing the same emphasis on social and emotional learning in the classroom as we do on memorizing facts and problem solving.
—Lou Cozolino, Professor of Psychology at Pepperdine

Brain science is defining a new era in learning. The science, data, discipline, practice and tools have reached a critical mass with compelling conclusions about how kids best learn. That new science also documents the damage inflicted on the brains of our kids by socioeconomic disparities, technological disruptions, outdated schools and teaching methods, social fragmentation, and the unrelenting pace of American life.

We clearly need more emphasis on social and emotional literacy. But that also presents the practical challenge of retraining close to 3.8 million teachers in America, as well as helping to retool an over-driven society.[3] This is not a training challenge as much as it is a cultural challenge. Social and Emotional Literacy requires both a new mindset and hands-on experience. Alyssa, the teacher featured in Chapters 9 and 10, told me that she wished she had a basic orientation to some useful methods of intervention, or even a bio on her kids in order to see them as individuals and not simply as students. From other conversations, I believe that is a common concern. During our research for this book, I also heard the following comments from teachers:

Research suggests that our kids are highly influenced by their teachers' personalities. Let's make sure our teachers are emotionally and socially healthy!
—Lisa Miller, Homeschool Educator

"No one ever prepared me for this."
"I am not qualified to deal with some of the challenges that erupt in my classroom."

"I had to just figure it out and for the first six months of my class I came home in tears many times. I at least figured some of this out and now have more good days than bad days."

Science is also reconfirming what common sense once told us:

- Kids need to be active during the day.
- They need safe and nurturing environments in order to learn.
- They learn best in social and engaging classrooms.
- Each student is unique; each one learns differently.
- Pressures and stress outside school affect the classroom.
- Healthy diets and healthy habits improve attention and engagement.

That's why the learning process must be personal, not bureaucratic. Just as medical care should focus on the patient more than on its own system, so education must care for and about each student. Brandon Busteed, Executive Director, Education & Workforce Development at Gallup, sums up what Gallup has researched as the core elements for student success: ". . . having someone who cares about your development and having an opportunity to do what you do best every day."[4]

Dr. Cozolino reinforces Gallup's research with brain science and says if we view learning as a process for growing the capacity of the brain, it grows best in an environment of supportive relationships, low stress and emotional arousal, balanced between thinking and feeling, and through the creative use of storytelling.

"Go Settle Your Glitter"

The Momentous Institute began in the 1920s as a therapeutic outreach to at-risk communities in South Dallas. Today, the Institute serves about 6,000 kids and families every year.

According to Michelle Kinder, the Executive Director of the Institute, many of these kids will fall under a mental health category called Adverse Childhood Experiences. These are divided into three categories: physical, emotional, and sexual abuse. A child coming out of these conditions will most likely experience disruption in neurodevelopment. That leads to social, emotional, and cognitive impairment, leading to destructive and risky behaviors. Without intervention by those who care, these journeys do not end well. Such interventions must start early, engage the family, and be led by teachers well trained in social and emotional literacy.

The Momentous Institute provides a safe, positive, and connected environment for their kids, from three years old to fifth grade. But they also recognize that unless their environments outside of school are positive, the gains will be short lived. Michelle took me to the parent resource room. There, she explained, "Parents are welcome to come at any time. Once a month there is a box of books and educational toys. The parents can take them home for their child's continued use. The box also has a journal, so they can describe how they used the material and read what other families wrote."

The space kids learn in is a vehicle for knowledge. It communicates a tone, encourages curiosity, and can set a child at ease.
—Christy Sharp, Art Love Magic

Parents also receive coaching and training so that they are equipped to work on improving the family and the home environment. Michelle took me to the vision wall, where parents and their kids draft their visions for the student's education. Some were simple, many were hopeful, but some were very specific and quite moving. Some stories just took my breath away.

Throughout the tour I found numerous subtle details that reveal the "momentous" attention to each child and the environment. The hallway walls were painted in textures that invite kids to sweep their hands along the wall as they walk, stimulating their senses. Photographs of the brain, highlighting different areas and brain functions, are posted throughout the school. I met three-year-olds who told me they had a brain and it was in their head and was very, very important. Five-year-olds know where frustration, anger, and sorrow come from in the brain. They also knew the coping skills that calm the brain down.

A glitter ball is a clear rubber ball filled with liquid and glitter. Shaking it up clouds it with a swirl of glitter. Of course, it takes a few minutes for it all to settle back to the bottom. If a student is acting out another student will hand them the ball and say, "Go Settle Your Glitter."

Michelle said that a lot of these kids come out of traumatized situations. Their emotions are on a hair trigger. When a child acts out they call it an "amygdala hijack." "You don't logic them out of their trauma. You have to calm them down, settle their glitter; then you can talk about consequences."

On down the hall, I saw a display of each kid's graduation in the future, including the date and a picture of him or her in a graduation gown. Near that display is another one, featuring pictures of kids who have graduated and the flag of the college they attend or attended.

Even though the institute teaches the kids only through fifth grade, Momentous graduates go on to perform at a much higher level than kids in typical school systems. Ninety-nine percent graduate from high school, 86 percent go on the college, and 87 percent of those students graduate from college. In other words, this kind of learning experience matters!

Throughout their 90 years of service, the Momentous Institute has trained over 5,000 teachers. The Institute is clearly a school with a well-integrated learning framework designed around social and emotional literacy. The one thing that seems to be the cardinal difference between Momentous and more traditional schools is *intentionality*. They care enough to actually think through the lives of students, and then to intentionally build the learning experience around that life.

The institute is a great model of empathetic design. They view their job through the lens of the students' emotional and social literacy from the time they arrive. They pay attention to how students arrive and are greeted, the effect of the opening breathing and centering exercise, student instruction, discipline, and so forth—the entire day is designed to provide a safe, nurturing, stimulating, empowering, and successful experience—every day. And, to the best of their ability, the Momentous Institute expands that intentionality into the family.

By contrast a traditional school experience seems to focus on specific disconnected class periods, a small part of that student's time and interaction in school. How might we rethink schools if we viewed learning as an integrated cumulative journey throughout the student's day, semester, and year? Could we move away from our batched, boxed, assembly-line school models to a more fluid and integrated learning community mindset? "The implications of this research suggest that

> *I saw a display of each kid's graduation in the future, including the date and a picture of him or her in a graduation gown. Near that display is another one, featuring pictures of kids who have graduated and the flag of the college they attend or attended.*

whatever differences children come to school with can be impacted by subsequent experiences in the classroom, especially teacher-student attachment relationships. Teachers can have a powerful influence on changing the brains of their students for the better."[5]

Early Warning Systems for Students

Dr. Lynn Frickey specializes in early warning systems and interventions for at risk kids. Right out of college, she started working at a Colorado treatment facility for boys who were victims of sexual abuse and violent crimes. That program, similar to an Outward Bound experience, took the boys for three weeks of survival training in Yellowstone or into the boundary waters of Minnesota. The boys were typically urban kids with no exposure to the outdoors and certainly no experience in wilderness conditions. Those three-week ventures in the wilderness created something magical: kids who up to that point "didn't give a damn and had no reason to care" were transformed into a connected, cohesive, and confident team.

She saw magic happen when kids got outdoors, were physically challenged, and encouraged to rely on one another.

After that experience, Lynn transitioned into education, where she continued working with at-risk kids. Once again, she saw magic happen when kids got outdoors, were physically challenged, and encouraged to rely on one another. Since her school was near a base for the Colorado National Guard, she invited active and retired military personnel to celebrate an upcoming Veteran's Day. When she saw how the kids responded to those in uniform, she continued to build on the experience.

"I sought them out to partner on leadership activities and mentoring. That led to coteaching the leadership course I created for kids who needed credits to graduate from high school."

Her father, a retired army colonel, was the emcee for the Veterans Day ceremony. He also spoke on other occasions and cowrote a reader's theater script to actively engage the kids in learning Vietnam history.

Lynn told me, "I told the military base brass how we were engaging the kids, using the reader's theater with my partners from the Colorado Army National Guard. They offered to turn it into a live simulation at the base. One of the sergeants created a rescue/survival mission simulation for a downed Huey helicopter. We scheduled these events on the base on Saturdays. The kids also experienced drills and eating MREs (Meal, Ready-to-Eat). It was voluntary but, even though the events were held on a Saturday, every kid showed up."

Dr. Frickey knew if at-risk kids could be identified early, there was a good chance for positive interventions. However, up until 2000, accurately identifying kids at risk was subjective at best. But there were well-established metrics for what an engaged student looked like. So Dr. Frickey reverse-engineered that research to test the signs of dis-engagement that lead to dropping out,[6] and that led to a breakthrough assessment tool: The Scale of Student Engagement/Disengagement, or SOS ED.[7] The assessment looks closely at demographic factors, connections and relationships, academic interests, habits, ability, skill levels, and future goals.

Hoosiers

I visited Washington High School in Washington, Indiana, where they had implemented Dr. Frickey's SOS ED early warning system. The school is about two hours southwest of Indianapolis. Washington looks like a typical Midwest semi-abandoned small town with a small town square. Once a factory town, the factories have now been closed a long time. The city has about 2,400 families; most are white and unemployed.

LeAnne Kelley, the principal, and Captain Neil May, Navy Reserve and science instructor at Washington High, are two unusually talented, experienced, and committed leaders in a community that is a faded and wounded image of its past. LeAnne is on a mission to transform the school and was, at the time of my visit, in the second year of the turnaround.

She explained that just getting to school is a struggle for many students. Most parents are unemployed. Meth addiction is a major problem. But LeAnne and Captain May were committed to changing the social landscape. They found that Dr. Frickey's assessment helped them build an early warning system that allowed teachers to see under-neath the masks and pinpoint kids needing intervention and support.

Captain May showed me their "war room." The walls were lined with student information (see Figure 11.1, which pictures an example of a "war room," showing names and grades for each subject). They even

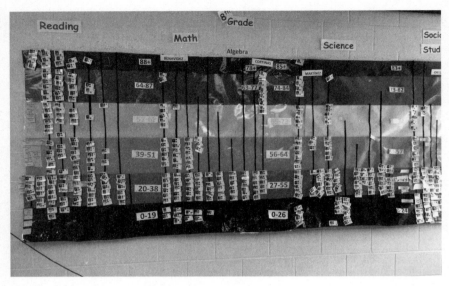

Figure 11.1   Tracking At-Risk Students

have a large spreadsheet listing different factors they track, in addition to the SOS ED results—truancy, grades, failing, disengagement, and disruptive behavior (see Figure 11.2). Their system ranks these in order of digression. When a student reaches a certain threshold it activates an intervention. The intervention begins with a meeting of that student's teachers and the creation of a shared living Google Doc and tracking device. Each teacher records his or her interactions and conversations with the student. The journal allows the root issues to slowly emerge through the iterative nature of capturing the evolution of progress.

For example, they told me about Melinda (not her real name), a student who started missing school, getting poor grades, acting out, and developing a harsh personality. She measured as "high risk of dropping out" on the SOS ED. When the teachers set up an "Intervention

When the teachers set up an "Intervention Journal," they learned that her parents' car had been repossessed. Melinda wanted to be at school but lack of transportation had become a daily and often unsurmountable hurdle. Their attention to the problem got everyone on the same page, and also developed a deeper appreciation of Melinda as a person and the challenges of her situation.

Figure 11.2   Student Risk Categories

Journal," they learned that her parents' car had been repossessed. Melinda wanted to be at school but lack of transportation had became a daily and often unsurmountable hurdle. Their attention to the problem got everyone on the same page, and also developed a deeper appreciation of Melinda as a person and the challenges of her situation. Teachers banded together to make sure that she got rides to and from school. Melinda's behavior changed; her anger and passion were channeled to becoming a leader and helping other kids who were starting to disengage or veer toward bad behavior.

Melinda's new outlook, and the development of a community of support at Washington High School began with a tool that provided early warning and direction for taking positive intervention.

A Teacher's Lesson in Emotional Literacy

Glennon Doyle Melton writes a blog called "Momastery." Through her personal life stories, Glennon opens the door for her readers to explore, unmask, and connect. Her January 30, 2014, blog presented an astounding story of her son's teacher.

Every Friday afternoon Chase's teacher asks her students to take out a piece of paper and write down the names of four children with whom they'd like to sit the following week. The children know that these requests may or may not be honored. She also asks the students to nominate one student whom they believe has been an exceptional classroom citizen that week. All ballots are privately submitted to her.

And every single Friday afternoon, after the students go home, Chase's teacher takes out those slips of paper, places them in front of her and studies them. She looks for patterns.

Who is not getting requested by anyone else?

Who doesn't even know who to request?

Who never gets noticed enough to be nominated?

Who had a million friends last week and none this week?

You see, Chase's teacher is not looking for a new seating chart or "exceptional citizens." Chase's teacher is looking for lonely children. She's looking for children who are struggling to connect with other children. She's identifying the little ones who are falling through the cracks of the class's social life. She is discovering whose gifts are going unnoticed by their peers. And she's pinning down—right away—who's being bullied and who is doing the bullying.

As a teacher, parent, and lover of all children—I think that this is the most brilliant Love Ninja strategy I have ever encountered. It's like taking an X-ray of a classroom to see beneath the surface of things and into the hearts of students. It is like mining for gold—the gold being those little ones who need a little help—who need adults to step in and TEACH them how to make friends, how to ask others to play, how to join a group, or how to share their gifts with others. And it's a bully deterrent because every teacher knows that bullying usually happens outside of her eyeshot—and that often kids being bullied are too intimidated to share. But as she said—the truth comes out on those safe, private, little sheets of paper.

As Chase's teacher explained this simple, ingenious idea—I stared at her with my mouth hanging open. "How long have you been using this system?" I said.

"Ever since Columbine," she said. Every single Friday afternoon since Columbine. Good Lord.

This brilliant woman watched Columbine knowing that ALL VIOLENCE BEGINS WITH DISCONNECTION. All outward violence begins as inner loneliness. She watched that tragedy KNOWING that children who aren't being noticed will eventually resort to being noticed by any means necessary.

As Chase's teacher explained this simple, ingenious idea—I stared at her with my mouth hanging open. "How long have you been using this system?" I said.

"Ever since Columbine," she said. Every single Friday afternoon since Columbine. Good Lord.

And so she decided to start fighting violence early and often, and with the world within her reach. What Chase's teacher is doing when she sits in her empty classroom studying those lists written with shaky 11 year old hands—is SAVING LIVES.[8]

For millennia, the social and family networks caught and saved those who wandered toward the cliff. But those networks are now seriously weakened and even nonexistent for many. But new systems are now emerging that will help us better see, assess, feel, and respond to those in need.

Tribes

So we have this kind of—I don't know—sort of like an antiquated notion of the professionalization of human relationships that doesn't really work. And it especially doesn't work for kids that are stressed or marginalized or traumatized. Love is the bridge for them to open up their brain to new learning. So I believe love is at the core of everything that all of us do.
—Lou Cozolino, Change the Odds Conference 2015

We all naturally gravitate to tribes. Barn raising, fighting forest fires, military action, Facebook, DaVerse Lounge, and The Momentous Institute are all examples of tribes.

Dr. Frickey's class became one, Melinda's teachers created a tribe for her and so did Chase's teacher. Dr. Cozolino defines a tribe as super-organism. It is a group of individuals who form a collective identity, and that identity makes them stronger than they would be as individuals.

This may be why Cozolino wrote, "We have to figure out ways to embed tribe building into the curriculum, weave it into classroom management, and find time to dedicate to tribe building."[9]

We believe, and research supports, that re-tribalizing school is one antidote to the Education Machine. Our proposal is not to simply allow more extra-curricular activities but to see and build re-tribalization as a holistic design feature into the culture, curriculum and facility. Our research has revealed that when several schools simply changed class format to small group face-to-face, learning and learning behavior improved, fun returned and teachers felt rejuvenated.

Restoring Common Sense

The Gutenberg worldview created institutions in order to gather individuals for collective outcomes. And that served societies well for more than 400 years. But, as institutions grew increasingly complex, people and cultures lost the tribal experience of community, connection and collective purpose. The Gutenberg mindset for learning has also emphasized rational intellectual learning over creative and craft learning.

The escalation of brain science and social and emotional literacy is rebalancing this bias. In addition, the Social-Mobile media shift is repatterning our perceptions of time and space and quickly reconstituting us into virtual tribes. All of this is helping us to reclaim the power humans have to grant one another worth. Through intimate connections and tribal formations we are all becoming more together than we can be on our own.

Will Richey invites his audience at the beginning of a session to repeat,

I want to see you . . .
I want to hear you . . .
I want to feel you . . .
I want to acknowledge you . . .
For you are worthy . . .
I am worthy . . .

With a short pause AP, his partner, comes out and says, "I love that statement but I think there is something missing. I believe that if we give everyone a melody to go with this, they will remember it."

Within a few minutes, all those gathered with Will and AP became a tribe; our brains became open and curious. We learned. Together.

Finding the Flow

Social and emotional literacy is the healing art that provides an open and adaptable brain, a brain that is eager and able to learn. The science that restores the over-stressed and traumatized mind is the same science that prepares all minds for deeper learning. This leads us to a discussion about student engagement, which describes the shift from externally motivated learning to the internal joy of learning. Engagement can also lead to a deeper level of absorption called flow. The next chapter describes how the open and curious mind becomes the engaged mind and can lead to flow.

CHAPTER 12

Creating a Healthy Learning Culture

Culture is the invisible attitudes, values, habits, and behaviors that run the place when you're not there.
— Rex Miller, Mabel Casey, and Mark Konchar, *Change Your Space, Change Your Culture*

M ost of my work helps organizations to define their strategy, culture, vision, purpose, and values—and then put those into practice. Leaders are typically good at developing clear vision, a reason for existence and an effective strategy. But when it comes to values and culture they struggle. What leaders often think are distinct and gripping values are usually very common and easily found. Many sound like Hallmark cards.

> *Culture is simply what happens when you're not there.*

Culture and values go hand-in-hand so it is not surprising that fuzziness on one end will produce fuzziness on the other.

Culture is simply what happens when you're not there.

It is the natural default of your organization, team, or classroom when authority is not around to direct, troubleshoot, and require accountability. Clear culture answers very fundamental questions: What is expected of me? How do we treat others? How do we get things done around here?

Following my lunch in the cafeteria of a Silicon Valley high-tech company I took my tray to the dishwashing conveyor belt. Before I could set it on the belt I was confronted with five different receptacles—blue, yellow, green, gray, and red. Each one had a symbol. But I'm from Texas where we have two different-colored waste receptacles; I had no clue which items were "compostable" rather than "biodegradable." I stared at the different bins and felt stupid; I did not want to make the wrong choice and get kicked off this magical planet. An employee quickly rescued me, "Let me show you where each item goes and I'll tell you why."

That is exactly what culture provides: an unprompted, unscripted *what, when, where, why,* and *how* to help me fit in and sync with their culture codes.

In our classroom visits across the country, we have seen many teachers help their students define class and school values in tangible ways and sometimes at a very early age. In one classroom of first graders we found them busy in small groups working on their "bucket filling" exercise. One of the groups was cutting out pictures from magazines and putting them into two different categories (see Figure 12.1).

When I asked about it, the teacher showed me a copy of Tom Rath's book, *How Full Is Your Bucket?* Rath provides research and examples about how we all fill or drain our emotional buckets. So I crouched down to ask one of the children for an example of bucket filling or draining.

"Like when you say 'thank you,' that fills someone's bucket."

"When you don't share... that's bad."

Fuzziness invites what we describe as "shadow culture." Fuzzy culture requires managing; the fuzzier the culture, the more management is needed."

The kids were learning the school's core values. Incredibly, this school focused on behavior and character work in kindergarten and first grade! What a great way to keep a certain cultural calibration. We saw some schools weave character training and reinforcement into all of their work and activities. But those were rare. Rarer still were the teachers and staff who work on these among themselves. So often, what we say we value begins to be crowded out by competing values. That's when it all becomes fuzzy. That fuzziness invites what we describe as "shadow culture."

Figure 12.1 Emotional Bucket Filling Exercise

Fuzzy culture requires managing; the fuzzier the culture, the more management is needed. Fuzzy culture requires constant attention for the 50 percent of teachers (or students) in the middle of the boat watching and waiting for "management" to give direction. More time is required putting out the fires created by the 20 percent in the back of the boat.

Values are simply the attitudes, habits, and behaviors you reward or tolerate.

The MeTEOR Makeover

John and Bill own and run MeTEOR Education.[1] Their mission is to inspire and support communities in providing world-class learning environments. When we first met to discuss updating their mission, values, purpose, and strategy they provided me with a list of 10 values. I went through each one of the 10 values and asked:

- What does it look like, in practice?
- What decisions or actions can I independently take based on it?
- Are these really the values that run the place when you're not there?

My last question opened up a lengthy conversation. When Peter Drucker said that, "Culture eats strategy for breakfast," he was referring to *shadow culture*. Most leaders know the Drucker maxim but few actually appreciate its significance and application.

The Shadow Culture

Values are like plays in a sports competition. They get executed in the heat of the moment under high pressure and rapidly changing conditions. Sometimes they are brilliantly executed, sometimes not. If the coach doesn't have first-hand experience of being in the heat of the moment as a player, then his or her instructions will come across fuzzy, wooden, and scripted.

Without building that level of reality and tangibility that the first graders were engaged in earlier, their shadow culture will prevail. It says, "This is how we really do things around here." If a new plan, program, teaching model, or software program cuts across the shadow culture it says, "No, thank you. We're happy doing things the old way."

Shadow culture is happy to outlast, outlive, act out, passively resist, and even sabotage a new strategy to preserve itself.

Shadow culture is happy to outlast, outlive, act out, passively resist, and even sabotage a new strategy to preserve itself.

"Change management" has become the institutional solution for getting "buy-in" and dealing with resistance. But that approach never addresses the field of play. When organizations start with strategy they assume they can coax the culture to buy in or, if met with resistance, simply drive the change they want. These are big mistakes. Shadow culture is far too savvy and knows when it is being patronized or manipulated. It is also too powerful to underestimate.

Instead of investing hours and dollars building a 100-slide Power-Point presentation and scheduling a road show of town hall meetings, we recommend that leaders get to know their organization's shadow culture.

Dining Room and Kitchen Culture

The next step for Bill and John was to meet together with the MeTEOR leadership team and set up a project-based learning assignment. I used Chef Ramsay and his show *Hell's Kitchen* to describe the difference between the dining room culture (the published values on the back of the menu) and the kitchen culture.

The dining room is what the public sees and experiences. It reflects best behavior. But the kitchen is where the work actually gets done. If you've watched an episode of *Hell's Kitchen* you know that what happens in the kitchen is messy, often nasty, and sometimes a train wreck.

The "kitchen culture" helped the MeTEOR leaders to see and talk about the unvarnished truth. It revealed some behaviors and attitudes that run the place and sometimes run rampant.

When I left, I gave them a simple assignment: Keep a journal over the next month. Observe and capture two kinds of behaviors. First, those spontaneous behaviors that impress and make you feel proud. Second, those that make you shake your head and wonder, "What were they thinking?"

That assignment is also a vital exercise for every teacher. As a coach it puts you back in the field of play and lets you experience the expectations that seem to be clear and consistent to the coaches, but may be fuzzy to the players. It will also help you see where they cut across the shadow culture.

After a month the MeTEOR team reconvened. The session began by sitting in a large open circle with each manager sharing overall observations, including highlights and lowlights. The team then spent the next 15 minutes discovering the top five behaviors in each category, writing them on sticky notes and then posting them on the wall. When they finished, the wall had more than a hundred sticky notes. The next step grouped all of the sticky notes into five categories. We used different-colored sticky notes for positive and negative behaviors.

The main themes included The Quality of Our Work, How We Treat Each Other, The Client Experience, and others. The next step refined the lists further by ranking each of the behaviors as positive or negative. The top positive behavior was "cheerfully going the extra mile." The top negative was "running support staff over."

It was then time to reflect on where the behaviors came from and how the current culture reinforced them. That took the leaders to the mirror.

A Look into the Mirror

There are four sources for *kitchen culture* behavior.

1. The actions of (and messages sent by) leaders and teachers.
2. Behaviors that are rewarded or punished (formally or informally).
3. Behaviors that are tolerated.
4. The physical environment.

One of the unspoken messages (source #1) that the MeTEOR leadership team identified was, "We're very busy and it had better be very important to interrupt us!" How did they uncover that? No one openly said it. But the receptionist noticed that every one of them usually entered the office building talking on their smartphone and walking straight to their office and shutting the door behind them. The leadership office locations, at one end of the space, also sent a message: "You are now entering a gated community; walk very carefully and check in with our gatekeepers."

So, what changed as a result of the makeover?

The management team first set an expectation for themselves. No manager could be on their cell phone when they came into the building. Instead, they would spend time strolling through each department and conversing with the employees.

They also changed their space away from the "us and them" message by distributing managers throughout the office, taking away gatekeepers, and changing their roles to help make managers more accessible.

Never naming the shadow culture is why so many mission and value statements sound and feel hollow.

When I asked the team, "What did you find that you value," Bill answered, "I guess we value numbers. You will be recognized for good numbers and spanked for bad ones."

Bill's candor and clarity about that shadow reality was rare and refreshing. Few organizations actually reach or are willing to acknowledge the reality of their shadow culture with that level of clarity. But without speaking the truth there is no foundation to build on. Never naming the shadow culture is why so many mission and value statements sound and feel hollow.

Adjusting Boat Behaviors

The management team used the boat analogy to define what the different engagement levels looked like (Figure 12.2). They took a close look at the range of behaviors from their "ethnographic" research, and from that defined front of the boat behaviors, middle of the boat behaviors, and back of the boat behaviors. For the first time MeTEOR Education had clarity and a taxonomy to set expectations around specific valued and unacceptable behaviors.

With the project completed, it came time to present the findings in a company-wide meeting. The management team took turns sharing the journey. The employees responded well; the company was in the middle of a three-year growth cycle. This meant that structures, roles, and people were navigating change and working hard to keep up. Managers were stretched and expectations had gotten fuzzy and sometimes contradictory. Clarity was welcomed.

After the presentation, it was time for one-on-one meetings with the "back of the boat" members. The power behind this conversation lie

Figure 12.2 Three Kinds of Boat Behavior: (1) Engaged, (2) Along for the Ride, and (3) Drilling a Hole.

partially in the new question: "Where are you in the boat and where do you want to be?" Defining the three kinds of boat behaviors gave tangible and specific definitions and examples. They were not simply handed a list of generic traits such as respect, honesty, integrity, and world-class service. The original list of 10 value statements was reduced to five short headlines, a corresponding icon, followed by a brief description and supported with several examples of what the behavior looks like.

Here is one example:

Headline: We travel in one boat together.

Icon: A boat with 10 people in it showing the front rowers, a middle group observing and two in the back drilling a hole.

Description: The family cares about each other and succeeds together.

Examples:
- We use the language of "we."
- No scapegoats.
- We know each other's professional and personal pain points.
- We celebrate together and mourn together.
- We produce artifacts of our success, like family portraits.

So what happened to the five? The final necessary piece to shifting this boat was the actual observed examples of back of the boat behavior. The managers had reconnected with the employees through first-hand observation and by leading by example and changing their own behaviors and habits.

This is one of the dilemmas of leadership, teaching, and parenting; when faced with two competing values, which one wins?

Bill and John did not know what to expect and actually concerned because these five people represented top revenue producers. If the values and observations were not clear it would have been easy to fall back into acquiescence, slapping wrists, and within a few days, the whole thing would fall back into old and negative behaviors. The message would have been, "We say everyone is equally important, but some are more equal than others. And they get a pass when they misbehave."

This is one of the dilemmas of leadership, teaching, and parenting; when faced with two competing values, which one wins?

The process created a clear, clean, and healthy approach to the next crucial set of conversations. Each employee heard what was observed and clear explanations of why their behaviors were unacceptable, and so on. It led the conversation to considering the pressures that these employees felt and how they were trying to live up to those expectations. The conversations once again verified that it is never a one-way street. Mature managers know that they set the tone and that they are part of the needed change.

With that insight and humility Bill and John found that most of the boat members were completely unaware of the impact of their negative behavior. Some appreciated the feedback and wanted to be seen as front of the boat members as well as respected leaders. Not everyone, however, received it well. The good news is that three of the five quickly moved closer to the front of the boat. The other good news is that the other two left.

Bill, very excited, called to share progress after a couple of months of the new changes settling in, "I wish we had done this months ago. John and I were really concerned that we might lose some of our heavy hitters. But we haven't missed a beat in our numbers. The headaches those employees brought are gone and the morale has never been better!"

Many leaders make a mistake by assuming that they can somehow create culture, as if it is the simple result of a brainstorm session. "Let's choose values *we* like, values that reflect who *we* think we are, and values that employees can get excited about." Without going back onto the field of play to see and feel the competing pressures that employees face, the shadow culture will swallow it all whole. And very possibly swallow you with it.

Culture is never created brand new; it grows out of what already exists. Culture already resides deep within the school or other organization. It lives along a simple quadrant with one continuum of healthy or unhealthy and the other continuum of by design or by default. You can move a culture, shape it, and even transform it, but you can't invent it during a work-shop or strategic planning session.

> *Culture is never created brand new; it grows out of what already exists.*

The Right Brain Side of Change

During my experience at TAG Consulting we saw many organizations struggle with change. Because our focus was cultural change, we saw these struggles through a different lens. In one case a company followed one of the renowned eight-step methods from Harvard Business School. The steps roughly follow this progression.

1. We have a burning platform. If we don't change we perish.
2. We need a small committed cadre to take up the cause.
3. If we do change, here is a picture of our better future.
4. We will find early adopters who can empower others; they will lead our first efforts.
5. This map will make those first steps easier.
6. We will reinforce and return with the message to stay focused and committed.
7. We will focus on early wins to build confidence and experience.
8. We will celebrate wins and progress to solidify our new direction.

All of the steps above are what we might label as left-brain elements of change. They are rational and sequential. But that is not how you or I experience deep change. We lose our balance, feel insecure, question our worth, feel anxious, and go from feeling confident to having to relearn all over again. These are right-brain elements. Deep change is emotional.

The health and strength of the shadow culture determines its adaptability and the pace of change that it can embrace (or digest). Resistance is simply a symptom or a barometer. When we overlook (or refuse to address) the sense of loss people feel leaving the familiar or feeling disconnected or incompetent in the new world, then we send a deeper message to the whole organization (and our kids). If we overlook building bridges for people to see and feel what it will be like in the new world and see for themselves that they can make it, they will resist and feel left behind.

What about Education?

The Education Machine also has cultures that will eat the best strategies. When the shadow culture in Newark was ignored, it ate over $200 million. The shadow culture at Chicago's Fenger Academy saw "super-stars" in education like Paul Vallas, Arne Duncan, and Liz Dozier proclaim bold strategies and spend several million dollars to make a difference. Fenger's performance has not improved during those 20 years. All three individuals, however, have moved on and up in that strange world where image trumps results. Culture ate their strategy. The November 15, 2015, *Politico* headline told readers, "Here's Why $7 Billion Didn't Help America's Worst Schools." I repeat, "Culture eats strategy!" For some strange reason, that seems to be the single most ignored truth in business and education . . . and if ignored it leads to failure.

> *The Education Machine also has cultures that will eat the best strategies. When the shadow culture in Newark was ignored, it ate over $200 million.*

The Leadership Triangle

I am one of those people who sometime use a hammer to attack a problem that needs a wrench. I will look at a people problem and quickly and naturally take action to move everyone toward the goal. My natural bias is toward what are called strategic solutions. And it serves me well. . . most of the time.

But I have a friend and colleague who will look at the same people problem and break it apart to look for the underlying process, a checklist, or its logic to help move a group onto the same page. That has served him well.

Then there is Joe, a Jungian psychologist. He will look at the same people problem and see the unspoken behavior dynamic. Joe sees hidden patterns that reveal incongruity, entitlement, low trust, ego, manipulation, or suppressed anger. He is gifted at seeing the hidden values that govern conversations. These require not only a change in behavior, but also a deeper shift in being. That is because they are adaptive or transformational issues.

All three approaches are important. Most people have a natural bent toward one, but we all need to develop a more layered awareness of the kind of problems we are really dealing with, and some skills that may not come naturally, in order to be effective. Most of us know the line "If all I have is a hammer then every problem looks like a nail."

These examples describe the three sides to a model that TAG Consulting created called the *Leadership Triangle*. They developed it because their consultants consistently encountered leaders who implemented programs that resulted in bigger problems and unintended consequences. Let's look at the three legs of the triangle:

1. *Tactical problems* are solved through technical expertise and good execution. About 80 percent of challenges fall into tactical or technical decisions. Examples might include bringing in specialists to support kids with learning differences or to implement new education software.
2. *Strategic problems* address direction and priorities. Perhaps 10 percent of challenges are strategic in nature. When external change or demands challenge the status quo, leaders must consider the competing values and interests. He or she must solicit open and candid feedback, set a direction, rank priorities, and then lead alignment. An example might include, "Which learning model do we want to adopt for the future, Project-Based Learning or becoming a STEM-focused school?"
3. *Transformational challenges* (also about 10 percent) address problems that question fundamental assumptions about the values and purpose of the organization. Or, they work with the culture shift needed by choosing a new strategy like Project-Based Learning. Examples include a school being placed on academic watch, a school scandal, a new principal, the unforeseen death of a student or teacher or a safety breach. These all raise basic questions about who we are as a school, what we believe, and who we need to become.

If the underlying problem is a lack of understanding or experience, then training and coaching are probably the best solution. If the underlying problem is a lack of focus and clarity, then the strategic questions should be addressed.

But if underlying problems are due to misaligned values, negative attitudes, and bad habits, then applying more training (a tactical approach) will only make the problem worse. Furthermore, that approach will create greater disengagement and resistance. Convening a visioning session to inspire (a strategic approach) will also make the problem worse if the underlying causes are misaligned values.

Most leaders do not consider what kind of problem they face. I would recommend that those leaders design meetings by identifying agenda topics as tactical, strategic, or transformational (changing behaviors and attitudes). Tactical or technical challenges can often be addressed in less than 10 minutes. Because they have a finite range of options, discussion can be limited to picking one, implementing it, and tracking progress.

Strategic challenges require dialogue, debate, and some form of getting on the same page with support for moving forward. Strategic topics normally range between 30

But if underlying problems are due to misaligned values, negative attitudes, and bad habits, then applying more training (a tactical approach) will only make the problem worse.

and 90 minutes. In most cases, setting a realistic time limit adds the right constraints to guide the group to a decision.

A sign that you may have a transformational or adaptive challenge is when you reach a point in the meeting where you decide to decide, but don't really decide. In other words the issue becomes tabled for future discussion. A second sign is when the same problems keep recurring and keep resisting all solutions.

Transformational challenges raise questions about what an organization really values. They will reveal deeper questions about relevancy or values misalignments. These discussions often lead into a series of meetings that allow deeper discovery, reflection, and debate. If leaders artificially cap the process or curtail vital conversations, they will inevitably drive a manufactured decision that is guaranteed to backfire and generate a ripple effect of unintended consequences.

We have found that teams that use the Leadership Triangle as a framework for identifying issues reach decisions with greater clarity and speed. It also helps them tackle those deeper transformational issues with realistic expectations and an understanding of the change agent role.

Agents of Change

If we apply the lens of culture to the larger challenge of the Education Machine we clearly see its true shadow nature. The machine values high test scores, following instructions, sitting still, and conformity. It consistently produces anxiety, insecurity, unfairness, loneliness, boredom, inflexibility, and gaming the system. The machine is impatient, unforgiving, and capricious.

In an upcoming chapter, titled "Leading Change at Your School" we provide examples, lessons, and principles for changing culture so that it will support you and not eat your new vision and strategy.

This next chapter reveals how to get your investment in technology to actually work and deliver on its promise of transformational learning. Most people tend to use new technologies inside a Gutenberg framework of learning. I know a man who actually used his first computer as a typewriter for printing voluminous studies; he never hit "save." Like him, we've all treated digital tools like caged animals in a zoo. They draw our curiosity and imagination but until we see them in their natural habitat we will never really understand those creatures. You will learn how the natural habitat of learning with digital tools moves us out of a caged *push* mode of education into the free-range experience of *pull* learning.

CHAPTER 13

How Technology Is Supposed to Work

. . . technology keeps moving forward, which makes it easier for the artists to tell their stories. . . .

—George Lucas

Our family drove to the Grapevine Theater in order to support Emily and Daniel as they gave their final piano recital pieces. But, for them, it was more closure than celebration. They were both just worn out by the tedium of lessons and practice.

Our youngest, Caleb, sat quietly with us in the auditorium as we all listened to the student performances. When the recital ended, the parents hugged and congratulated their kids and then filed out of the theater. But that recital changed Caleb's life. That was our first indicator that he was an artist; he was reaching for the tools necessary for telling his story.

One of the performers at the recital played Solfeggietto in C Major. It is one of C.P.E. Bach's best-recognized pieces: few chords, almost exclusively single notes played rapidly to an ancient and (what some consider) mystical progression of tones. When we got home that night, Caleb (who had been learning piano from Lisa) bounded upstairs to his keyboard. He found the Solfeggio on YouTube. After a few days he was playing the piece accurately from memory. That's when Lisa called: "I think we need to find a piano teacher for Caleb."

"Really? He just started; how much are lessons?"

"Four hundred dollars a month."

"Why don't we wait a few more months to see if he's really serious?"

"You need to listen to this." Then she asked Caleb to play the number for me over the phone.

"Okay, I think he needs lessons, too."

We were fortunate to find good instructors who understood that Caleb was not there to fulfill his parent's wishes. They prepared him and set him on a path to turn that passion and willingness to work hard to gain mastery. Today, six years later, Caleb has become an accomplished composer and musician. He took second place in a North Texas competition for high school seniors and has been accepted to the Berklee College of Music, but regardless of which school he accepts, he will study film-score composing.

Who can explain why the switch flips for one kid and not another? We know a lot of what turns that switch *off*. Thankfully, Lisa and I saw that a switch had turned on and we chose to channel it instead of trying to control it. We both saw, in our own home, how technology equipped one individual for great engagement with, and ownership of, his learning.

But what about technology-equipped peer-to-peer engagement?

Sugata Mitra won the 2013 TED Prize in education. His Hole in the Wall experiment with kids in a New Delhi slum demonstrated the great potential of learning, even without formal education structures, using simple technology, curiosity, and the agency of peer-to-peer learning.

Pete Dugas, the owner of TSAV, a Georgia technology firm specializing in education, tells the story of a Monday morning rollout of new laptops to a group of third graders. The school had planned a typical day of class orientation by teachers to the kids on how to use new equipment.

Pete had a different idea.

With the laptops in one corner of the classroom and the new, but unassembled, furniture in the other, Pete walked into the class and said, "I'm your teacher for the day but I need to step out for a few minutes. Your login is on the board so go ahead and start getting the room set up."

Pete's firm had installed a camera to see what the kids might do. They quickly and naturally began working together, dividing up tasks; within 10 minutes they were ready to go. When Pete came back, he gave them an assignment to create a collage from Harriet Beecher Stowe's work. Then he left again.

"By the time I came back, the kids had created a shared Google Doc with photographs. The kids went far beyond what I and the teachers thought they could do."

So we've seen technology empowering an individual to commit to his learning. And we've just looked at peer-to-peer engagement. What about technology assisting student-to-teacher engagement?

Tools that provide simple ways of creating groups lead to new groups . . . and not just more groups but more kinds of groups.
—Clay Shirky, Here Comes Everybody: The Power of Organizing without Organizations

Dr. Eric Hamilton, Professor of Education at Pepperdine, looks and sounds a bit like Indiana Jones with his wide-brimmed sable fedora and stories of taking technology into remote African villages. Eric specializes in research that uncovers where the magic in technology lies for engaging students, especially around STEM disciplines.

When I first met with Eric I found him conducting an international student-teacher workshop. I watched teachers and students paired together creating instructional videos to explain different math equations. I asked what he thought this kind of research would yield.

Our country spends millions of dollars supporting research and teacher professional development to get teachers more deeply immersed in content, more deeply immersed in understanding how their kids think. What I discovered was that, as good as the curriculum creators were, they were never as good as the teachers creating their own content.

. . . instead of relying on university people to come up with clever ways of doing things, we put teachers in a space where we gave them tools to be imaginative, tools that they never had before. You notice [he points to teachers and students] that they get completely lost in doing it. I mean completely immersed, completely absorbed. Everything we are interested in, that we've spent millions of dollars trying to figure out, is happening right in front our eyes. I was not the agent of the magic. The teachers were the agent of the magic.

I asked Eric how other countries approach math. He noted that, in addition to taking a deeper dive into the content, their curriculum provides more "coherence." The subjects and topics are more tightly linked and that integration leads to more rapid comprehension and mastery. "When you're a school teacher creating a video, you have to be coherent. We see a deeper immersion in the content in order to synthesize the concepts into an instructional video. You have to make each frame consistent to the prior and linked to the next. In our model, editing is where the action takes place because you repeat and rehearse ideas all the time. Editing is more than a final technical detail but represents the sweet spot of learning when you're creating. "In other words, you can't treat the subject like a slide presentation, where each slide is a stand-alone thought. Video production adds narrative to the learning.

> *The teacher says to the students, "Will you help me make videos?"*
>
> *The kids say, "You want us to help you teach the class?"*
>
> *The kids begin to see themselves differently. They see the teacher differently. Math is no longer something you have to learn to pass a test. It is something you have to learn in order to explain to other people.*

> *The way we set up the work for teachers is to not provide enough time to finish. That led to recruiting students to help. We noticed a cross-generational dynamic that is off the charts.*
>
>   *The teacher says to the students, "Will you help me make videos?"*
>   *The kids say, "You want us to help you teach the class?"*
>   *The kids begin to see themselves differently. They see the teacher differently. Math is no longer something you have to learn to pass a test. It is something you have to learn in order to explain to other people.* [1]

I said, "Wow—this reframes the whole experience."

Eric sees this approach as a variation of the maker movement, producing the same energy and enthusiasm around tinkering and doing it yourself. Making videos also introduces the Silicon Valley notion of fast failure, efforts that fail but teach. Eric is concerned that the fear of failure in our school culture acts to block higher-level learning. "You can't make good videos until you make bad ones."

These stories demonstrate the power of technology to facilitate new dimensions of engagement. They are also examples of a new dynamic in learning, called Pull. The authors of *The Power of Pull: How Small Moves, Smartly Made, Can Set Big Things in Motion* describe it as ". . . the ability to draw out people and resources as needed to address opportunities and challenges. Pull gives us unprecedented access to what we need, when we need it, even when we're not quite sure what 'it' is."

> *If you want to teach people a new way of thinking, don't bother trying to teach them. Instead, give them a tool, the use of which will lead to new ways of thinking.*
>
> —Buckminster Fuller

Technology: Crossing the Border

Technologies—think of the printing press, the wheel, firearms, electricity, semiconductors, the internal combustion engine, and so on—always mark the borders between eras. Those who continue to hold onto the technologies of a past era pay a very high price for their procrastination or blindness.

For example, in Chapter 7, I tell the story of a college that needed to increase student enrollment, at $30,000 per school year. They had no idea how technology had changed the rules. For example, they could not understand that an iPod (now a smartphone) is a personalized, on-demand, content provider, and that this device virtually negated their business proposition because it could deliver the best content on earth for free. Their challenge was how to compete with *free*.

And Pete's experience with third graders setting up a classroom reveals the dramatic shift—a technology-driven shift—from traditional education to the new learning platform. This story also explains why so many technology rollouts fail. New tools—the tools of a new era—combined with old thinking leads to failure and waste. Ultimately it all sinks back into old ways.

Want to see what is really at stake here? Shannon Buerk captures a major burning platform issue for K–12 education in America: "As long as time stays a constant and the teacher-student ratio remains constant, public schools are not going to survive. The year-after-year increase in the cost of education is a crisis. Education today is a people-intensive business and that is not sustainable. It must become a blended model, leveraging technology, and one where students can be more autonomous."

Ken Robinson concludes, "The key to this transformation is not to standardize education, but to personalize it, to build achievement on discovering the individual talents of each child, to put students in an environment where they want to learn and where they can naturally discover their true passions."[2]

> *The key to this transformation is not to standardize education, but to personalize it, to build achievement on discovering the individual talents of each child, to put students in an environment where they want to learn and where they can naturally discover their true passions.*
> —Ken Robinson

To make the necessary strides in performance and to close the widening equity gap, *we see only one solution—individualized learning through technology*. This is major, an historic shift. In other words, new technologies are confronting old and sclerotic ways of modern education just as refrigeration once confronted icehouses or sailing vessels challenged propulsion by oars.

Or consider the farming revolution from a horse and plow to the tractor: "It took a farmer an hour and a half to till an acre of ground with five horses and a gang plow. With a 27-horsepower tractor and a moldboard plow, it took only a half-hour to plow an acre and only 15 minutes with a 35-horsepower tractor and a moldboard plow. Today, using a 154-horsepower tractor and a chisel plow, a farmer can till an acre in five minutes."[3]

Most traditional schools would not consider their system as a horse-drawn plow approach. And most cannot imagine digital tools as having the power to transform learning. But when we consider that we are all digital immigrants our lack of imagination makes sense. We, too, often approach digital technology like print natives. *Our comfort zone acts as the choke valve controlling the fuel of learning to our students.* Pete Dugas' experiment in letting students set up the furniture and technology for a classroom demonstrates the power of a "tractor over horse" approach. Just provide a small amount of instruction and structure and let the student's curiosity and engagement fuel the learning.

Disrupting Class

Usually the first problems you solve with a new paradigm are the ones that were unsolvable with the old paradigm.
—Joel Barker, *Paradigms: The Business of Discovering the Future*

In 1971, Alvin Toffler predicted a kind of change that would create psychological and sociological culture shock: he called it "future shock," in which disruption is a major and inevitable component. A quarter century later, Clayton Christensen tested those observations in his best-selling book, *The Innovators Dilemma: When New Technologies Cause Great Firms to Fail* (McGraw-Hill, 1997).

Years later, Christensen and Michael Horn wrote *Disrupting Class* (McGraw-Hill, 2008), applying the same theory of the *Innovator's Dilemma* to education. Charter schools are not the threat to public education that many portray them to be. If anything, charters push public schools to improve the quality and efficiency of their education platform.

The threat is at the low cost end of the spectrum. The kind of innovation that upsets the apple cart starts by solving a problem no one else is interested in, or one that is better than nothing for those who can't afford anything else. Just remember that Khan Academy looked like the rotary phone of education in 2004.

Why Is Change So Complicated?

While the examples of Pull learning discussed earlier—my son's immersion in music and Pete Dugas' story of third graders setting up their classroom—seem simple, perhaps even heartwarming, the issue is more complex. Here is what it really looks like: Exponential change and obsolescence, moving vast amounts of static content to a dynamic and interactive medium, linking these to a centralized infrastructure, establishing and managing security protocols, scaling the rollout to thousands of students and teachers and then coordinating facilities, procurement, curriculum, human resources, and IT—now it is no longer simple or heartwarming.

This complexity means our whole approach to selecting, implementing, and maintaining technology has to shift from departmental silos, making detached decisions, to an integrated process of stakeholders. *Buying systems is different than buying things.*

> *This complexity means our whole approach to selecting, implementing, and maintaining technology has to shift from departmental silos, making detached decisions, to an integrated process of stakeholders.* Buying systems is different than buying things.

Pete Dugas told a story of one school district that passed a billion-dollar bond for new technology. The funding for the capital equipment was assigned to the facility budget. So, Facilities issued their bids and awarded the technology contract to a well-known tablet computer supplier. That was the most visible piece to what became a disconnected puzzle. A smaller portion of the budget went to IT for set up and maintenance. However, the classrooms were not equipped with enough electricity to charge that many tablets, and the servers were not designed to integrate or process the new volume of data. Because the tablets ran their own software and were not cloud-based, no one considered what it would take to continually update software one tablet at a time. No one included the teachers or considered the affect on the curriculum. The only professional development provided was on how individual students could use the tablets; not one dime or detail was provided on how to redesign lesson planning, the flow of the classroom, or empower the students.

The Los Angeles school district iPad fiasco followed a similar narrative. Consider Michael Horn's assessment of where Los Angeles went wrong, "LA is emblematic of a problem we're seeing across the country right now. . . . Districts are starting with the technology and not asking themselves: 'What problem are we trying to solve, and what's the instructional model we need to solve it?' and then finding technology in service of that."[4]

Buzzwords Are Fuzzy Words

Shannon Buerk's firm, Engag2Learn, has worked with more than 150 school districts implementing active learning strategies. That almost always involves technology. So they have learned to ask a vital question at the front end, "What is it you really want?" That question is, of course, essential when schools request something that is trendy or contains a hot buzzword.

So I asked, "How would you explain personalized learning?"

Personalized learning is a current favorite. As with all buzzwords, there are multiple interpretations. Technology vendors are pushing the concept because of the way that group defines personalized—they mean each student in front of a computer. Parents and others want to see education become more personalized, because to them it means individualized. The danger is that personalized education, by itself, does not have a collaborative component. The best models for learning include both individualized and collaborative learning. That strategy has worked. Test scores for those schools jump significantly in the first year. If we move to just "personalized" learning, we will lose the humanizing social component of education, which for us is the heart of learning.[5]

Another buzzword phrase, "one-to-one," has come to mean that each student has his or her own tablet. When Page Dettmann was executive director for Sarasota Middle Schools she did not follow the trend but adopted an active learning STEM model in her math and science classrooms that had a four-to-one ratio (see Figure 13.1). Their team-based teaching model drove that strategy. Page's team saw the interaction and socializing of learning as crucial. Handhelds allowed each student to have individual interactive abilities.

Figure 13.1   STEM Classroom, Sarasota Middle School
Source: Photo by David Hansen, Jacobs Engineering.

> *We all know that technology and programs should adapt to serve those ends. But too often we become enamored of the romance of technology. Or, schools may secure funding for a program and bolt it on without integrating it into the overarching approach to teaching.*

Sometimes purpose becomes obscured by the attraction of shiny objects and the desire to simplify. Asking, "Why" repeatedly will either lead to the true reason or reveal that they don't know what they want.

STEM is another popular buzz-word. When I asked Shannon to explain more about what makes STEM different, she asked, "What do you mean by STEM? Are you talking about a STEM course, a STEM pathway, a STEM cluster, or a STEM culture? Each of those means different things."

I simply said, "Uh, I'm not sure what I mean."[6]

Neither do most people when they use buzzwords. We found the schools with strong positive results began by clarifying their teaching strategy, one that was grounded in, "What kind of experience will engage kids most and prove effective?" We all know that technology and programs should adapt to serve those ends. But too often we become enamored of the romance of technology. Or, schools may secure funding for a program and bolt it on without integrating it into the overarching approach to teaching.

Why Is the Timing Right for Transformation?

> *Communications tools don't get socially interesting until they get technologically boring.*
> —Clay Shirky, *Here Comes Everybody: The Power of Organizing without Organizations*

Why is this transition taking so long? We see two reasons.

1. One obstacle is called the innovation adoption curve.
2. Those in leadership today are digital immigrants, not digital natives.

Digital devices and applications have yet to become second nature for today's leaders (that includes me). That's why most teachers confess that they find it challenging and stressful to feel proficient with multiple devices and software platforms. As Clay Shirky points out, we're just beginning to get to that socially interesting phase as tablets, personal devices, Facebook, Wikipedia, Khan Academy, Google Docs, and other cloud applications become boring.

Jeff Wacker, former EDS Futurist and Fellow, sees that information technology adoption follows an approximate 20-year cycle. The first 10 years of the cycle is called Growth and Innovation. The second decade is called Refinement, Design, and Application. The first phase breaks new ground with a lot of ideas. The second phase builds stable and useful applications.

Let's look at some examples.

Sergey Brin and Larry Page launched Google in 1998 and took the company public in 2004. Today, Google represents the standard for search. More important, search capacity turns information into a commodity. We no longer need to spend time memorizing facts. So why is the search for information still the primary mode of teaching and testing?

Jimmy Wales introduced Wikipedia in 2001. In 2005, I told a group of professors that Wikipedia would be the new model for gathering information, and that it would replace the expert peer-review encyclopedia model. That was shortly after *Nature* magazine compared the accuracy of Wikipedia to Britannica and concluded that it was a statistical dead heat. That idea was understandably offensive to the professors. That offense has been experienced with other educators and librarians I have addressed since then. But today most people assume Wikipedia's accuracy.

When Mark Zuckerberg started Facebook in 2004 he set the standard for social media. Facebook has entered its phase-two growth period and is expanding more deeply into organizing our social worlds.

In 2004 Sal Khan began tutoring his cousin in math, making short YouTube videos. As those demonstrations got passed around the Internet, he attracted a sufficient following to launch Khan Academy in 2006. As late as 2014, I heard an executive for one of the large textbook publishing companies criticize the quality and value of Khan's "homemade YouTube videos" for education.

She obviously had not seen one recently.

Khan Academy has attracted funding from the Gates Foundation, Google, AT&T, NASA, and other major American institutions. It is now in its phase-two cycle of growth. In 2015 the College Board partnered with Khan Academy to provide free SAT training. With its current

Google, Wikipedia, Facebook, Khan Academy, and smartphones have dramatically changed the way we think and live. So why does this most important consequence of digital technology go missing when we consider technology for the classroom?

trajectory and the analytics it is collecting, Khan Academy could conceivably overtake many curriculum providers. If the College Board doesn't radically reinvent, it, too, is vulnerable. Now imagine the disruption and transformation for education if curriculum and all assessments were virtually free? In Texas alone testing costs over $1 billion. Over dinner one night, Bill Latham and I projected that shifting that billion dollars could modernize 20,000 Texas classrooms.

The iPhone was introduced in 2007; we now see the hardware growth and innovation cycle slowing. That means it is poised for phase-two expansion into pervasive applications. The iPhone marks a new mobile era of digital living and learning. Smartphones provide a new and potentially game changing personal learning platform for schools because of their low cost, cloud storage and broad adaptability of applications.

Google, Wikipedia, Facebook, Khan Academy, and smartphones have dramatically changed the way we think and live. So why does this most important consequence of digital technology go missing when we consider technology for the classroom? Our imaginations and personal experiences somehow get shoved aside as we narrowly focus on devices, features, applications, and budgets.

Flow: The Creative Zone

It is when we act freely, for the sake of the action itself rather than for ulterior motives, that we learn to become more than what we were."
—Mihaly Csikszentmihalyi, *Flow: The Psychology of Optimal Experience*

As already referenced, Eric Hamilton began studying what happens when teachers can ascend from simply delivering content to creating content. But this work actually began in the 1980s soon after Mihaly Csikszentmihalyi began releasing his research on the phenomena called flow. When a teacher can step into that immersive creative zone they achieve what is called a peak state or peak performance. It is magical for them and their students. Using video as a medium for engagement, content immersion and synthesizing learning has proven effective globally, including remote villages in Africa.

Eric Hamilton summarized, "We're trying to figure out if there is something that we can tap into, is there a vein of activity or pursuit that is replicable without requiring a magical teacher, or is there a vein that we can pursue where teachers can become magical in their own way? And that's what we think we've found."

Blended Learning

Christensen and Horn address how to leverage the disruptive power of technology to personalize learning, and how to avoid the common mistakes made over and over again in district wide rollouts. "Too many schools miss the potential that technology offers to personalize learning at a scale never before imagined," Horn explained. The cart is far ahead of the horse when educators look at technology solutions. *They fall in love with devices and software without beginning with a grounded theory of technology-based learning tied to strategic learning goals.*

> Too many schools miss the potential that technology offers to personalize learning at a scale never before imagined.
> —Michael Horn

Horn notes that the growth in blended learning is climbing at an exponential rate, but still not approaching its potential with personalized learning. The Clayton Christensen Institute has collected the most robust repository of schools and districts that have been successful in their adoption of blended learning and improved student results. Their synthesis of lessons learned and best practices provide an essential resource for a leader considering a blended model.

Gamification and Financial Literacy

Game designers are obsessed with emotion. How do we create the emotions that we want gamers to feel, and how can we really make it this intense, emotional experience?"[7]

—Jane McGonigal

Brian Cahill, the California Division President for Balfour Beatty, and a member of our MindShift team, carries a true passion to equip our nation's youth with financial literacy skills. That passion goes back to the influence Junior Achievement had on him when he was in high school.

He currently serves on the board of directors for the local Junior Achievement (JA). JA's mission is "to inspire and prepare young people to succeed in a global economy." A few years ago he collaborated with them to create a facility that would teach them students basic financial literacy and how the American free enterprise system works.

The facility includes two high-tech training centers. BizTown is a 10,000-square-foot facility where elementary students learn the basics of personal financial management. Every day approximately 150 elementary school students spend four and a half hours in training. As the BizTown website states, "Elementary school students are not old enough to drive, work, or vote. But that doesn't stop them from managing businesses, operating banks, opening bank accounts, and writing checks."

Finance Park is designed to give high school students a realistic window into the future by walking them through the process of picking a job and career track, selecting a lifestyle they desire, and then revealing if the job or career they've chosen will live up to their expectations. More than13,000 San Diego High School students experience the JA Finance Park annually. In addition, it is open to family and adult financial literacy classes on evenings and weekends.

Brian's role and leadership made it possible for us to hold a three-day summit at the facility. The summit provided us with a unique behind-the-scenes look at BizTown and Finance Park (Figure 13.2). It was also a great view of how technology is changing the face of learning.

One afternoon our MindShift team got to play in Finance Park. The exercise was so enjoyable and winning that many of us lost track of time.

For example, I learned that my "Life Situation" scenario (a personal profile with all the details of a real life) made me married, a father with two kids, a public works water maintenance worker making $35,000 a year, and facing an unexpected expense of $1,500 to provide braces for one of my kids.

First, I had to create my budget for several predetermined categories; housing, utilities, a car, groceries, insurance, savings, retirement, and so forth. The program automatically deducts taxes. As I watched taxes erode my money, I felt that universal constriction of feeling behind the eight ball.

Figure 13.2   Working with a Junior Achievement Student Ambassador

I decided to set aside savings and retirement first (10 percent for each) and force myself to work with the rest. As the software kept a running tally of what I had left, I quickly found that I was only about 70 percent through my budget and out of money! Then the trade-offs began. I cut a lot of stuff, went barebones with my cable and phone costs, and slashed my savings and retirement funds in half. Eating out and entertainment vanished. When I finished it was time to test my budget against the real world.

My decision to buy a home gave me three options. I chose the lowest cost house. When I entered my choice I was told to go to the bank and apply for a mortgage. After filling out a brief application, I learned that I did not qualify for a mortgage. My tablet then gave me three choices for apartments.

As you can see, the exercise gives a student an idea of the reality of budgeting.

Once we completed the exercise we asked what the experience was like for the students. They told us:

- "I never realized how hard it is to create a budget and then to make it work. Wow."

- "I appreciate what my mom and dad go through—I don't buy stuff or eat out the way I used to."
- "I thought I wanted to become a vet-tech until I found out how much they make and how little that will buy."
- "I decided I want to be an engineer because I'm good at math and engineers make a decent living."
- I want to wait to have kids until I finish my education and am in a good financial position. Kids are expensive!!

And the MindShift team also had many revealing comments.

- "I'd love to bring my kids here; they could sure use it."
- "No one ever taught me any of this when I was in school. It sure would have helped." Real-life simulation is a powerful way to transform teaching into learning.

Finding Our Groove with Technology

Technology has an ethos, a set of behaviors and a mindset that release its potential. It is the kind of mindset that spontaneously takes place in a state of flow that Dr. Hamilton has extensively researched. When your mind overcomes orienting to the novelty or strangeness of the experience it will synchronize with that ethos. This is what good jazz musicians or improv comedians experience when they "find their groove."

Google's Jaime Casap has been involved in the design of a unique school, The Phoenix Code Academy. He described a very different mindset that drives the academy's mission, design, and curriculum.

> One of the challenges I face working at Google is how do I convince Latino kids that this is a path they can take and succeed in? My mother still wants me to be a lawyer, right. Like, I'm not successful until I'm a lawyer. What does she know about computer science? How do you go into a community of Latino kids, low-income Latino kids, and say to a student, "You should be doing programming and computer science." Parents don't understand. The community doesn't understand. They don't know that's where their future is.
>
> One of the key missions for the Academy is educating the community about the college and career potential in learning to code and focusing on

Latino students. The school will graduate 120 Latino kids a year, fully qualified to work as computer scientists.

I was at one of my board meetings and a lot of the board members just came from a robotics competition. They were talking about how fascinating it was to see these kids, about how engaged they were, and how they were collaborating even with opponents to fix pieces on their robotics thing and they were all into it. It's a Saturday and they were there for 14 hours and they're like fascinated by all this.

> *They were talking about how fascinating it was to see these kids, about how engaged they were and how they were collaborating even with opponents to fix pieces on their robotics thing and they were all into it.*
>
> *I'm listening to this conversation and finally say, "None of this is fascinating. What's fascinating is that we've been able to trick kids into sitting still and not moving for the past 100 years."*

I'm listening to this conversation and finally say, "None of this is fascinating. What's fascinating is that we've been able to trick kids into sitting still and not moving for the past 100 years." That's fascinating because moving and interacting is kids' natural state.[8]

The Path of Change to Blended Learning

Page Dettmann had some old and tired school buildings, a high percentage of free and reduced–cost–meal students, discipline challenges, a declining interest in math and science, and an increasing dropout rate.

Mark Pritchett, the CEO of the Gulf Coast Community Foundation, completed a study that revealed Sarasota ranked barely average for students' interest in STEM careers in a city that was trying to attract more science, medical, and technology companies. Their studies also showed student scores and interest in math and science dropped in middle school, and that is where intervention could turn the tide. "What if we could transform the way teachers teach and students learn?" With this question in mind, the Gulf Coast Community Foundation launched a five-year initiative they branded STEMsmart and offered a partnership to the secondary schools.

This common interest forged an alliance between Page and Mark that led to a remarkable transformation and national recognition. Our team spent three days in Sarasota listening to the different stories and observing the students' experiences.

Page is a seasoned and savvy teacher and administrator. She knew that the system, left to its natural bent, would revert to entrenched silos, politics, and turf. One of the first steps she took was to bring all of the departments together along with her administrators and teachers to begin a dialogue and begin asking some fundamental questions. They were well aware of the data. It was not a surprise that change would be on the horizon. The difference is that change was not handed down—it was developed together.

Page asked the teachers to engage the kids and ask them to write essays on what they thought twenty-first-century learning could look like and how they best learn. They got responses such as the following.

- The teacher should not be in the front of the room. Put the teacher's desk in the back.
- I'd like it to be hands-on style.
- I'd like to be part of a team
- Learning from kids is easier than learning from adults.
- The chairs should be comfortable, with padding.
- It would be great if our chairs were on wheels
- Have round tables with built-in computers.
- Just reading about things is not the same as doing them.

Page brought all of the departments together to take a day and ask, "If we could create the best experiences and environment for learning, what would it look like?

"What does learning look like in the next five years?

"What will our roles look like?"

That conversation led to identifying the four Cs for future-ready kids: collaboration, communication, creative thinking, and critical thinking.

After this work they brought in a graphic designer to illustrate some of the ideas for learning. John, the Director of Construction, created cardboard mockups of tables, custom designed by the kids and teachers, ideas of what the classroom might look like, and simulated how instruction would take place. A local architect took these ideas and developed a concept plan that would provide a budget for converting a classroom. The cost estimated was approximately $50,000 per classroom—$25,000 for environment and $25,000 for infrastructure.

Figure 13.3   High Impact Learning Classroom—Designed by the students, teachers, and the architect
Source: Photo by David Hansen, Jacobs Engineering

Page took this vision to the Gulf Coast Foundation. Initially they were willing to invest $100,000. However, it was clear that the vision was much bigger. Additional local businesses and individual donors were invited to take part.

When the team and support was fully in place, Page began a deeper discovery process.

The outside of Sarasota Middle School looks like a tired 1980s designed and built structure. The stand-alone pillbox-shaped buildings house three classrooms. The STEM classrooms, however, were completely transformed (see Figure 13.3). Each room had six half-moon shaped tables that seated four students. The monitor hung on a monitor arm so students could position it for viewing or presenting. The teacher stayed in the middle of the room with a custom-built table to house his or her equipment. This allowed them to be three steps away from every team and any student.

Teachers and students had earlier simulated what instruction might look like but the rehearsals needed to become codified into culture, protocols, and a playbook. One example of protocols is Accountable Talk. The kids in previous years never interacted to this level: they usually had very little face-to-face interaction; they just stared at the back of the head in the next row. The teachers quickly learned that face-to-face engagement and working in teams would create more friction. So the teachers had to teach the students how to engage with the idea, not the person.

We also learned that discipline problems in the STEM Active classrooms dropped dramatically. Kids reported that bullying disappeared within their STEMSmart classes. Each classroom was branded as STEMSmart Tech-Active, giving the classrooms and program a distinct identity. Both kids and parents felt proud walking into the rooms. The tables had names, allowing each class to personalize their space.

The school provided tours and many open houses so the kids were able to share their experience. Reinforcing the vision, ongoing training, and continuous communication with the community and key stake-holders has sustained the momentum and growth. Page collected the stories and student testimonials in order to engage the community. That has also helped to expand the effort.

Our team heard a beautiful and powerful story of an autistic sixth grader who would not speak. In seventh grade, however, he stood up in front of his team and presented to the class.

Their strategic direction was in response to the Foundation's report and district data. Page began communicating a new vision very early; she built both community and internal alignment before they moved forward. The success of their tactical execution came from cross-departmental integration at the front end and building a solid, clear, and coherent teaching approach based on the science of engaged learning. The adaptive element became an ongoing effort of leading by example, creating a safe atmosphere to experiment and learn. That built transparency with parents and the community and reinforcing the new values and behaviors they defined essential for student-engaged learning.

The Golden Triad of Pedagogy, Technology, and Place

During the 1500s the innovators of our current education system designed a learning approach that would take advantage of the powerful new technology, the printing press. Print media and subject-trained teachers provided, for the first time, standardized learning. They created an institutional machine to replicate and scale those standards. Naturally that standardized system had to be facilitated by standardized buildings. We are still using that same technology of learning.

This chapter examines the learning technologies that represent a new era of preparing our children for a new future.

New pedagogy, new technology, and new environments form a triad for the new era of engaged, individualized, and future-ready learning. These new learning environments are often referred to as the "Third Teacher."

New schools don't look like schools. Why? What is so dramatically different about these new learning environments, and what difference can they make? In the next chapter, we look at some of these magical schools and see how their new pedagogy drove their design.

CHAPTER 14

Designing a Place That Inspires and Equips

Plainly, the environment must be a living one, directed by a higher intelligence, arranged by an adult who is prepared for his mission.
—Maria Montessori

Naturally, it was hot when we arrived in South Texas for our September Summit. Our theme for that particular summit was school turnarounds and community engagement. Shannon Buerk, MindShift team member and President of Engage2Learn, served as our host. She arranged for our team to spend a day with an elementary school that had ranked in the bottom 2 percent in Texas for the past several years. But the school had a new principle and half the teachers were new. Engage2Learn was selected to introduce and train the school in an active learning model as the foundation for the turnaround. While we were on campus, the school was still operating at a frenetic pace because of the massive changes.

When we arrived at the school, shortly after the morning bell, the sight of the two-story stucco windowless bunker of a building built in the 1960s sobered and disappointed us. Our walk through the parking lot seemed slower and quieter than in previous site visits. The muted chatter seemed to reflect our group's doubt about the value of this field trip. The Teacher's Lounge, the site for our orientation, seemed to be an old and unloved utility space; it would comfortably fit a dozen people and our group numbered 35.

Figure 14.1   Dramatic Change in Engagement from the Previous Year

But then we broke into small teams and began touring the classrooms (see Figure 14.1). And our impressions quickly improved: we saw kids fully engaged in their learning. They were active, eager, and talking to one another. Despite the 1960s feel of the building, we saw no rows of desks. Some rooms were arranged in a semi-circle around a teacher. Others were distributed in small pods of students. David Vroonland, Superintendent for Mesquite (Texas) ISD, observed that every classroom vibrated with the "collaborative hum." He contrasted this to typical classrooms, which are mostly silent except for a teacher lecturing.

The Building Has a Voice

When we returned to the teacher's lounge to debrief with the new principal and superintendent, Amy Yurko, an architect on our team, could not stay silent. She and her company, BrainSpaces, focus on the neuroscience of design and educational spaces.

"This building has a powerful voice over these kid's education," she said before she listed the building's offenses—no natural light, visual clutter, poor quality florescent lighting, "temporary" buildings that were rusty from age and overuse. She pleaded the case for the kids who had to spend up to 1,000 hours a year subjected to these conditions.

Bill Latham and Page Dettmann use a model to find the sweet spot for engaged learning that I've refer to as the golden triad: sound pedagogy, effective technology, and active learning environments. All are focused on student engagement in the center. This school was clearly missing an important side of that triangle.

The superintendent acknowledged the conditions and said that the obsolescence and conditions of several old buildings was a huge challenge for the school district. This is common for many districts, in Texas and across the United States.

There are more than 100,000 public schools in America. Schools are the second-largest public investment our country makes each year. Almost 50,000 of those schools were built for the baby boomer generation and now require modernization. The ASCE[1] estimates that to stay current with growth, upkeep, and modernization our country needs to invest $58 billion for upkeep, $77 billion in modernization, and $10 billion in growth (new schools). Current spending levels are $46 billion short.[2] The Center for Green Schools estimates that schools spent $211 billion on upkeep between 1995 and 2008, but this was less than half the $482 billion that was needed, based on a formula included in the most recent GAO study."[3]

> *Eighty percent of our work still supports the factory model of education . . . our first design for a progressive school was only seven years ago.*
> —Dan Boggio, PBK Architects

Dan Boggio, the Principal and CEO for PBK Architects in Houston, says that, "Eighty percent of our work still supports the factory model of education . . . our first design for a progressive school was only seven years ago." He sees growth and interest in twenty-first-century design as positive but recognizes there is a long way to go in convincing communities and administrators to change.

Simple Math

If we have an annual $46 billion shortfall and we are short an estimated $271 billion in infrastructure and maintenance, it will take an *additional*

$73 billion a year for the next 10 years to bridge the gap. Now consider that 80 percent of the capital dollars spent today are for building outdated schools. Clearly, we will not catch the runaway train anytime soon with the current mode of thinking and operating.

We've got to think differently. To help us see things more clearly, this chapter focuses on:

- The vital partnership space plays in engaged learning.
- How space can become a catalyst for transformation.
- Moving from traditional building design to applying Design Thinking.
- Using neuroscience to inform design.
- Investigating how "micro-environments" can economically transform an older building.
- Tips and observations from building and design experts.
- Understanding the emerging trend toward wellness and the Delos Well-Building standard.

The Magic of Playgrounds

Wonder is the beginning of wisdom.

—Socrates

In her TEDx Talk, "The Wonder of Wonder: Stimulating Curiosity in Children," Amy Yurko asks if our learning environments are creating those stimulating opportunities of curiosity and play that are essential to learning. She contrasts the perfunctory factory model of classroom design to playgrounds. Well-designed playgrounds release the imagination in play. Why? Because the playground designer has a singular focus, the *play experience*.

Well-designed playgrounds release the imagination in play. Why? Because the playground designer has a singular focus, the play experience.

School design, like many institutional building models, is driven by budgets, standards, square-foot requirements, and schedules. The pedagogy and learning experience is squeezed at the end of all of the big decisions if included at all. We will show you why and how placing pedagogy and the learning experience at the forefront of the process improves the schedule and the budget.

Paris, Illinois: A School Building That Spoke to the Community

Paris, a small farm town of about 8,900 people and 2,300 students, is located on the Illinois/Indiana border 100 miles due west of Indianapolis.

Paris is similar to many Midwest towns that peaked in the early 1970s, but have bumped up and down in a stagnant growth pattern since then. The high school was housed in a 100-year-old building. Jim Blue, a school board member, said the school building was out of date, cramped for space and symbolic of the stagnation in the town. The town was ready to face the transition required to move from being a small farm town with an old and outdated high school into one that could attract new families and businesses.

Thankfully, some town leaders saw the need to change. While some had ideas of what it would take to make the transition, it was clear they needed strong partners to guide them through the process. Paris selected an experienced team for help in envisioning the future of learning: BLDD and FMG architects, MeTEOR Education for the interior design, and Bretford as one of the key furniture suppliers.

The Mayor, Craig Smith, recognized that Paris must become a community that looked to the future in order to keep businesses and attract families. "The best way you can show you're a progressive community is to have a state-of-the-art school. It shows that you buy into what's important to this generation and the next, the education of our children." That is the same conclusion J. Irwin Miller reached in 1950—a healthy future begins with our kids and the quality of their schools.

Some in the town questioned if they really needed a new high school and if the cost would be worth it. Bill "Beetle" Bailey, a school board member, said that one of the community members came up to him after the first meeting on the project. "He was kind of against it." He didn't have kids in the school anymore and pushed back on the vision. But after a bit of discussion he said, "Beetle, I got to thinkin' about this real hard . . . somewhere a hundred and some years ago when they built Paris High School, I am sure there were critics then . . . but someone pulled their boots up, jumped in, and did it. I guess I oughta be the one to help do that today."

With the help of the state, Paris raised the $23 million needed to build a new high school, an innovative and sophisticated learning environment similar in design to the active learning environments we saw in Columbus, Birdville, Coppell, or many of the other project-based-learning environments that are leading the way into the future. I was also interested in the school and community benefits.

Kristy Rodriquez, an English teacher, told the story of a student who could not focus on his reading in the old, traditional environment. Since they have added the comfortable seating and community tables in the "Extended Learning Area" right outside her classroom, this student has become one of her best readers. The kids feel comfortable moving chairs and tables around and gathering in small groups.

Most architects and contractors know what a future-ready school looks like and how to deliver one. But too few are brought in early as partners in the process, the way the Paris community engaged their architects, designer, and furniture suppliers.

Kristy sums up her observation of the student experience now: "In this new school, the students are happier and more relaxed."

Zach, a student, said that that kind of support from the community made him want to step up and do more. *This is what engagement begins to look like: pride, gratitude, and ownership.* Paris shifted stagnant thinking into a virtuous cycle that will refill the reservoirs of social capital. Listen to Jenna, another student, "For once the community believed in us enough to grant us a new school so we can better ourselves."

The improved environment spoke a clear message to the teachers, the students and the community. Craig Smith summarized their pride, "We can show anyone in the United States that if they are thinking about coming here to hire people or build . . . they will not find a better school than here."

Paris had the foresight to not only build a new school, but to do so with guidance and help. Most architects and contractors know what a future-ready school looks like and how to deliver one. But too few are brought in early as partners in the process, the way the Paris community engaged their architects, designer, and furniture suppliers.

Change Your Space, Change Your Culture

The workplace becomes the catalyst, the stage, and the enhancer for new values to emerge and grow.
—— Rex Miller, Mabel Casey, and Mark Konchar,
Change Your Space, Change Your Culture

Our last MindShift project and book looked closely at several companies rated as some of the most engaging places to work: they included Google, CBRE, Zappos, Harley Davidson, W.L. Gore, Red Hat, and many others. Our conclusion was that space, to them, was a proxy for culture. In other words, it reinforced the values, attitudes, behaviors, and habits that signaled what was important to them.

When new strategy is needed it also requires a new set of priorities (values), new attitudes, behaviors, and habits. Those don't simply change because an organization decides it wants to go in a new direction. In fact research shows that more than 80 percent of new strategies in business fail because leadership wants to go one direction and the culture says, "No, thank you. We'll continue as we were."

If changing space is *not* executed with the new desired culture in mind the new space will get eaten by the shadow culture.[4] Bill Latham tells about an award-winning high school in Connecticut. They decided to create an active learning campus with open spacious classrooms that would push casual seating out into hallways. Traditional student desks were replaced with tablet chairs on wheels. The school was bathed in natural light; the windows allowed the landscaping to feel like an extension of the corridors. But there was just one problem. *Teachers who held onto the shadow factory culture lined those mobile student chairs in rows and columns.* They stood in the front of the class and taught the same way that teachers have taught for more than a hundred years.

If we design with the learning experience in mind, we will see a cascade of change. By redesigning how we would like kids, content, and teachers to interact, we change their relationships. Changed relationships change the learning experiences.

How are we approaching design and how are we influencing the learning experience? If we design with the learning experience in mind, we will see a cascade of change. By redesigning how we would like kids, content, and teachers to interact, we change their relationships. Changed relationships change the learning experience.

Engaged Leaders Lead to Engaged Schools

"In 2010, Facebook founder Mark Zuckerberg appeared on Oprah's couch with Newark Mayor Cory Booker and New Jersey Governor Chris Christie to announce a $100 million matching grant for Newark's troubled school district. At the time of the announcement, Booker promised to transform the face of urban school reform."[5]

That, of course, did not happen. Why? Dale Russakoff's book, *The Prize* (Houghton Mifflin Harcourt, 2015), painfully chronicles where it all went wrong. A primary problem was the lack of frontline engagement by the key decision makers and champions. It is the same common error that business leaders make during big corporate shifts that present bold new strategies.

As the CEO of Engage2Learn, Shannon Buerk has worked with more than 150 school districts. She finds the lack of addressing all three sides of the Leadership Triangle a common struggle when districts adopt new strategies. Leaders tend to excel at vision (the strategic side of the triangle) but do not lead the culture shift (adaptive change) or integrate the tactical components in a coherent plan of execution. In fact, they often suffer from an overabundance of initiatives that lead to organizational paralysis and confusion.

There are structural reasons for this leadership gap that are not entirely the fault of leaders. One structural challenge is the layers between the Superintendent and how the work of educating really gets done.

A second challenge is the departmental silos where each lays claim to a piece of the decision, the process, and the budget. Instead of an integrated team focused on the learning experience, each silo constricts and protects its domain. Because self-interest becomes the loudest voice in the ear of each leader, the voice of the student gets completely lost in the complex, highly segregated machine.

Tiffany Anderson in Jennings, Missouri, and Jeff Turner in North Texas are visionary superintendents who stayed engaged; they eventually won over the shadow culture and built relational bridges for old mindsets to cross over into unknown territory. They also actively developed cohesive leadership teams and broke down silos in their schools. They were all serious about creating consensus and partnership around their kids.

They also approached new ideas and new design differently. Innovation requires exploring unorthodox approaches, asking the right kinds of questions and moving beyond simply repackaging common practices. By first stepping into the real-life experience of the student, the ultimate customer of education, you gain a deep understanding of what engaged learning looks and feels like. By doing the same through the eyes of the teacher you gain appreciation for the learning choreography that takes place in an active and participative classroom. This process is designed to give room to experiment, prototype, test, and refine ideas.

The Cardboard Classroom

After Page Dettmann's team conducted field trips and developed their teaching strategy for their STEM Active initiative, it was time to simulate a day-in-the-life of a class and test their furniture and equipment ideas. They tossed out the traditional approach of searching images on the Internet or asking their architect to create digital renderings. They started from scratch.

Page brought in students, teachers, members of their facility team, their designers and even their furniture suppliers to reimagine an empty classroom. Their only starting point was a large pile of cardboard in the middle of the room. The project for the day? To build the classroom of their dreams and simulate the new active learning model.

The kids positioned the teacher in the middle of the room at a standing work surface. The desks were designed for collaborative inquiry, with four students at each station. The shape they cut out was a new concept that resembled a large "D." They envisioned a touch screen monitor, connected to the table. In a second iteration, this monitor would be required to swivel and allow access from numerous angles to adjust for presenting and easier input from students.

Nothing in production at that time fit their unique needs, so they created their environment from scratch. The kids changed the standard height and the standard top dimensions to better facilitate sitting and frequent standing.

That exercise produced several benefits. The most important was the common experience, sense of accomplishment, and ownership the students and teachers felt by participating in such a process. They realized that someone actually cared about how their environment would best support them. The second benefit was the shift in student-teacher relationships; they became partners in designing their classroom and practicing in the new environment. They became co-creators of their future educational experiences.

The third benefit was the furniture modifications that the manufacturer was able to accommodate. Nothing in production at that time fit their unique needs, so they created their environment from scratch. The kids changed the standard height and the standard top dimensions to better facilitate sitting and frequent standing.

Legacy High School and the Flex-Mod Schedule

If you were to walk through Google, LinkedIn, or CBRE headquarters you would notice many different kinds of unexpected spaces. Imagine turning every imaginable traditional single-purpose space into work, think, gather, ideation, conferencing, presenting, eating, and casual places. CBRE, the largest real estate broker in the world, does not have any permanently assigned spaces in their headquarters. Instead they have neighborhoods (accounting, sales, legal, etc.) open to anyone. There is one private office for their CFO and its walls are glass. Their old office included standard private offices, cubicles, small conference rooms, and large conference rooms. When they redesigned the new space CBRE went through a discovery process to arrive at their cocreated office. They applied a design approach called Activity Workplace Design. AWD first looks at how work actually flows through the organization and then designs the space to support those particular tasks. CBRE's existing space made work fit into four traditional boxes: a private office, a cubicle and a small and a large conference room. After their AWD process they arrived at sixteen distinct work venues that are staged seamlessly throughout the office. There appears to be no demarcation of where areas begin or end.

Employees migrate through the workspace throughout the day to work as needed with different people, in different settings. Moving away from permanent assigned work areas allowed much more space for informal meeting areas and accommodates 40 percent more employees without feeling squeezed and uncomfortable.

Imagine this kind of thinking for a school; an activity-based design that looks and feels like a high-tech work culture and encourages students to choose where and when to do individual or group work. That is the strategy that Legacy High School in Bismarck, North Dakota, followed. Having chosen a bold new concept in scheduling known as "Flex-Mod," the school set itself on a path of student agency and control over many hours each week that would, in traditional environments, have been structured and allocated for them. In order to see this vision through, the facility and its environments had to support a variety of group and independent activities. Working with MeTEOR Education interior designers and Amy Yurko, principal of BrainSpaces, the school was able to fully realize and support their vision and integrate Flex-Mod scheduling. This enabled students more influence and discretion in owning and adapting their work in a needs-based system.

Imagine this kind of thinking for a school: an activity-based design that looks and feels like a high-tech work culture and encourages students to choose where and when to do individual or group work.

A growing body of solid research verifies the benefits of Flex-Mod scheduling. Based on 20-minute time blocks, classes are assigned a certain number of modules, depending on the subject and kind of learning students are engaged in. While it may seem intuitive that not all subjects require the same time allotment to be taught, it may be even more important to consider that not every student requires the same amount of time to assimilate the information and gain mastery over a topic. Some learning is better chunked into smaller bites or extended for deeper immersion.

This strategy moves toward more personalized learning, greater relevance, and increased student power. This approach gives breathing room in the schedule to accommodate more flexibility; this could never be accommodated in a traditional school setting. The building has to be equally adaptable and open.

Legacy High is a magical place to visit. Faculty and students are clearly engaged. When you walk through the halls it is not unusual to see a small group of students, or a teacher with a few students in a small room with writable walls and a projector so fully engrossed in their conversation that it's clear some are experiencing creative "flow."

Traditional schools don't have to be very smart. They are cookie-cutter templates with rigid fixed-wall, single-purpose classrooms, halls, cafeterias, gyms, and so on. These new buildings or upgraded and modernized schools require smart design. They need to intuitively convey the kinds of behaviors, the imaginative uses and permission to break out of passive learning and compliance into fully accessing the facility as a learning resource. These new patterns require a lot of time in order to become the habits and attitudes of a new culture.

The Shelton School: Intelligent Space

Children want to learn to the degree that they are unable to distinguish learning from fun. They keep this attitude until we adults convince them that learning is not fun.

—*Gina Shapira*

Over the years I've known that Shelton School in Dallas is renowned for its work with kids with learning differences. But when I recently met with Shelton's Amy Kelton I realized that Shelton's success also depends on intelligent spaces.

Amy, an energetic, positive, and fast-moving guide, opened our conversation with an intentional and direct gaze, "You're going to find I get passionate when I begin talking about our kids." Throughout our tour, I became fully engaged as a "systems guy," but also as the father of a son diagnosed with ADHD and a daughter with Asperger's syndrome. I quickly saw that all their methods and the environment were designed to support their students' unique wiring and individualized learning needs.

Shelton is designed with three foundations:

1. Piaget's theory of cognitive development: Amy walked through the reasoning for the different activities in each grade classroom based on this theory.
2. The Montessori method.
3. Brain science and emotional literacy.

Amy Kelton's tour reminded me of the design mindset that Amy Yurko described, designing for the essential elements of learning: curiosity and play. So it didn't surprise me that Shelton is built on the Montessori method. I knew that Maria Montessori developed her model for mentally challenged kids and that she produced extraordinary results.

The question I've been reflecting on since that tour is: Do solutions that address the extremes and those on the margins hold insights for us all?

The Lean Classroom

Many know about the Lean model of manufacturing because of Toyota's success. That kind of thinking has expanded into other fields and disciplines that must focus on reducing waste and errors. But I never thought of it as a principle for designing a classroom. Amy walked me through all of the areas in an empty classroom and the reason for its organization, artifacts, signs, and placement of materials. Within a few moments I realized that I was standing in a Lean learning factory.

I saw, for example, that setting up a work area on a factory floor (or in one of Shelton's classrooms) is to make the work and workflow intuitive (see Figure 14.2). Anyone who walks into the area will quickly see the nature and flow of the work, and the staging of the needed materials and just-in-time access to those materials.

A small kindergarten classroom is divided into seven learning zones—language, association, math, culture, practical life, sensorial life, and oral language—and it does not feel cramped or cluttered. A small white rug defines a child's work area. They roll it up and take it with them from zone to zone. A specific icon for each zone communicates the kind of work they will be doing. The supplies needed, including a kit of parts, are placed in the same zone so each child can make one trip.

Inside the door of each child's locker is a small plastic envelope that holds badges for each of the different zone icons. Each student can choose any of the badges to work on. They take the learning zone badge from the envelope and their little white rug from the locker and move to set up in that learning zone. The outside of the locker features a ribbon badge. When the student masters a zone they place their badge on the ribbon (see Figure 14.3).

That self-selected and self-paced learning approach evolves in form as the students get older.

Figure 14.2   Student Learning Mat at Shelton School

This classroom is an example of integrating pedagogy and the unique learning experiences of the age or cognitive development of the child, and creating a self-paced learning environment that provides agency, curiosity, and play. For example, in the Math Learning Station (see Figure 14.4), all the supplies are assembled, easily accessible, and intuitive.

> *So many progressive schools reflect design thinking—designing with the user in mind.*

This is just a sampling of the schools we visited that follow similar principles. I also learned about the Joy School in Houston, a Balfour Beatty project that also serves kids with learning differences. They faced the additional and very unique challenge of taking an old estate that had been adapted beyond coherence and capacity rethinking the learning experience in a fresh way, and then applying those insights into building a new facility from the ground up.

The Da Vinci School in Los Angeles is specifically chartered to prepare future-ready kids through project-based learning and college

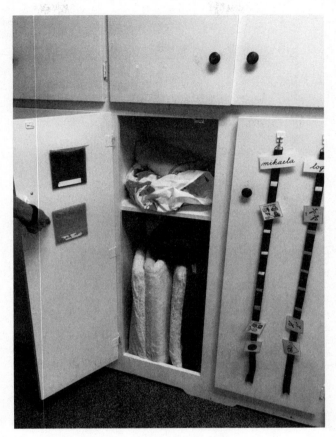

Figure 14.3   Student Locker at Shelton School

preparatory curriculum. In a true student-centered approach the kids came up with the school name in a design charrette exercise intended to capture the cross-functional learning approach. The school is unique because of the way the platform of learning is expanded: they have a 13th-year university transfer path as well as a blended learning option available through their Da Vinci Innovation Academy. Da Vinci is moving forward to an integrated life-learning mindset that can take place anywhere, at any time—for life. No wonder they are graduating kids who are academically, emotionally, and culturally well rounded.

So many progressive schools are designed with the user in mind. We saw that in the way Sarasota modernized old traditional classrooms or how Paris High School engaged the community in a collective vision and

Figure 14.4   Math Learning Station at Shelton School

tangible expression of how they envisioned their future. Legacy High used design thinking to build a school to reflect the kind of agency required in a flexible work-world. Shelton's environment reveals design thinking in its pedagogy, in the deep understanding of the unique needs of the students and applied brain science.

50,000 Schools and the Micro-Environment Solution

> There has been a shift with decision makers gaining greater recognition . . . of the role microenvironments play in creating positive, high-performing learning environments.
>
>   —*Bill Latham*

Half of today's schools—about 50,000—were designed for the baby boomer generation. That means they must be modernized in order to support active learning and the development of future-ready skills.

It can be done. We saw it in the dramatic improvement at Sarasota

The challenge for many other older schools is not primarily funding, it is a lack of imagination and the failure to empower teachers, administrators, and the community to make changes.

Middle School. The challenge for many other older schools is not primarily funding: it is a lack of imagination and the failure to empower teachers, administrators, and the community to make changes. No one walking through Sarasota will mistake it for a new state-of-the-art campus like Paris or Legacy. But you will see student engagement and effective learning in these places.

And, just like people, school districts can get used to things being the way they are—or always have been. Paris, Illinois, had fallen into that state until some of the leaders got tired of a slow demoralizing decline.

At the beginning of the chapter I describe a dilapidated 1960s-style elementary school in Texas. We asked our architects, designers, contractors, and cognitive consultants what they could do to this school's microenvironments that would create a more positive experience. They went to work reimagining the possibilities. The actions they recommended may be helpful to other schools.

Reimagine real estate: Half of the library space contained stacks of unread books. The other half contained folding tables with desktop computers (in a school where every child has a tablet). We learned that the banks of computers were for kids who were being disciplined by having their tablets taken away (one of our members wondered if the school would take textbooks away as punishment).

Neither the stack of books nor the banks of desktop computers were necessary. The school could reclaim the space and make an engaging multiuse learning lounge with comfortable seating and moveable furniture.

This school also maintained a separate computer lab and multiple storage areas. If repurposed all that space could also be captured for new and creative learning spaces.

Declutter: Part of the reason that the school facility felt cramped was the many objects stashed and stored on the floors, items that had no place or were being kept "just in case" someone might need them.

Transform the cafeteria: The two-story cafeteria occupied the center of the building. The second-floor open corridor ringed the cafeteria and was the only space in the building bathed in natural light. The long gray cafeteria tables and benches made the space look like a prison mess hall. Our team quickly sketched ways the room could be transformed with a variety of table shapes, seating options, and booths.

Lighting: Few things can transform institutional environments like lighting, and its relatively inexpensive. The new LED lighting technologies certainly create better learning and working environments for everyone. And the white "outdoor" color of bulbs is much brighter and friendlier than fluorescent lighting.

Walls: The barren prisonlike walls in the corridors of the Texas school could easily be reimagined to showcase student work, school conversations, or student works of art.

Entry: A large overhang created a compressed and sterile entrance into the building. We saw the possibilities for a renovation that could feature plants, a large wall mural, and even benches to soften and make the area inviting.

Gardens: The landscaping around the school was also reminiscent of a prison: lots of dirt and scrubby and isolated patches of grass. These were perfect areas for the creation of gardens. They would not only transform the campus, but could also provide an engaging horticultural learning experience.

Active furniture: The school furniture was old, heavy, and dented, made of steel with attached brown desks. The teachers were trying to create small learning clusters or semicircle configurations, but it was clear the furniture worked against an easy and enjoyable reformatting of the room. New furniture would achieve a great recapturing of space.

These suggestions reveal some of the possibilities for finding brand-new space within any existing building.

New Thinking in School Design

In addition to the example of the Texas elementary school, MindShift has explored the new thinking in progressive school design, construction, and furniture. We continue to ask experts about trends. Their answers blow the doors right off the possibilities.

What Is the Biggest Change You See Taking Place in the Classroom?

I see the departure of the four-walled rectangular classroom. It is evolving into open, transparent spaces that recognize learning does not stop when the bell rings. The new 'classroom' spills out to the hallways, stairs, and outdoor spaces and creates active learning zones throughout the school."
—Irene Nigaglioni, PBK Architects

Irene Nigaglioni, Partner at PBK Architects: "I see the departure of the four-walled rectangular class-room. It is evolving into open, trans-parent spaces that recognize learning does not stop when the bell rings. The new 'classroom' spills out to the hall-ways, stairs, and outdoor spaces and creates active learning zones through-out the school."

Gil Fullen, Vice President of Education for Balfour Beatty: "The rate of technology change has a direct effect on classroom design. It must be flexible in order to adapt to future applications."

Kris Hammer, Vice President of Business Development for Moor-eco: "The biggest change in classroom design is the integration of technology into a flexible space. Because older facilities have fewer power outlets, the migration to one-to-one use and moveable furniture makes getting power to everyone a major undertaking."

David Stone, Project Executive Balfour Beatty: "The new learning models like project-based learning, personalized learning, smaller learn-ing communities, and advanced career and technology centers all require different kinds of learning spaces."

Bill Latham, CEO, MeTEOR Education: "Naturalness—light, sound, temperature, air quality, and links to nature (outdoors). The corporate world has taught us that setting up cages under fake lights with no views to the outside world is devastating for morale and retention."

What Change Can Have the Biggest Impact in a Traditional Classroom?

Irene Nigaglioni: "The way the teacher personalizes his or her space and the use of the furniture. Too often teachers, even with flexible furniture, revert back to traditional lecturing. A little creativity goes a long way."

Gil Fullen: "Teachers themselves have the biggest impact. Their ability to connect and tailor learning makes it personal, not traditional."

Kris Hammer: "The mobility of furniture and a mobile teacher's station in the middle so there is no front or back of the classroom will make the most immediate impact."

Bill Latham: "Aligning the classroom microenvironment to support the specific local priorities of teaching and learning. A daily fight is ensuing in learning environments all across the country where the space actively works against the students and teacher—physically and cognitively."

David Stone: "If teachers take a fresh look and think about how to creatively use their 550–1,200 square feet, they will find a lot of changes they can make."

Page Dettmann: "Nothing is more important than the new role of the teacher to help students become collaborators and thinkers and to give them the opportunity and support to thrive in this new way of learning. This transformative culture shift can happen in any classroom, new or traditional, and is enhanced when a High Impact Learning Environment wraps around the teacher and students to provide an interactive experience."

What Are Some Means to Classroom Improvement That Teachers Often Miss?

Irene Nigaglioni: "Most schools feel like prisons where autonomy is stripped and students feel controlled. I believe that teachers some-times overlook the power they have to impact their classroom environments."

Gil Fullen: "Teachers sometimes miss the value of new technologies and don't adapt and learn so they can deliver an effective experience for the kids."

Kris Hammer: "They can miss that teaching has shifted to creating learning experiences. Many still feel more comfortable lecturing; they just hate leaving that behind."

David Stone: "Teachers tend to be tethered to their individual classroom. Some have had the same classroom for 10 or more years and still teach like they did 10 years ago."

Bill Latham: "The work is about the students, so the environments should be about the students. Teachers too often miss that. They think it's about control, classroom management, and the teacher's sense of order and preference."

Reversing the Rising Health Risks in Schools

The concerns of childhood obesity, poor air quality in schools, daylight deficiency, stress and passive learning (sitting all day) mark a rising crisis in the workplace and in schools. Only a small percentage of our schools have been designed to address these challenges.

A large body of research underwritten by the federal government, Carnegie Mellon, Lawrence Livermore Labs, Cornell University, and the Academy of Neuroscience for Architecture (part of the Salk Institute) have studied the effects of different kinds of lighting, air quality, ergonomics and acoustics on the health and performance of people in office spaces, schools, and hospitals.

That is why our nation will begin to hear more discussions about evidence-based design, salutogenic (the source of health) design, circadian rhythms, sleep, and the value of physical activity and recess on physical and psychological well-being. The benefits and practice of mindfulness have already been in use in many at-risk schools and schools for learning differences. Now, it is expanding into the mainstream of learning. Our growing understanding of the brain through FMRI brain scanning and what seems like an epidemic of different conditions have raised the alarm. The good news is that we know our environments and lifestyle are key causes—and we can do something about that.

In our research on workplace disengagement, we ran across a startling issue: sitting is the new smoking. Consider this summary: "The takeaway (from a Stanford conference on the dangers of sitting) was simple: Sitting is not only harmful because it represents a lack of exercise, but also because sedentary behavior initiates a unique cascade of physiological changes that lead to a higher concentration of fat in the blood, insulin resistance, type-2 diabetes, heart disease, and obesity—even in those people who meet the recommended 150 minutes per week of moderate to intense aerobic activity."[6]

In earlier chapters we addressed the importance of safe and stress-free learning environments, especially for at-risk students. Wellness is now a hot social topic because of the ripple effect of the Affordable Care Act and increased health insurance costs.

The rise in chronic health issues and the social and emotional health challenges in underserved communities will force all districts to include their facilities as a key part of their holistic strategies in tackling this problem. New design standards will emerge to guide schools and their architects and designers in creating facilities that promote wellness and well-being. Delos is an organization that has developed a Well Building Standard. The WELL Building Standard® is an evidence-based system for measuring, certifying, and monitoring the performance of building features that impact health and well-being. Their work is one of the catalytic forces in this conversation.

In the convergence of need, understanding, and our ability to act, school buildings will become a major arena for rethinking design and use, space as a catalyst for healthier behavior, and an environment that fosters wellness and well-being.

Future Ready

If our mission in education is to prepare future-ready students, we will need a dramatic shift in our approach to designing our learning environments. Our school buildings can be used as catalysts for positive change and reinforcements of a future-ready culture, or they can impede our best intentions. Achieving this transformation will require administrators, principals, teachers, parents, and citizens to be full stakeholders in the process and the outcome.

The job of administrators and teachers balances on a razor's edge of maintaining an old system's standards while transforming their schools to prepare kids for a 2040 world. This is the volatile, uncertain, complex, and ambiguous (VUCA) world of leadership. None of us were trained or prepared for walking this razor's edge. We have found several examples, however, of leaders who are accomplishing both. The next chapter tells some of their stories and distills their lessons in leading change.

CHAPTER 15

The Power of Positive

Knowledge is power and enthusiasm pulls the switch.

—Steve Droke

Several years ago I was asked to work with a toxic and high-conflict leadership team ranked at the bottom of an organization's metrics for engagement. We used the Clifton Strengthsfinder assessment and CoreClarity[1] to provide a framework for the team to better understand themselves and one another and to identify the natural areas of friction.

I would be doing all of that over a four-day workshop, and I only had two days of material. This looked like it would be a tough and hostile group. I barely finished my introduction when a hard-nosed engineer to my left said, "So *they* think we need someone like *you* to fix us? Good luck."

This group was not eager, willing, or cooperative when I opened the session. I knew the aggregate talents of the individuals and understood where the group drew both positive and negative energy. Their top two Strengthsfinder talents were Deliberative and Analytical. Both talents are energized by questioning and often killing new ideas. They saw new and untested ideas as risky. And to them "team building" was anecdotal at best, and manipulation at worst.

I asked, "How many of you think we are about to engage in fuzzy-wuzzy, horoscopy, psychobabble BS?" Twelve out of 19 participants raised their hands. I promised them, "If I don't have your attention by noon, then I will shut this down." By mid-morning we had reset expectations and created interest.

Except for Bob.

The Clifton Strengthfinder 20-minute assessment is a Gallup tool that identifies what people naturally do best and enjoy most. The results of the assessment, when used with CoreClarity, helped me gain insight into what activities were naturally motivating for this team and what activities drained that motivation and could create friction.

The team sat around a large U-shaped table in the center of the room. I like that configuration because it allows me to engage them from the middle of the U, getting up close to everyone. Bob sat at my far right-hand corner, arms folded and head down. He struck me as a "C.A.V.E. Dweller: Consistently Against Virtually Everything" (see Figure 15.1).

I tried every trick I knew to engage Bob, including walking right up to him and getting inside his personal space. He did not budge and he was not asleep. Although the morning went fairly well, Bob's disengagement frustrated me.

Figure 15.1   C.A.V.E. Dweller

When we broke for lunch, Jim Osterhaus, a colleague and a clinical psychologist, and I invited Bob to go to lunch with us. He accepted. I had one agenda and that was to find out what might unlock Bob's participation.

When we sat down, I said, "Bob, what do you get to do during the week that taps into your talents and energizes you?"

"Nothing."

"Okay, what do you do after work that taps your talents? What do you enjoy?"

"Nothing."

"Wow, Bob, how long has this been going on?"

"Twenty-five years. I hate my job and I hate the people I work with!"

I was definitely in over my head at this point and a bit desperate to find a way out; we still had forty-five minutes of lunchtime.

"Bob, I have just one question. What does this look like in five years if nothing changes? Health? Happiness? Career?"

Bob dropped his head and shook it as if saying, "I don't know."

Fortunately Jim was able to rescue me and shift our conversation.

When we got back to the workshop I was still a bit shell-shocked. We didn't see much of a change in Bob's demeanor over the next three days.

Three months later I returned for a second phase of the training. Bob was one of the first people I saw. He smiled and said, "Good to see you." During the training he was active and engaged. On the second day, Bob stood up after one of the exercises and blurted out, in tears, "This is the best place I've ever worked, I love you guys!" About half the people in the room and I all lost our composure. At the break I went over to his supervisor and asked, "Dave, what just happened?"

Dave told the story, "After you and Jim had lunch with Bob three months ago he asked if he could talk. He said he finally understood why every day was so hard, why he always felt like he was always swimming against the current. He saw that his talents were completely constrained in his role. He could just barely make it through a day. I was able to see it, too, after the training. So we redesigned his role to tap into his strong analytical and creative talents. He's like a new guy."

Ninety days from being a C.A.V.E. dweller to an engaged, happy, considerate, and productive team member. Most C.A.V.E dwellers are good people, but locked into roles that do not tap into their strengths.

Imagine something you just hate to do; in fact, just the thought of it drains your energy. Now imagine that you are stuck in a job that has you doing what you hate all day, every day.

At first it would feel difficult and frustrating. You would be emotionally drained by the end of the day. Your work would never receive any recognition at all. Finally, you would work under great stress and pressure. In order to cope, you would mentally check out and survive by simply going through the motions. Over time your attitude would go from disengaged to angry. Finally, you reach the C.A.V.E. dweller stage and rage against the machine.

Imagine having the opportunity to do what you naturally do best, and to do that every day.

Now, imagine your favorite activity, relationship, place, or topic. Remember a time when you were so absorbed that you lost track of time. That experience was an example of flow.[2] Imagine having the opportunity to do what you naturally do best, and to do that every day.

The Gallup Organization's Brandon Busteed wonders why ". . . instead of using a strengths-based approach in education, we have created a system that approaches everything through a deficit-based lens: what's wrong with students, what they don't know, and how ineffective teachers are, for example."

I wonder that too.

Do you think that utilizing strengths might have application in learning? What would happen if we unlocked the natural curiosity of students? What if we could determine each student's strengths and release him or her to do that every day? What if teachers and students could develop life and learning skills through these unique abilities? To look further into these questions, let's look at the story of Del Norte (Colorado) Middle School.

"Mrs. B! I Have Talents!"

Candace Fitzpatrick is the founder of CoreClarity, the system I used for Bob's team. Her sister Terry was the Bully Prevention Coordinator for the Colorado Trust (a foundation dedicated to the health of Coloradoans). She was naturally familiar with Candace's program and wanted to test it with one of the state's at-risk schools. Terry picked Del Norte Middle School, in a low-income community. The school was also on academic watch and in jeopardy of being taken over by the state.

All of the teachers were interviewed for the pilot project. And they all took Gallup's Strengthsfinder assessment. Candace and her team provided a two-day summer workshop with the whole staff and teachers. Denise Benevides, a sixth-grade teacher, was selected as the school's lead for the experiment. The teachers held a parents' night to explain the vision and process. The parents were told that the experiment would focus on their child's strengths and talents, on what is already right about them, not what needs to be fixed. These parents usually heard the opposite about their kids. The proposed pilot received 100 percent buy-in from the parents.

All of the kids took Gallup's Strengths Explorer assessment, specially designed for 11- to 14-year-olds (the same assessment Lisa and I used with Caleb in our decision to homeschool him). Denise said it was an eye-opener.

"When Nicholas came to school after taking the assessment he could hardly wait to tell me the news. 'Mrs. B, Mrs. B, I have talents, it's not blank!' "

While Denise rejoiced for Nicholas, she also knew the harsh reality of the world that he and the other kids go home to. It's the same story so often repeated, ". . . stuck in what they know, experience, and are surrounded by . . . These kids have grown up with a victim mindset. They are told over and over they don't have a chance. We send a message that they are less and so we expect them to do less."

The class went through team-building and personal growth training for 40 minutes at the end of each day. Teachers experimented with different groupings. They discovered that putting kids together with others with the same or similar talents was not as effective as putting them together with students with different and even colliding talents.

They also found that the new language, the different kinds of groupings, and the active learning model broke down cliques. Instead, these practices created a common, inclusive foundation where everyone fit it.

The kids quickly incorporated the language into their everyday work. "Mrs. B, I forgot my homework, I need an Organizer, I'm not an Organizer." And so this student was paired up with another who had the Organizer talent.

They also found that the new language, the different kinds of groupings, and the active learning model broke down cliques. Instead, these practices created a common, inclusive foundation where everyone fit it.

The experiment produced successful results and exceeded expectations. The school had the best attendance in the district, bullying dropped dramatically, and test scores improved to a level that Governor Ritter recognized the class publically. In one year, Del Norte Middle School went from academic watch to recognition for achievement.

Denise's biggest surprise was how the community bonded through a common language, common mission, and common journey. They became Mrs. B's tribe. But, despite the success, after three years the funding was discontinued.

Positive Psychology

> Intelligence is not to make no mistakes, but quickly to see how to make them good.
>
> —*Bertolt Brecht*

According to Dr. Amit Sood, Professor of Medicine at Mayo Clinic College of Medicine and Chair of the Mayo Mind-Body Initiative, our minds have a negativity bias. The police car we drive by catches our attention and raises our pulse but the red Toyota is invisible. This conditioning, however, is reversible and part of the path to building emotional health.

Dr. Sood's research at the Mayo clinic found (among other things) that the brain is restless. It easily gets bored; the mind wanders. We all know the experience of doing a simple chore as our mind drifts away from the task at hand. While trying to read a book, especially in the evening, I can "read" several pages before I stop, realizing I cannot remember what I had just read. I developed my hobby of simple cartooning during boring classes in school. Mind wandering also happens after something we learn becomes habit, like driving a car. This is the brain's default mode; it's a little scary to know that it makes up from 50 to 80 percent of our thoughts!

Two-thirds of this kind of mind wandering travels into emotionally negative territory. Excessive mind wandering is often related to depression. It is easy to see how kids can mentally check out of a class that is content heavy unless they are kept engaged through active learning.

That is why more schools are moving to active learning models like Project-Based Learning, EdTech, and Expeditionary Learning. They can see the difference in engagement levels and how that leads to mastering the material. These approaches are physically and socially engaging whereas lectures quickly become routine, boring, and fatiguing.

Traditional classroom lecture-style teaching (see Figure 15.2) also falls victim to what Dr. Sood calls hedonic habituation. This is the experience,

Figure 15.2   Set Up of a Traditional Class

The brain requires brief periods of rest every hour to 90 minutes. That is because it has no pain fibers and won't send a signal when you are overworking it.

for example, of being served your favorite dessert. The first bite is wonderful, the second is good, the third is okay, and by the fourth and fifth bites the magic is gone. Kids experience the same habituation in schools that follow a structured routine. The first week of school is fresh, novel, and engaging. By the second and third week the combination of routine, sitting in rows of desks, in the same seat, and attempting to absorb lectures of content-heavy material sends the brain into unproductive mind-wandering.

Focused attention, engagement, takes place when a person is confronted with novelty, a topic of high interest, or is in a changing dynamic social setting. Even in an engaged mode, and especially in an engaged mode, the brain requires brief periods of rest every hour to 90 minutes. That is because it has no pain fibers and won't send a signal when you are overworking it. These rest habits can be learned just like practicing a backhand in tennis, learning arpeggios in music, or following the breath in Yoga. The operating principle is intentionality versus default mode. As we saw in Chapter 11, the Momentous Institute provides an example of integrated intentionality throughout the school schedule, building design, the instruction, child and staff interactions, and is extended to families. Their holistic approach is the result of applying 90 years of therapy and brain science. They recognize that every moment and interaction through the child's day is a learning experience. The more those encounters can happen with intentionality, the deeper and more permanent is their learning.

This means that rest must also be done with intentionality. Dr. Sood recommends that a break can be from 10 to 15 minutes in a relaxed posture and by shifting the mind to positive and motivating thoughts.

"What Do Successful and Happy People Do Differently?"

Dr. Donald Clifton developed the Strengthsfinder assessment, a tool for identifying your strongest natural talents and areas of interest. It was the fruit of over 50 years of research.

Positive psychology is the scientific study of human flourishing, and an applied approach to optimal functioning. It has also been defined as the study of the strengths and virtues that enable individuals, communities, and organizations to thrive.[3]

While in college during the 1950s he asked a different question. "What do successful and happy people do differently?" After 50 years of research and more than 2 million interviews, in 1989 he and a team of Gallup scientists created an assessment that identified 34 talent themes that consistently surfaced in happy and successful people.

The research also found that these people focused more of their energy on "playing to their strengths." This strategy yields much greater growth, satisfaction, and success than attempting to fix areas of weakness. Conversely, they found that people who put great effort into trying to improve secondary talents found it difficult and stressful to make marginal improvements, especially ones that could not be sustained. This is a profound insight that seems to go counter to our practice and experience with others.

While he was with Gallup, Marcus Buckingham used to ask parents if their child brought home grades with three "A's" a "C," and an "F," which grades they would focus on. Seventy-six percent picked the "F." Six percent claimed they would focus on the "A's." I've asked the same question in my workshops. From 4,000 people I've met only two who said they would focus on the "A."

When I grew up it did not take an "F" to get a third–degree interrogation from my six-foot-two, World War II veteran father. When I was in eighth grade I was all of four-foot-eight, 83 pounds, and still had a high squeaky voice. The eighth grade was my bonehead year of growing up. I can remember my dad standing over me in the kitchen with my opened report card; he pressed his finger on one of the grades and asked, "What happened here?"

Of course, I froze. I mumbled the universal deer in the headlights answer, "I don't know."

During a workshop in Atlanta I shared the research and my story. The next day Pete, one of the directors asked to share. He said, "I'm that dad who gives his child the third degree. I got a call from my 17-year-old son yesterday afternoon during the workshop. We've been having a tough time. So when he said, 'Dad, when you get home we need to talk,' I knew what that meant, because semester grades were just issued."

Pete went on to say that when his son began to share the grades he went right to one of the low grades and began to apologize.

"I stopped my son and asked if I could see the card. He had several A's, so I asked about those. I know it surprised him. We then talked about all kinds of stuff for close to two hours."

Then, in tears, Pete told all of us, "I can't remember the last time I had a two-hour conversation with my son."

Three Stanford researchers looked at group hedonic balance and at team performance.[4] Hedonic balance is the ratio of positive to negative interactions. They found that a ratio of five positive to one negative produced superior performance and that a single factor could explain a 35 percent variance in performance. This, coincidentally, is the same ratio recommended for healthy marriages.

The NIH conducted research in 2014 on the long-term health effects of a positive hedonic balance in marriage. They concluded, "Evidence is accruing that positive emotions play a crucial role in shaping a healthy interpersonal climate."[5]

The research is clear. By focusing on what people do naturally well, they flourish and perform. However, that is not our natural tendency. Remember Dr. Sood's statement that our brains have a built-in negativity bias. Our institutional structures reinforce finding the flaw, fixing the weakness. And, of course, high-stakes testing and punitive accountability push the problem into the zone of emotional stress, anxiety, and even depression. And, according to Dr. Cozolino, "The brain shuts down neural plasticity at very low levels of arousal to conserve energy and at high levels of arousal to divert energy toward immediate survival."[6]

In tears, Pete told all of us, "I can't remember the last time I had a two hour conversation with my son."

The work in the field of positive psychology has reached a critical mass of both depth, breadth, and accessibility.

Posttraumatic Strength Syndrome

Dr. Seligman has picked up the mantle from Dr. Clifton as the "father" of positive psychology. His several books and array of free online assessments provide a comprehensive and accessible resource. His particular work with the U.S. Army stands out in our research. The Army contracted Dr. Seligman to tackle the problem of veterans returning from war with Posttraumatic Stress Syndrome. In the tradition of Dr. Clifton he looked

> *Teachers are dead last among all professions Gallup studied in saying their "opinions count" at work and their "supervisors create an open and trusting environment."*
> —*Brandon Busteed, Gallup*

for those who actually became *stronger* through the trauma. He called this ability, "Posttraumatic Strength Syndrome." In his book *Flourish*, Seligman recaps their research and the intervention training they implemented with the acronym PERMA: purpose, engagement, relationship, meaning, and achievement.

My firm has been working with these tools and integrating them into organizations since 2006. We have trained more than 8,000 people during that time and used the tool for personal development and coaching, team building, crises resolution, high-stakes negotiations, role development, team design, and shaping or shifting culture.

The ability to shift or shape culture in positive ways and create tribal identity such as Mrs. B and Linda Anderson have accomplished using the tool is a large untapped opportunity that is within anyone's reach.

The Cost of Disengaged Teachers

According to Brandon Busteed at Gallup, "Teachers are dead last among all professions Gallup studied in saying their 'opinions count' at work and their 'supervisors create an open and trusting environment.'"

Gallup's 2015 survey on teacher engagement shows that 7 out of 10 teachers are disengaged.[7] If you had an average sampling of 10 teachers rowing in a boat together you would find 3 at the front actively rowing, in harmony, and happy in their work. There would be 5 in the middle of the boat, also happy, but for different reasons. They are watching, not rowing. They will row, with a good attitude, if someone tells them what to do, how to do it, and follows up to make sure they actually did it. I've come to call the middle-of-the-boat teachers *The Managed*. In the back of the boat there are 2 teachers that I've labeled the *Toxic 20 Percent*. They are drilling a hole in the boat and draining the motivation out of those around them (Figure 15.3).

Figure 15.3   Front, Middle, and Back of the Boat Behavior

The *Toxic 20 Percent*—remember, the C.A.V.E. Dweller, "Consistently against Virtually Everything?—are often burned-out teachers who are simply not able to do what they do best. Dr. Cozolino notes that, "Teachers don't burn out from working hard; they burn out because they are frustrated, unappreciated, or hopeless about making a difference."

Sandcastles

One of the major engagement killers develops when detached leadership makes decisions without understanding who is affected and how. I call this the *Undercover Boss* dilemma. *Undercover Boss* is a reality television show that sends the boss out in disguise to do frontline work. The storyline typically depicts a boss who thinks they are making good decisions for their employees, but once they are in the field, he or she discovers that they had little or no awareness of how tough the job actually is and how difficult many of those detached decisions are for their frontline employees.

Could that be why 70 percent of teachers and administrators would rather be anywhere but in their school? And why are so few even asking about the effects of disengagement and burn-out on the students they are supposed to help?

So many of the innovative, caring, committed, engaging teachers who are working heroically on the front lines feel like they get the rug pulled out from them when promising programs are killed before they can be fully implemented. One reason these programs succeed is because of the blood, sweat, and tears willingly offered by administrators and teachers. Many go to sacrificial lengths just to have the opportunity to make a difference.

These often-heroic efforts end up as "Sandcastles": they take a lot of effort and look wonderful until the tide of new leadership, new agendas, and new budgets washes them away.

For example, when a chronically low-performing school was reconstituted in Texas, its principal and at least half of its teachers were reassigned to other schools. Of course, that meant a new principal and new teachers were brought in from other schools throughout the district. You can imagine the damage to the culture and continuity. But teachers and principals had no voice in the matter. The Education Machine only operates with a mandate and a formula; it cannot care or even think.

Of course, such a structure and approach increases disengagement and burn-out. Could that be why 70 percent of teachers and administrators would rather be anywhere but in their school? And why are so few even asking about the effects of disengagement and burn-out on the students they are supposed to help? Dr. Cozolino emphasizes, "A demoralized or burned-out teacher cannot be a positive guide or a model of heroism."[8]

Disengaged Teachers Reproduce

> The drop in student engagement for each year students are in school is our monumental, collective national failure.
>
> —*Gallup*

In his book *Out of Our Minds,* Sir Ken Robinson passionately argues that schools are killing the creativity in our kids at a time when creativity and innovation are crucial for business and society. He cites a famous NASA study on creativity that revealed:

- At five years of age, 98 percent of the kids tested at genius levels.
- By age 10 it had dropped to 32 percent.
- The genius level dropped to 12 percent by age 15.
- By the time we get through school and into work there is virtually no creativity left in us. Adults tested at genius levels of 2 percent.

Gallup's annual 2013 engagement survey tracks the steep decline in levels of student engagement as they progress through the Education Machine. In the fifth grade 80 percent of students are engaged. By eighth grade it is 60 percent; by graduation it has dropped to 40 percent.[9]

Common Traits of Engaged Learning Environments

In our work across the nation, we identified eight common traits evident in highly engaged learning environments.

1. They created close-knit tribal communities, thereby providing a safe, positive, and personalized learning environment.
2. They provided hands-on active learning activities and environments.
3. Teachers embraced their new roles as *learning experience designers* and learning facilitators.
4. Several of the schools include multiage classrooms and kids with learning differences within an atmosphere of acceptance and mutual support. It was marvelous to see and hear directly from the kids what they valued from an inclusive classroom experience.
5. Each school had a central philosophy that built on kid's strengths. Teachers were trained to focus on bright spots instead of an emphasis on where their students fall short. Two schools, Birdville and Del Norte, took this to the next level, using assessment tools to better understand each child's unique mix of talents.
6. The curriculum was designed to use relevant and often local topics and issues.
7. All used a variation of a "maker" approach to learning. They required students to design and produce content integrating several modes of learning; research, team dynamics, prototyping, testing, analysis, complex problem solving, script writing, videography, design, lab testing, production, and presentation.
8. The Momentous Institute, Joy School, Shelton, and DaVerse Lounge succeed by creating a holistic experience of social and emotional learning: they apply brain science in practical and accessible ways to the teaching of at-risk and traumatized kids.

The common threads in all of these approaches include student-centered, active social learning in tribal classrooms, affirming environments, and a culture of engagement.

In the past two decades leading change has gone from a specialized course in management to a necessary skill for a volatile, uncertain, complex, and ambiguous (VUCA) world. The successful change leaders we met all focus on the power of the positive as their starting point. In the next chapter you will see why they also take a very intentional approach to building a positive and healthy culture. They know that this is what empowers new strategies and supports deep changes. The fact that most leaders still don't approach change in this manner explains why more than 80 percent of change initiatives fail. It also explains why this next chapter may be the most important one that you will read.

CHAPTER 16

Leading Change at Your School

Every system is perfectly designed to get the results it gets.
—Don Berwick, past president and CEO
of the Institute for Healthcare Improvement

The front page of the December 14, 2008, Sunday edition of the *Atlanta Journal-Constitution* ripped the lid off the story about Atlanta Public School (APS) teachers changing test scores. That story became the pulled thread that unraveled the culture of cheating in the APS.

The final report, hand delivered to the governor in June 2011, summarized the scandal: ". . . institutionalized corruption of standardized tests, directed from the central office, for a decade. Teachers and administrators gave children answers, erased incorrect answers, hid and altered documents, offered monetary incentives to encourage cheating, and punished employees who refused to cheat.[1]"

Beverly Hall, the superintendent at the time, had become a nationally known champion reformer. In her more than 10 years of APS leadership, test scores improved—dramatically. The district had become a national model and Hall was named National Superintendent of the Year.

In March 2012, Damany Lewis, a math teacher at Parks Middle School, was the first to fall in the scandal. He was a good teacher, but the No Child Left Behind (NCLB) legislation set new rules for test scores in 2002, and imposed new consequences for failing to achieve those results. The APS layered it's own local and tougher expectations on top of that, making the mission for Parks and other left-behind schools impossible. Signals from top leadership communicated that new ends justify new means. Finally, for Lewis, a new principal willing to game the system turned the implicit expectations into explicit ones. In Lewis' mind it was either play the game or the school would be closed, taking away whatever hope remained in this community.

The Perverse Logic of a System

Every system develops a culture that helps to achieve what that system values. NCLB, signed into law in January of 2002, established that our nation valued test scores above all other outcomes of from education. With grand intentions to improve opportunities for at-risk kids and raise national achievement levels, it was implemented with no piloting or flexibility for local adaptation. The Machine's one-size-fits-all plan to improve education created, instead, the opposite. The communities that needed improvement the most were the ones least able to comply.

> *Every system develops a culture that helps to achieve what that system values.*

Schools or communities that had cultural values of personal responsibility and accountability already in place succeeded. Those caught in the vicious cycle of poverty, with broken social structures and starting behind from day one never had a chance in the new system.

After the *Journal-Constitution* article in 2008, investigations began rolling. In 2010, the Georgia Bureau of Investigation assigned more than fifty agents to the case. They found that 44 out of 56 schools and 178 teachers and principals changed answers to tests. In the fall of 2014 22 teachers and principals were brought to trial. Eleven received criminal sentences.

The Battle of Atlanta, or How to Move from What's Wrong to What's Strong

In April 2014 Dr. Meria Carstarphen took over as Superintendent. She believed that a good culture can overcome a bad system. K–12 MindShift found that, in two years of research, APS was the first large urban turnaround effort that placed culture before strategy.

That's why "The Battle of Atlanta" is a story worth telling.

Brandon Busteed, Executive Director of Education and Workplace Development for Gallup, had been working with Dr. Carstarphen in her previous position as Superintendent of Schools in Austin, Texas. "Dr. C," as Carstarphen is known, adopted Gallup's strengths-focused philosophy, their Q12 engagement assessment, and their Clifton Strengthsfinder tools. Her Strenghtsfinder talents include: Achiever, Self-Assurance, Learner, Deliberative, and Responsibility. She is a goal-oriented, unrelentingly confident, life-long learner who carefully plans, is deeply considerate of others, and committed to the well-being of her team and students. In other words, she was the perfect candidate to lead a turnaround effort.

To understand the story better, I flew to Atlanta and interviewed several people. Their story offers some guidelines for leading change. Consider the following planks in the "Leading Change at Your School" platform.

Start Over

I asked Angela Smith, Special Assistant to the Superintendent, "Where do you even begin? How do you present hope within a devastated and publically humiliated organization?"

"I remember Dr. C asking a room full of teachers and principals, 'Do you guys know the little bird on your emblem logo? It's a phoenix!' She continued, 'Y'all need to rise. You have to rise out of the ashes. It's time for us to stop with the burning. We had the fires and all of the other distractions for the past two years, but now I need you to rise. We've gotta do this for the kids. Atlanta, we are moving from what's wrong to what's strong. And what is strong is each of you.'

"For all the people in that room, that was huge. They needed to start over and she called them up to it."

Model Expectations

According to Angela, Dr. C. hit the ground running to help change the culture; "She was out talking to everyone. She was out with the bus drivers at 4:00 or 5:00 in the morning. I was with her, carrying the doughnuts. She was out with the Facilities folks. She could say, 'I was in this school at this time and the bathrooms are dirty. I'm going back in two days and I need the bathrooms to be cleaned.' "

Creating New Structures Transforms Relationships

APS restructured their schools based on a cluster model that Dr. C had used previously in Austin. A cluster is based on a flagship high school and the different middle and elementary schools that feed into it.

Each cluster featured a community-designed "signature program" that linked all students to a larger vision. From kindergarten students and their families could clearly see and join a building momentum toward graduation from the flagship high school. The cluster concept also brought the school principals into alignment around common purposes.

Reinforce the Message of Stakeholder Engagement

Dr. C continually stated and fortified her expectation that everyone must work together. In so doing, she slowly changed an atmosphere that encouraged unilateral actions into "a caring culture of collaboration." She made sure that the decision making process included all stakeholders.

> Dr. C. slowly changed an atmosphere that encouraged unilateral actions into "a caring culture of collaboration."

Design and Build New Roles

Dr. Emily Massey, Associate Superintendent, knows her focus is developing APS's human resources. In addition to getting people who fit the function, her role also looks at the cultural fit. She helps to craft roles that tap into what people naturally do best and enjoy most. She also focuses on what's strong in individuals. Dr. Massey loves work that is motivated by higher purpose and that serves others. She also enjoys dealing with the unpredictable and tackling APS's in-the-moment demands, which can be challenging to more routine-minded administrators. Dr. Massey is able to communicate ideas in a way that make them memorable and personal. Riding with her for my tour of Martin Luther King Middle School gave me another window into their change strategy of developing Teacher/ Leaders.

Because principals are *the* leverage point for changing a district, APS is taking theirs through an intensive "boot camp" process, redesigning their role into (my words) the Chief Education Officer for each school. For the strategy to work the principals need to have mastered the teaching model and be both the example and coach for high-level teaching. Paul Brown, MLK Middle School's principal, is built like a linebacker. He radiates a welcoming smile, quiet manner, and deep conviction about a respectful, responsible culture and engaged and competent teachers. He was one of Dr. Carstarphen's *first followers*; he already modeled that behavior while principal at a neighboring district.

Each morning Paul stands in the foyer welcoming kids, shaking hands, patting them on the back, joking, and handing out personal encouragements or exhortations. He goes to every classroom during the first period. When he returns to his office he'll send a message over the public address system with a theme, news, and then a comment based on his impression of the tone or energy of the kids when they filed through the entrance. "Okay teachers, there must be a full moon because the kids feel energized and eager to put that energy into learning."

Build a Culture

Dr. Donyall Dickey, the Chief Schools Officer for APS, is impeccably dressed, articulate, and keenly focused on raising the competency of the teacher core. More important, he and all the leaders I met came from successful turnaround schools in embattled communities. I saw the same unrehearsed clarity and conviction that can come from years of working together, but they hadn't. Somehow, they had learned common principles through their experiences in common crucibles. They know that the ingredients for education are students, culture, content, competency, consistency, coherence, communication, collaboration, and community. Repeat.

> *They know that the ingredients for education are students, culture, content, competency, consistency, coherence, communication, collaboration, and community. Repeat.*

Donyall was born in poverty and never knew his parents. "My mother was a drug addict; my father I didn't know. My grandmother raised me." He found school to be a ladder up and out. "So when I taught the kids in Baltimore, I was really reflecting on the idea that I may represent their only hope; their only chance to get educated." He worked with third graders and found language (more specifically vocabulary) a key to accelerating learning. That became his obsession, and for good reason. "Because we know, the prison systems are built based on a kid's ability to read at the end of grade three. That's how prisons project their new construction needs—based upon reading level![2] I knew I had a task and so it was the third-grade teaching position that shaped who I am as an educator."

His success for building a process to accelerate reading resulted in advancement in Baltimore, then Philadelphia, and now Atlanta. His job is to build the framework and mastery among APS teachers to replicate this success. "Improvement is no mystery," he told me. "You cannot transfer what you do not have, right? So if kids have to analyze U.S. seminal documents of historical and literary significance with a focus on themes, purposes, and rhetorical features, teachers better know what that means. And, don't make the mistake of assuming everyone knows."

"Charlie has special needs. He could also take your wallet while he's grinnin' at you. He was neglected and underserved for years, and you saw that in his performance. I worked on phonetics with Charlie, as his principal, for two years. I then insisted that he participate in class and learn grade-level subject matter like the other kids."

One of my assistant principals was covering a class for a teacher, and I sat in, too. He said to the kids, 'Can you define the word transdermal?' Charlie raised his hand and the AP ignored him. Charlie, raised it again and spoke out, 'I know. *Trans*; when you see trans in a word, it means across. When you see *derm*, it means skin. It's referrin' to across the skin. When you see "a-l" at the end of a word, it means related to. Sir; I think transdermal means something that goes across the skin.' Blew them out of the water!"

"Kids don't understand what they read in a chapter because they don't understand what they read on a page; because they don't under-stand what they read in a paragraph; because they don't understand what they read in a sentence; because they don't understand an individual word; because they don't understand individual word parts. A kid reading at third grade level has learned 25,000 words compared to 2,500 words for a kid far below grade level. How do you multiply that? Through learning word parts. There are thirty prefixes, thirty roots, and thirty suffixes that if learned provide them with 95 percent of the working words they need to master. When you build Charlie's knowledge of word parts, you build Charlie's knowledge of *anything* that he reads."

The APS story demonstrates what leading change in a school looks like.

- Culture before strategy
- Reframe the old story
- Build on strengths and bright spots
- Be visible and model behavior
- Remind leaders how "we" make decisions and treat one another
- Engage *all* stakeholders
- Create relational eco-systems
- Practice well what you preach
- Invest in roles that have high leverage in the system
- Grow teachers from competency to mastery
- Embrace first followers
- Build an "A" team at the core
- Stabilize with a surge of support
- Don't make assumptions regarding teacher skills
- Support and train
- Refocus and rebuild the fundamentals

Stakeholder Engagement

Columbus, Indiana, school officials were shocked in 1996 when a commissioned Hudson Institute report declared that Columbus schools were the weak link in Columbus's economic development. Their "aha" moment, however, was the report's conclusion that K–12 education *is* economic development. The challenge was not simply better schools but a different kind of community.

Columbus' past experience with many public-private partnerships created habits for how to come together to address a big and, in this case, embarrassing report. The community had sufficient social capital (trust and respect) that enabled them to step up together, instead of reacting to the bad news and pointing fingers. Jack Hess, the Executive Director for the Institute for Coalition Building, explained the extraordinary instinctive response from the community. In time, the response became the framework for their *Stakeholder Engagement Process*.

How Did "We" Get Here?

According to Jack, "No one looked for blame. The questions that were being asked were basically, 'What can we do to improve the K–12 piece?' Columbus possesses an imbedded philosophy; responsibility precedes accountability. In other words, *"We should be willing to accept personal responsibility before we ask for accountability from others.*

"This atmosphere allowed the Superintendent to open his remarks with, 'I know this is bad news, the data is not great, and we can all point fingers, but the bottom line is that I can't get this done alone.' Employers acknowledged they had not given enough direction about the kinds of skills and careers they needed. The postsecondary schools recognized they had no degree programs that lined up with the community's strengths. There was no working relationship between the postsecondary and K–12 system. There were no career pathways defined and the schools had neglected their career/tech-education departments."

"Everyone invested a lot of time doing personal inventories over months, discussing how they cocreated the situation. They used this time to build a key component to the stakeholder process called *shared understanding,* which leads to *collective action.*

The Stakeholder Engagement Process[3]

The Institute for Coalition Building has since mapped what the community learned into a process that takes the shape of a four-quadrant wheel (see Figure 16.1). The right half of the wheel explains the steps for reaching Shared Understanding. The left half of the wheel explains the steps for Collective Action.

Transforming the system is ultimately about transforming relationships among those who shape the system.

—Jack Hess

Once there is a shared understanding and resolve, action begins around a series of small projects. According to Jack, "This is a system thing, not a single issue, and you can't attack a whole system."

"You can strategically shift a system through multiple small interventions that also change the nature of the working relationship among stakeholders. This is a subtle but significant difference in approach. Instead of the natural focus to tackle issues and solve problems, the process shifts the emphasis to working on relationships in the system through collective efforts to address issues and problems. Transforming the system is ultimately about transforming relationships among those who shape the system."

The Atlanta Public Schools discovered this same truth when it adopted its cluster strategy. Clusters created a structure that brought principals together who had never before had common interest or common cause.

Columbus used small projects in a similar way, as a structure to bring entities together with common interests to create common cause. One team in Columbus worked with the high school to create better linkage to the postsecondary schools. A second project worked with the post-secondary degree programs to align with business needs. One effort led to another until these efforts numbered more than 30 projects.

Jack said, "Early on, the process is the structure and the structure equals relationships. Good collaboration processes create new conversations . . . and slowly shift the values of the system." That's why linking cluster principals or project teams to work together produced new relationship dynamics.

The problem also gets distributed. Jack recapped how employers, educators—K–12 and postsecondary—and community leaders recognized, far more than only their piece of the problem, how their relationship to the whole created the situation. This also means the solutions are distributed. In other words, programs, funding, and initiatives without distributed decision-making will fail.

Who?

The upper right quadrant of the wheel defines the "who" questions. It begins with, "What is the collective issue *we* face?"

What is the problem that is too big for any one entity to tackle? What is the story that conveys its complexity and importance? What group of stakeholders is willing to take responsibility for the success of the system? Who are the right participants?

During this phase, which can extend for several months, a sponsor-facilitator works to bring people together, hear divergent perspectives, and clarify the complex issues or problems "we" face. Each stakeholder is like a blind sage trying to describe an elephant. Their passionate descriptions of the problem captures only a limited and small view, even though, to that person, it looks like the whole beast.

Why?

The bottom right quadrant works to establish trust and shared understanding. The first step asks, "What outcomes and benefits do the stakeholders collectively desire? What creates value for each stakeholder?"

The "why" quadrant of the wheel works to create common interest and common cause by developing "two to three themes that would align the interests of the stakeholder group." A lot of the work in this phase is determining what information is needed, what projects are of interest, conducting and listening to "voice of the customer," mapping social assets, and mapping the different networks and nodes in the system. This phase reaches closure when participants arrive at a shared understanding of the research and data and its implications.

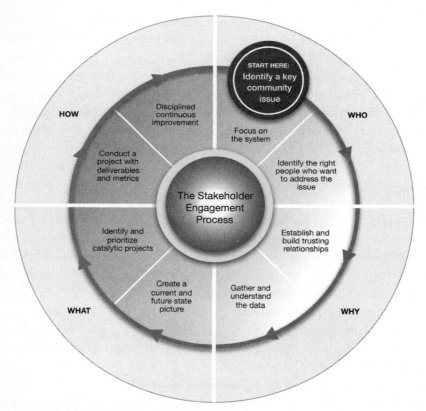

Figure 16.1 Stakeholder Engagement Process

What?

The alignment achieved through the "who" and "why" leads to grounding the work. "What is?" and "what is desired?" are fleshed out in a current state and future state mapping exercise. The mountain ahead is what lies between. The "what" quadrant is on the bottom left of the circle. It has moved from the Shared Understanding and Alignment to Collective Action.

Jack explains, "The initial work looks like coordinating and aligning what is already in place and working. Identify where the strongest interests reside and tap that energy, which leads to small initiatives that test the system's resistance and leverage points. Small wins, pilots, and experiments set the stage for a broader effort to scale."

How?

The fourth phase is the upper left quadrant of the circle. Collective action is taking on a self-directed life of its own. This activity begins to shift system outcomes. Restructuring key relationships to tackle common interests is one of the most effective means for changing the system. Aligning the Atlanta Public Schools' principals in a cluster model restructured their relationships. The different relationship structures changed the nature and focus of their work, leading to a more integrated curriculum that creates a more cohesive learning experience. It also shifted a model of school autonomy to a community with a Signature Program. That identity, pride, and social capital is now cascading into the neighborhoods.

> *"The initial work looks like coordinating and aligning what is already in place and working. Identify where the strongest interests reside and tap that energy, which leads to small initiatives that test the system's resistance and leverage points. Small wins, pilots, and experiments set the stage for a broader effort to scale."*

I Moved Here Because of Your Schools: Don't Change Anything!

In 2008, 35 Texas superintendents led a study and issued a report on the future needs in education.[4] Jeff Turner, superintendent of Coppell ISD, was one of the organizers. They concluded that fundamental change was

> *"It doesn't matter that we're the best. The last typewriter that Smith Corona made was its best. But we don't use typewriters anymore!"*

necessary to educate future-ready kids. They and other Texas leaders clearly saw the radical overhaul needed to replace a factory education model. But with schools excelling on the standardized tests and in college placement, there was no burning reason to gather support and drive change.

So, naturally, the initial message from parents was, "Don't mess with success!" Jeff responded: "It doesn't matter that we're the best. The last typewriter that Smith Corona made was its best. But we don't use typewriters anymore!" The emotional risk to parents of letting go of proven success in order to try an untested strategy on "my" child outweighed reason and evidence.

Jeff and his team, including Assistant Superintendent Shannon Buerk, knew that the real challenge they faced was bored students who were mostly going through the motions of learning. They also knew that there was a growing new focus on the need for future-ready skills.

So Shannon reframed the challenge by asking, "What if we're really not competing with the schools around us? What if our real challenge is preparing kids for the future and providing an engaging learning experience?" Then she formed a group of about 50 people, half school staff and students and half community participants, called Pinnacle 2020. They met every other Thursday for about two years. Shannon stated their mission, "What can we do to address the growth issue but also an opportunity for students to gain twenty-first-century skills?"

The question addressed Coppell's immediate need and the city's future. Everyone is curious about the future. Jeff and Shannon knew that in order for the community to reach the same level of conviction reflected in the Superintendent's report it would require more than simply transferring that information. Attempting to adopt those recommendations, without the process, would have been too abstract and too risky to consider . . . a bridge too far.

Designing the "Aha" Moment

Shannon needed to engage their stakeholders in a collective discovery that would lead to an "aha" moment. So she designed a discovery process that included the following elements.

Day in the Life

Administrators and community members followed a student for a day. They quickly discovered a normal day was boring, unchallenging, passive, and focused on preparing for the next test.

Student Work Audit

When the principals reviewed student work from around the district, they were shocked that most of it was low-level disconnected busy work.

Homework Audit

The staff collected two weeks of homework from several students, made copies of everything, and simply stacked it in piles on a desk. That, of course, created a visual and visceral "wow!"

Student Survey

A survey was sent to students; one question simply asked how much of their school time is boring. The average was over 50 percent.

Book Club

At the same time the committee read *Windows in the Future* and viewed videos like Ken Robinson's TED Talk, *Do Schools Kill Creativity?*. All of these experiences helped to reach a tipping point.

Future Summit

Shannon's team invited the community to participate in a Future's Summit. The questions about twenty-first-century skills were put on the table. One exercise looked into the future, using a scenario-planning matrix.

A yearning for change began rumbling through Coppell. Soon, the city heard a collective "aha." Everyone reached the same conclusion. The leaders heard a chorus of new thinking. "Even if we have top scores on current assessment measures, even if we're leading other schools we still don't believe we are doing right by our kids if we don't prepare them for the twenty-first century."

At this point the culture shifted from "preserve our rankings" to excitement about building for the future. As Jack Hess says, "A system is transformed when the type of system it is thought to be changes." The Coppell culture valued high-test scores and competing to win against other schools. But then, because of those leading change, it shifted to value kids learning twenty-first-century skills. That shift enabled radical changes.

Out of seven school options the committee narrowed them down to two, a ninth grade academy and a choice school. The board selected the choice school.

New Tech High

The board and school leaders invested considerable work in researching emerging pedagogy, visiting early adopter schools, looking at different schedule structures, redefining roles and designing a new learning experience and new kind of space. The same engagement approach was used for this phase as well. Their process mirrors the stakeholder wheel. Small groups addressed the campus strategy, learner outcomes, design principles, new teacher profiles, a hiring process, finance, technology, facilities, human resources, professional development, teaching methodology, restructuring the school day, learning pathway, and intramural activities.

Coppell chose a New Tech model for project based and team learning. They adapted a modular scheduling structure they saw working well at West Side High School in Omaha, Nebraska.

New Tech created a new process for Coppell's own version of the *Stakeholder Engagement Process*. When it was time to build a new school for Lee Elementary they partnered with Stantec and Balfour Beatty to create an equally innovative school in Coppell on the inside and out. It was the first Net Zero (energy consumption) elementary school in the United States.

Schools Within a School

Lee Elementary stretched even further into the future designing a building based on campus strategy and learning experience. That central strategy is to create community and continuity for kids during these early developing years. We shared Lou Cozolino's research on the value of chunking down the size of a school to recreate a "tribal" intimacy–or human scale–fostering safety and connectedness. The 550-plus students are divided into six vertical "houses," like schools within a school. Each house has a team of teachers that cover K–5. "The school itself is an architectural and design feat; it's completely flex space, with only a few movable walls and plenty of collaborative spaces and communal facilities."

How You Can Lead a Movement

Several years ago, when I volunteered for a nonprofit serving a local community, our growth meant that we had to relocate the organization's office from a personal residence to an actual office. So we decided to buy land that would be sufficient for an office and other community-benefitting possibilities. The land, zoned for agriculture, already had one building: a "pole barn," a three-sided, pole-supported structure for sheltering farm implements and equipment, bales of hay, and so forth.

The nonprofit bought the materials and the volunteers provided the labor for converting the barn to an office. The NFP had many people gifted in landscaping, masonry, carpentry, electrical, plumbing and other trades. Then there were the many, like me, who were eager to help and take part. But I probably used three nails for every two that went in straight. Turns out I was best at shoveling and hauling dirt.

Throughout the summer during the longer evenings and all day on weekends there were sometimes 30 or more men and women busy building, planting, and doing whatever needed to be done to bring a community asset into being. The process was beautiful: parents brought their children; kids roamed over the property, playing, chasing fireflies, and getting rides on a tractor driven by a volunteer named Gerald.

We had a gifted playground designer as a volunteer. One of the first projects completed was a truly inspired playground for the kids. With leadership from an architect, we completed the conversion of the pole barn and eventually landscaped the property and built several soccer fields. For the past 30 years the project has been a gift to the local community. The converted pole barn/office still stands and the fields are full of kids and parents along with a few dogs.

Communication led to conversation, then to common interest, and on to coordination and collaboration. The whole process led to a deepened sense of community.

The real "product" of that project came from an idea that grew into a conversation and led to our collective action and built a sense of community for those who volunteered. We built something of lasting value, and with values that lasted as well and made a solid contribution to a sense of community. That sense of community expanded to the adjacent neighborhoods that still enjoy the beautiful fields. Much of that is because it was not a public works program. It was their neighbors who made the investment.

Social capital is the most overlooked but most powerful asset that schools and communities have. Leading change helps people find their common interests! From that, they come together and find a common cause for action. To paraphrase the Stakeholder Engagement Process, communication led to conversation, then to common interest, and on to coordination and collaboration. The whole process led to a deepened sense of community.

First Followers

When we think of leading change, our focus goes to the person standing out in front. We often overlook those first followers, a role that all of us have played and any of us can do today.

This is the point of Derek Shiver's viral TED Talk video, "How to Start a Movement." Shivers says that the arrival of first followers "turns a lone nut into a leader." If you're the lone nut Shriver recommends that you embrace first followers as equals. They play a vital role because people follow followers.

I often ask leaders, "Who were your first followers and how did they make a difference to you and your work?"

Without exception they instantly name those people and describe how vital they were. They offered a sounding board, encouragement, and sometimes provided a venue and a network. Most important, they spoke truth back to the lone nut.

The role of the first followers is to show others how to follow.

To Begin

My first MindShift group was birthed from the conversations at my Pancake House roundtable breakfasts. As I shared in Chapter 3, the breakfast group was composed of five business leaders, over a long time, have become trusted advisors and friends. Those gatherings have given us all permission to voice frustrations, ask questions, and present ideas. Although most of those ideas failed to germinate, there is something catalytic about sharing a meal, coffee, or a drink with others around discussing common interests, common concerns, and common causes. I've consulted with successful startup companies that began in a bar or around a kitchen table.

In his book *Where Good Ideas Come From,* Steven Johnson says that a diversity of voices is a common element for social, scientific or artistic innovation. My Pancake roundtable provides five very successful, distinct, and opinionated voices.

> *I've listened to parents' strong opinions about their schools. I've also listened to teachers in the teacher's lounge and administrators at conferences. There is no shortage of opinions. However, they can become echo chambers when isolated from each other.*

I share this because I've listened to parents' strong opinions about their schools. I've also listened to teachers in the teacher's lounge and administrators at conferences. There is no shortage of opinions. However, they can become echo chambers when isolated from each other. Successful change leaders bring different voices together in order to find common interest.

The stories of success almost always include some mention of the conversations that evolved over *time*. A lot of time together. The two most common "if I had it to do over" comments I hear are "I wish we had started sooner" and "I wish we had put more time into working together."

The work of transformation is not a program. It is attracting hearts and minds through vision, trust, and engagement. The Institute of Coalition Building says that change begins with an individual or "a group that wants to take responsibility for the success of a system."[5]

Anyone, anywhere can organize—to do anything. Once upon a time, it took an organization with a charter and a mission or a blue ribbon committee with authorization to coordinate people and resources to accept a challenge. However, just as bloggers have overthrown much of the platform of official journalism, today is the day of the person with a dream and audacity. Credentials not required. I had an idea I had incubated for almost five years. I found three first followers who were willing to host a small workshop to test the idea. The rest, for me, is history.

Where We Go from Here

Kids first come to school eager to learn and highly engaged with life; they get excited about almost everything. But, very soon, after arriving in the artificial environment called "school," they discover that passing tests are what matter. Remember Candi's grandson Elisha in Chapter 5?

In his 2010 TEDex talk, Dr. Michael Wesch, Associate Professor of Cultural Anthropology at Kansas State, described the disengaged students in his lecture room. That led him to more deeply explore what learning looks like through their eyes. His simple measure for engagement is the questions students ask. A good question leads to a quest. But he realized that his typical questions had been like:

What will be covered on the test?

How many points is this worth?

How many pages does it need to be?

That led him to consider how to go from being a good teacher to creating a good learning environment.

He saw that students "associate learning with acquiring information. No deeper understanding. And the message of the classroom reinforces that message. The teacher is at the front of the room teaching the material and student's job is to absorb and recall that information."[6]

He also said that, in this Google world, kids are coming out of K–12 with questions that previous generations never addressed head on. But now all of us must wrestle with,

Who am I?

What am I going to do?

Am I going to make it?

Dr. Welch then laments, ". . . the tragedy of our times is that our schools are not speaking to these questions."[7]

The last chapter brings us back to our original question. How do we reimagine, in a Google world, learning that will turn disengaged students into inspired learners?

CHAPTER 17

Humanity High

The Movie

The black ribbon of four-lane highway curls up over and around the hills tinted with the light green of early spring. You glance at your dashboard clock: 9:53. Here in the Southwest, the heat is already climbing and it's still early in the morning. A few minutes later you see the sign: Humanity High School—3 Miles.

A couple of miles later you top the ridge. And stop. The sight is so beautiful that you kill the engine and step out of your car. From the hill you can see the vast sweep of the Organ Mountains to the east, the arid desert valley below, and the beautiful campus of Humanity High (see Figure 17.1).

Space Design

As you drive down from the ridge, the sheer beauty of the three-sided cloister, enclosed by glass exterior walls, and the green carpet of roof grass galvanize your attention.

After parking, you walk toward the courtyard. You see students gathered around the dramatic and beautiful water pool. A freestanding glass-tapered cone rises near the pool. Then you enter the school building—immediately, you feel the atmosphere of peace, calm, and easy alertness that reminds you of an upscale office. Keeping with the concept of learning as a natural part of life, earth tones throughout the

PBK

HUMANITY HIGH SCHOOL   EXTERIOR VIEW

Figure 17.1   Humanity High School: Exterior View

Source: PBK Architects

building extend the muted colors native to the local desert and mountain environments.

The principal, Ms. Ortega, greets you and begins the tour. You like her; she seems to have all the time in the world for you. She is young, attractive, and wears a very comfortable, tailored, light green pants suit. As she walks with you, she clearly and softly explains the architecture.

"The building is so eco-friendly and was, in fact, built as a Living Building.[1] We generate a surplus of energy and capture and treat our water before it returns to the system. As you can see, the courtyard's glass walls push natural light deep into the building, giving our learning spaces transparent walls—light penetrates throughout. And the natural light eliminates most electrical lighting. The natural green roof not only forms an insulation barrier but also reduces the heat sink effect of hard surfaces. And the green roof also offers organic gardening space for students: they learn to cultivate plants and value food sustainability. As you can see, our learning space extends out onto the campus."

As you continue to walk, she points out other significant features:

> *The green roof also offers organic gardening space for students; they learn to cultivate plants and value food sustainability.*

The building's main student circulation pattern runs through a corridor adjacent to the three glass walls of the courtyard. Positioning the corridor a sufficient distance from the glass walls allows space for an active multipurpose learning commons between the corridor and the glass wall. The two-story learning commons accommodates a variety of learning activities: students working in groups of various sizes (and ages), students working alone, teachers and students interacting in a variety of informal ways. The commons design also encourages students to work between classes, eat lunch, and collaborate with their peers in different ways.

The multifunctional space also consists of labs, smaller spaces where students can comfortably collaborate, and larger spaces for group purposes.

Respect

As you and Ms. Ortega walk the corridors, step into the learning spaces, and stroll across the campus, you notice the banners prominently posted throughout the school.

AT HUMANITY HIGH, WE ALL STRIVE TO:

Pursue Knowledge
Discover the Joy of Wisdom
Live Courageously
Find Our Own Unique Voice & Then Speak Honestly
Serve Others & Demonstrate Kindness
Work & Play Well with Others
Live with Purpose
Make Tomorrow Better for People & the Planet

You ask Ms. Ortega about them.

"Yes, those values constitute our Humanity Code. We drew them from the research of Professor Martin Seligman."

"I'm not familiar with him."

"He is an author, professor—University of Pennsylvania, I think— who has done landmark work in the field of positive psychology. Others focus on what is wrong, but he studies what is right, what works. He studied a wide spectrum of cultures in order to codify some universal virtues. Using his list, we developed our own code."

"So, that's why you see the banners. And we also post them as the back cover of our publications, on our website, and even as our screensavers. I make sure that our staff models each and every line of the code in our relationships with each other, and with all the students, their parents, and everyone within the larger community. And we do that every day. We live these messages more than we speak them."

Curiosity

Explaining that she has an appointment to welcome a new student, Ms. Ortega invites you to explore the spaces, faces, and hearts of Humanity High. She asks if you're available for lunch. You agree to meet her in an hour.

Our students are free range; we have no cages, we inject no chemicals, and we reject conformity.

You begin walking the corridors between glass walls. You see students and adults, presumably "teachers," working together at group work surfaces. And the students, with wide-open and eager faces, are leaning into their work.

You notice that everyone listens when another person is speaking. As you watch, you remember what Ms. Ortega told you a few minutes ago, "Our students are free range; we have no cages, we inject no chemicals, and we reject conformity." Gazing into the young faces beyond the glass walls, you begin to get it. This is what curiosity looks like. It explores, pokes, and snoops through the nooks and crannies of its environment. It knows no fear. Students freely walk out of their learning space, into the corridor, and down to the large flat-screen monitors. They punch information into a handheld device and a Khan Academy video comes to life.

As you continue walking, you notice the silence and peace of the atmosphere. Minutes later, some (but not all) students begin pouring from the learning spaces into the corridor. They walk into other spaces down the corridor. Some go to the commons to get a snack or drink.

You stop a young girl; she appears to be about 13. "May I ask you a question?"

"Sure," she smiles.

"I did not hear a bell, yet students are obviously changing class. How do you know when and where to go next?"

Her grin reveals that she hears this question a lot. "Well, this school is like an office. My mom's office doesn't have bells. Mom knows how to find the space and the people she needs for her projects. I do, too."

Then, she turns to walk away, but stops.

"Did I answer your question?" she asks.

And then you see it. The administrators respect the students and give them the autonomy and freedom to take responsibility for their own learning pace and path. That kind of human respect is the gyroscope that keeps everything upright.

Now, you see, *really see*, The Code at work.

Encouragement

As you walk through the large, glass–walled learning commons (see Figure 17.2), you notice framed 11- by 14-inch photographs of students in caps and gowns. Each photo carries a name and a future date: 2019, 2020, 2017, 2018 . . .

Figure 17.2   Humanity High School: Learning Commons

Source: PBK Architects

You go to the desk and ask the lady wearing the "Concierge" nametag about the photos. She explains that they have computer-generated "maturing" portraits of each student (in fact, every K–12 student in the district). This way, every student can see evidence of Humanity High's encouragement toward, and full assumptions about, every student graduating. *Every* student.

You slowly stroll back to and down the corridor. You notice a class teacher—actually, a "guide"—standing at the side of the room as a student speaks. When the student sits down, another student begins addressing her class. All the while the guide remains at the side of the room; she does not speak or gesture. Although you cannot hear the words, another student speaks to the guide. You walk into the room as she steps over to the pod; you can hear her as she offers assistance. She reminds you more of a "genius" at an Apple store than a teacher. She is positive, empathetic, engaging, and *helpful*. No condescension, no eye-rolling, no impatience. Her voice and her entire demeanor are encouraging; you can see it in her eyes—she *wants* that kid to get it!

> *She reminds you more of a "genius" at an Apple store than a teacher. She is positive, empathetic, engaging, and helpful.*

Community

In a few moments, as you walk on down the corridor, you see a room of 13-, maybe 14-year-old, students listening to an elderly, wheelchair-bound, African-American man talk. You step inside the room as a student raises his hand.

"Mr. Bowles, we watched a video about civil rights, but how did you and others actually start the movement?"

"Well, son," the old man started, "We didn't start it; we never thought about it or referred to it as 'civil rights.' We didn't know them words. It wasn't like today, when TV cameras are everywhere. I don't think anyone ever, I sure never heard it, talked about bein' a movement. Less see, I was in my early 30s. Now I'm 91. We was fighting for our lives, for our neighborhoods, and the lives of those who would come later. We didn't know we was making history. Martin and the other leaders may have known; I sure didn't."

You see Ms. Ortega in the hall. Realizing it's time for you to meet her, you step out into the hall. "Ready for lunch?" she asks.

Over lunch you ask her about the elderly gentleman speaking about his civil rights days.

"Yes, his name is Athol Bowles. He grew up in Selma, Alabama, but retired here 30 or more years ago for the drier climate. He's almost faculty; he talks about what he saw in Alabama in the '50s and '60s. I think he's addressed every class of students for the past 10, maybe 12 years. Students love him. When his wife died a couple of years ago, over 300 students attended her funeral."

"Do you have other citizens who do that?"

"Oh, yes. We have a retired nuclear energy scientist, a Navy Admiral, former Governor, one of the first female airline pilots, and several others in the community who come in regularly and interact with students. We even bring some nursing home residents, like an elderly musician, a guy who played saxophone in recording sessions with Sinatra, here to talk to the kids. They bring views and voices that we, obviously, do not have on staff. They are essential to giving a good education to our students."

> *That is part of our Stakeholder Engagement Process. Everyone in town has an investment, a stake, in what happens with our staff and our students.*

"So, are you more like a community center than a school?"

"We are integrally related to our community. Like, a couple of our local banks take groups of students every month; they explain the idea and practice of banking, show them how it all works, explain the policies, how to get the most out of savings and checking; they talk about taxes. And other businesses and industries like the local police department regularly spend 1 or 2 hours a day offering tours, answering questions, and building relationships with Humanity High."

"Incredible. They come to you and you go to them."

"Absolutely. That is part of our Stakeholder Engagement Process. Everyone in town has an investment, a stake, in what happens with our staff and our students. We want their voices to be heard. And we continuously solicit feedback. We cannot effectively pursue our mission if we don't have strong ties with the community."

"Ms. Ortega, I also . . ."

"Excuse me, let me just say that our community base is also why we have so many parents and other adults on our campus. Our learning center is open to anyone. So on any night of the week, you will see adults here. Some are working with their children or grandchildren on projects, others are doing their own research or working with others, like maybe a church group, on a project."

Discipline

As you think about the community dimension, and while Ms. Ortega takes a few bites of food, you keep thinking about the faces of kids at Humanity High.

"I gotta ask you; I don't see any evidence of discipline problems, no behavior or attitude stuff. I grew up scared to death of our principal, Mr. Hammer. But that kept me in line. How do you *manage* this kind of, I guess, peace in the school?"

Ms. Ortega pauses and takes a bite of her salad. Then she speaks,

"When students are free to do what they do best and enjoy most, when they face other students rather than stare at the back of their heads, when they have influence and equity in their own learning, they don't act up. We honestly do not have discipline problems. We relate to the students as guides, not experts or cops. The atmosphere is, as you probably notice, *positive*. You wouldn't run into a heavy-handed, rigid attitude at a fine restaurant—the staff is there to make sure you get healthy and delicious food and within an atmosphere that supports your purpose for the meal. They are not there to control your arrival time, departure, or how fast or how slow you eat your food. We're the same way. We try to treat everyone as though they are our customers. Because they are!"

As you talk, you notice students walking across the courtyard or sitting on the wall of the pond. The atmosphere is casual, but as far you can see, no one abuses the freedom.

And the time with Ms. Ortega comes to an end. There were other questions to ask, like about technology, but they must wait for another time. She invites you to return; you will. But, for now, you bid her farewell and walk to your car.

What If?

What you have just read is "just a movie." Of course, it presents the future-ready, kid-centered school of the future in its best possible light. But we present it here as a way of provoking and releasing your imagination about the possibilities where you live (see Figure 17.3).

So imagine . . . what if your school started over? What if the Education Machine were to disappear tomorrow and you and other stakeholders in your community took blank sheets of paper to design a new school.

What if you had no funding problems, no battle with special interests, no legal issues, and a completely supportive community? What if you could begin again? What would you create? What would it look like?

What if the Education Machine were to disappear tomorrow?
What if you could begin again?
What would you create?

We live in one of the most exciting times in human history, a time marked by the transformation of every issue, tradition, and challenge. They are all being sifted and reconsidered. All the pillars of civilization are

Figure 17.3   Kids with an Equal Chance in the Race to Learn

under intense scrutiny. That certainly includes the way we prepare our children for the future.

We, as a society, seem to be stripping the modern artifice and mechanization of education away; we are questioning its core assumptions. Think about it: education's basic elements are very simple: students, wise teachers (or facilitators, guides, etc.), and a place to facilitate that. In other times and places, a school might be people sitting on a hillside, in conversation with a teacher. So what are the possible new relationships, shapes, symmetries, colors, and meanings?

Will school buildings become obsolete?

Will they disappear?

Will the Carnegie Unit[2] survive a world of continuous learning?

Do grades have relevance in a shift toward mastery?

How long will students be grouped by common age?

Will standardized tests be seen as dangerous, like smoking or fast food?

Clay Shirky said, "You can call social change a revolution when the members of the *relevant society* demand things that can't be provided by the existing institutions."[3]

You Don't Need Permission

The idea that learning is the elite province of experts is one of the single biggest deterrents to innovation in education. Generations have been trained to "get away and stay away from our silo!" Our busy schedules and our often-bad memories of our school experiences tend to distract us from the new realities inside the walls of the Education Machine. And schools don't make it easy, either. They do not engage their own stakeholders. Schools, like other social institutions, have become defensive in the face of change. The more radical the change, the more defensive and protective they become. That makes the shades go down tight!

As you saw in "the movie," education needs every voice. An open relationship with the community may end certain patterns of preference for interest and advocacy groups. Such a relationship will also expose obsolete practices and activities. But the openness would also revitalize community energy and support.

In Chapter 3, I explained that our K–12 MindShift never sought permission. We just walked in like we owned the place and knew what we were doing. And you don't need permission, either.

Finally . . . Remember the Collaborative Hum

Most authors have one phrase that captures what they intend to convey to the reader. "The Collaborative Hum" may be my phrase for this book. That is because humanizing the Education Machine begins with a group of kids completely absorbed in learning. The buzz, the hum that rises from that collaboration, is distinctive and haunting. It is the sound of curiosity bubbling from a group of kids in full pursuit of knowledge. It's the joy, the laughter of discovery, the mumbling of "hey, cool!" or "wow; look at this!"

The collaborative hum resonated deeply within each member in our K–12 MindShift group. When we toured schools our team members immediately spotted those kids who were *lost* in the play of curiosity and learning. We all gravitated to them. And after our tours, as we debriefed in the school library or back at the hotel, those were the stories that energized us. We asked one another: "Did you see those kids . . . ?" "Did you feel the energy in the room?"

> *"Humanizing the Education Machine" begins with a group of kids completely absorbed in learning.*

As the group leader, I must confess something. When I started the journey I didn't know what to look for. I had been so distracted by battles with the Education Machine in my own home that I had fallen into the trap of just reacting to its agendas and assumptions. I accepted that the standards, the goals, were test scores, completed homework and good teacher reports. If I had known what to really look for—"the collaborative hum—I think Lisa and I could have steered a much different course.

Unfortunately, too many teachers and administrators are also distracted by their own battles with the Education Machine; they have either given up or forgotten what the collaborative hum looks and sounds like. We love teachers and administrators. Every day they do the heavy lifting of training and preparing kids for a presently undefined future.

To all of them, I would say, as Mufasa says to Simba in *The Lion King*, "Remember who you are." Remember why you first yearned for the high calling of teaching. Whatever compelled you in that direction still exists! You have just been caught in the crunch of historical shifts of the societal tectonic plates. But those buried under the weight of the collapse will soon see a shaft of light, a tunnel that leads to a new landscape. Our story and journey met many

> *The thing that flipped me was when we toured our first classroom. I was frankly stunned; it was an emotional moment. I saw firsthand what engaged learning looked like.*

teachers who rediscovered the signal of engaged learning. They heard the sonar ping that first called them to education. Some found a way to shut out the noise of the Education Machine. The future possibilities are very exciting for those who can see and hear them coming.

I will never forget that the thing that flipped me was when we toured our first classroom. I was frankly stunned; it was an emotional moment. I saw firsthand what engaged learning looked like. And I saw what it did to my team of tough, even cynical, veteran teachers, professors, and consultants. They turned into kids. They got down on their knees to join in the joy of discovery. They walked through classes mesmerized by the sights and sounds of kids digging for knowledge. They lingered when it was time to move on. And the kids? They didn't even notice 35 grownups invading their room. No one looked up.

Anyone could see that the kids were enjoying the class. Getting kids to experience the kind of flow, described by Dr. Hamilton in an earlier chapter, is not the product of hard work or talent, but rather of design! My team was fascinated by the grace and fluidity of the kids and teachers worked together searching and creating.

I will never forget one of our intense working sessions in Columbus, when a long-time teacher just broke down and began to cry. She wept openly in front of all of us. Her emotions overflowed the banks because she *saw* the dawn of possibilities for children everywhere. In that moment, she reconnected with her original dream for childhood learning; it was still pulsating under the rubble of discouragement.

The collaborative hum became my compass, my signal, for recognizing those being schooled versus those absorbed in learning. The first time you see it will change your life. That hum could become your compass, too.

Where Do We Go from Here?

I hope we've reminded you—teachers, parents, administrators, and citizens—of the pure core of learning. That and remembering who you are will help you to pick up the signal again.

One of our team members, a principal, returned home from a summit determined to expand the walls of his high school into the community; he was excited to ignite the previously unrecognized knowledge, interests, and resources in his own backyard. He said, "I can see it! We are going to learn to think differently; we will expand our vision of learning!"

To you parents, teachers, administrators, community leaders, or other stakeholders, I hope this book will be a manifesto and a manual to bring a new vision and help your community to find new traction in humanizing the machine. I hope this book will take all of us, including you, down a new path. May we all learn to reimagine the dream of what learning can be.

APPENDIX
FROM ACCIDENTAL CHANGE AGENT
TO UP-FRONT GRIEF COUNSELING

When I present the work of culture change to organizations I often joke, "You thought your job was managing change . . . but it is actually grief counseling!" Of course, they laugh. But it is an important reminder about a serious consequences of change.

The textbook approaches to change deal with what I call the left-brain side, steps like:

1. Create the burning platform: If we don't change, we die!
2. Build an "A" team: Aligned, committed, and competent.
3. Provide a compelling positive vision of a better future: If we do change, we live!
4. Clear first steps, remove obstacles: The first steps are easy, just do it.
5. Go for quick wins: Tackle the low-hanging fruit to build confidence and momentum.
6. Recruit your champion: Find early adopters who are respected and can provide strong influence.
7. Repeat steps 1 and 2 often.
8. Let people have a voice and express their aspirations and fears.

These are all logical, linear, and left-brained.

However, deep change is a right-brain emotional experience. As those caught in profound change go through the process, they have to cope with a sense of loss, unbalance, insecurity, fear, and incompetence. Unless and until people see the positive potential of life on the other side of the disruption of change, they will resist.

Leaders make a great mistake when they rush from strategy to execution without factoring the right brain attempting to cope with the loss. The process of coping can often look like resistance. And if coping is read as defiance (as some of it will be) rather than loss, the reaction to the resistance will usually turn up the heat and pressure. That will turn vulnerability and grief into real defiance. That often leads to an unnecessary transition quagmire.

The boat analogy, used earlier in the book, may be helpful here. Remember there are three people in the front of the boat engaged and rowing, five in the middle watching and waiting for instruction, and two in the back drilling a hole in the bottom of the boat. The leverage point for leaders may be found in easing the transition for the five in the middle. That also more clearly exposes the toxic two in the back of the boat.

NOTES

Chapter 1. Numbers Don't Lie

1. William J. Broad, "Deadly and Yet Necessary, Quakes Renew the Planet," *New York Times* (January 11, 2005), www.nytimes.com/2005/01/11/science/deadly-and-yet-necessary-quakes-renew-the-planet.html? _r=0.

Chapter 2. Two Guys from Gainesville

1. Dan Aykroyd and John Landis, *The Blues Brothers*, directed by John Landis, Universal Pictures (1980).
2. M. Rex Miller, *The Commercial Real Estate Revolution: Nine Transforming Keys to Lowering Costs, Cutting Waste, and Driving Change in a Broken Industry* (Hoboken, NJ: John Wiley & Sons, 2009).
3. MindShift is the process I developed for assembling thought leaders to tackle large and complex challenges. That process will be described throughout the book.
4. A silo is a large, vertical, and often airtight grain storage tube. The term *silo* used in business and this book refers to a department or an attitude of a group that has a vertical hierarchical structure, is isolated, and avoids connection to or communication with other organizational agencies or offices.

Chapter 4. The Learning Manifesto

1. Merriam-Webster Online, www.merriam-webster.com/dictionary/manifesto (accessed March 18, 2016).
2. Steven Zaillian and Aaron Sorkin, *Moneyball*, directed by Bennett Miller (2011).
3. *A Nation At Risk: The Imperative for Educational Reform* (Washington, DC: The Commission on Excellence in Education, 1983).
4. The Cluetrain Manifesto. www.cluetrain.com (accessed March 24, 2016).
5. Robert Johansen, *Leaders Make the Future: Ten New Leadership Skills for an Uncertain World* (San Francisco: Berrett-Koehler, 2012).

6. Gillian Tett, *The Silo Effect: The Peril of Expertise and the Promise of Breaking Down Barriers* (New York: Simon & Schuster, 2015).

7. "Frequently Used Acronyms in Education/GreatKids," *GreatKids*, Web (April 2, 2016). http://www.greatschools.org/gk/articles/acronyms-in-education.

8. The Cluetrain Manifesto. www.cluetrain.com (accessed March 24, 2016).

9. Mike Ettling, "How to Attract Talent for Jobs That Don't Exist Yet," *Forbes Magazine* (October 13, 2015). http://www.forbes.com/sites/sap/2015/10/13/how-to-attract-talent-for-jobs-that-dont-yet-exist/#64effb3473d9.

10. The Clayton Christensen Institute maintains the most up-to-date data on successful blended learning implementations.

11. www.census.gov/content/dam/Census/library/publications/2014/demo/p60–249.pdf.

12. *Underprepared Students on the Pathway to Success*, Charles Cook, Austin Community College—EVP, Academic Affairs at the 2016 SXSWedu Conference.

Chapter 5. How the Road to Transformation Began in Failure

1. Author and professor Robert Putnam once identified social capital as "the features of social organization, such as networks, norms, and trust, that facilitate coordination and cooperation for mutual benefits." Robert D. Putnam, "The Prosperous Community: Social Capital and Public Life," *The American Prospect* 13 (Spring 1993), http://epn.org/prospect/13/13putn.html.

2. The chapter "The Power of Positive" is a vital but missing conversation in the reform movement about the role of social capital as an essential context for transformation to take place. It first comes out of a philosophical approach to the role and value of schools in a community context.

3. Rex Miller, Mabel Casey, and Mark Konchar, *Change Your Space, Change Your Culture: How Engaging Workspaces Lead to Transformation and Growth* (Hoboken, NJ: John Wiley & Sons, 2014).

4. Kyle Spencer, "The Uncomfortable Reality of Community Schools," *PBS* (July 14, 2014). http://www.pbs.org/wgbh/frontline/article/the-uncomfortable-reality-of-community-schools.

Chapter 6. Gutenberg to Google

1. Clay Shirky, "The Next 50 Years of Media Chaos," *Big Think* (2009), http://bigthink.com/videos/the-next-50-years-of-media-chaos. (accessed March 29, 2016).

2. "Top 10 Uses of Smartphone's," *Top10Nowcom* (2015). Web (accessed March 28, 2016). http://top10-now.com/2015/12/25/top-10-uses-of-smartphones.

3. IBM, *Leading Through Connections: Insights from the Global Chief Executive Officer Study* (IBM, 2014). http://www-935.ibm.com/services/us/en/c-suite/ceostudy2012.

4. "Total and Current Expenditures per Pupil in Public Elementary and Secondary Schools: Selected Years, 1919–20 through 2009–10" (National Center for Education Statistics). Web (accessed March 29, 2016). https://nces.ed.gov/programs/digest/d12/tables/dt12_213.asp.

Chapter 7. The Learning Matrix

1. Michael Schrage, *No More Teams!* (New York: Random House, 1990).
2. "Top 10 Uses Of Smartphone's—Top10-Now.com." Top10-Nowcom (n.p., 2015). Web (accessed April 24, 2016). http://top10-now.com/2015/12/25/top-10-uses-of-smartphones.
3. M. Rex Miller, *The Millennium Matrix: Reclaiming the Past, Reframing the Future of the Church* (San Francisco: Jossey-Bass, 2004).
4. The introduction of the written word or inventions like the telegraph and radio are not included because they never became the dominant platform for communication.
5. "History of Television." *Facts-Stats* (n.p., n.d.). Web (accessed April 24, 2016). http://www.tvhistory.tv/facts-stats.htm.
6. "Presidential Approval Ratings—Gallup Historical Statistics and Trends." *Gallup.com* (n.p., n.d.). Web (accessed April 24, 2016). http://www.gallup.com/poll/116677/presidential-approval-ratings-gallup-historical-statistics-trends.aspx.
7. U.S. Department of Commerce, National Telecommunications and Information Administration *Exploring the Digital Nation: America's Emerging Online Experience*, by Lawrence E. Strickling and Mark Doms (Washington, DC: US Department of Commerce, 2013).
8. Juliet Eilperin, "Here's How the First President of the Social Media Age Has Chosen to Connect with Americans," *Washington Post* (May 26, 2015).
9. Thomas Kuhn, *The Essential Tension: Selected Studies in Scientific Tradition and Change* (Chicago: University of Chicago Press, 1977), 234.
10. M. Rex Miller, *The Millennium Matrix: Reclaiming the Past, Reframing the Future of the Church* (San Francisco: Jossey-Bass, 2004).
11. Ibid.
12. Walter J. Ong, *The Presence of the Word: Some Prolegomena for Cultural and Religious History* (New Haven, CT: Yale University Press, 1967).
13. M. Rex Miller, *The Millennium Matrix: Reclaiming the Past, Reframing the Future of the Church* (San Francisco: Jossey-Bass, 2004).
14. Ibid.

Chapter 8. The Pandorification of Learning

1. Clay Shirky, *Here Comes Everybody: The Power of Organizing* (New York: Penguin, 2009), 105.

2. At age 4 students select from a number of learning pathways that include academic, career-tech, engineering, bio-science, agri-tech, and arts.

3. *Authentic Happiness* (n.p., n.d.). Web (accessed June 1, 2016). https://www.authentichappiness.sas.upenn.edu/learn/wellbeing.

4. "A City in Central Florida Is Subsidizing Uber." *Marketplace—NPR* (March 25, 2016). Web (accessed Mar. 31, 2016).

5. Alvin Toffler, *Future Shock* (New York: Random House, 1970).

6. Mike Perry, "Fortune 500 Firms in 1955 vs. 2014; 88% Are Gone, and We're All Better Off Because of That Dynamic 'Creative Destruction'—AEI." *AEI* (August 18, 2014).

7. Mary Cullinane, SXSWEDU (March 6, 2016), www.hmhco.com/media-center/blogs/2015/march/sxswedu-same-conference-different-bagel (accessed April 8, 2016).

8. www.khanacademy.org/about (accessed April 8, 2016).

9. Clayton Christensen Institute, www.christenseninstitute.org/blended-learning-definitions-and-models (accessed April 8, 2016).

Chapter 9. Changing the Odds

1. Children's Defense Fund, *Child Poverty in America 2014: National Analysis*, www.childrensdefense.org/library/poverty-report/child-poverty-in-america-2014.pdf (accessed April 12, 2016).

2. Pew Research Center, www.pewresearch.org/fact-tank/2014/01/15/college-enrollment-among-low-income-students-still-trails-richer-groups (accessed April 12, 2016).

3. Robert D. Putnam, *Our Kids: The American Dream in Crisis* (New York: Simon & Schuster, 2015), 189.

4. PS 111, Seton Falls Elementary was ranked 2,161 out of 2,311 in 2015, the bottom 6%.

5. Casap, Jamie. "Education Evangelist.": *My Speech for FLOTUS' "Beat the Odds" Summit at the White House July 23, 2015*. N.p., n.d. Web. 24 July 2015. http://eduevangelist.blogspot.com.

6. "SXSWedu 2015/Transforming Schools Using Brain Science," *Vimeo* (Mar. 2015). Web (Apr. 2, 2016). https://vimeo.com/130127224

7. Paul Tough, *How Children Succeed; Grit, Curiosity, and the Hidden Power of Character* (New York: Mariner Books, 2013).

8. Sean Reardon, "The Widening Academic Achievement Gap between the Rich and the Poor: New Evidence and Possible Explanations," http://cepa.stanford.edu/content/widening-academic-achievement-gap-between-rich-and-poor-new-evidence-and-possible (accessed April 2, 2016).

9. Joshua S. Wyner, John M. Bridgeland, and John DiIulio, Jr. "Achievement Trap: How America Is Failing Millions of High-Achieving Students from Lower-Income Families" (Lansdowne, VA: Jack Kent Cooke Foundation, September 1, 2007).

10. Ibid.

11. Hart, Betty, and Todd R. Risley. "The Early Catastrophe: The 30 Million Word Gap by Age 3." *American Educator* Spring 2003: 4–9. Print. http://www.aft.org/sites/default/files/periodicals/TheEarlyCatastrophe.pdf

12. Carol J. Carter, "Why Aren't Low-Income Students Succeeding in School?" *The Huffington Post* (May 19, 2013).

13. "Early Warning! Why Reading by the End of Third Grade Matters—The Annie E. Casey Foundation." The Annie E. Casey Foundation (January 1, 2010). Web. (accessed April 2, 2016). http://www.aecf.org/resources/early-warning-why-reading-by-the-end-of-third-grade-matters.

14. "Ensuring School Success: A Tale of Two Studies/Nieer.org." http://nieer.org/publications/ensuring-school-success-tale-two-studies (accessed April 2, 2016).

15. "Keeping Kids in School Preventing Dropouts." http://www.centerforpubliceducation.org/Main-Menu/Staffingstudents/Keeping-kids-in-school-At-a-glance/Keeping-kids-in-school-Preventing-dropouts.html (April 5, 2007). Web.

16. Robert D. Putnam, *Our Kids: The American Dream in Crisis* (New York: Simon & Schuster, 2016).

17. Busteed's presentation at SXSWedu2015. Austin, TX, March 13 – 22, 2015.

18. Barbara Barnes, *It's the Kids! Forty Years of Innovations in How We Educate Our Children* (Laguna Beach, CA: Creative Storytellers, LLC, 2011).

Chapter 10. Humanizing the Great Education Machine

1. Dale Russakoff, *The Prize: Who's in Charge of America's Schools?* (New York: Houghton Mifflin Harcourt, 2015), 57.

2. Ibid., 108.

3. Emma Brown, "Teach for America Celebrates 25th Anniversary at Washington Event," *The Washington Post* (February 6, 2016), www.washingtonpost.com/local/education/teach-for-america-celebrates-25th-anniversary-at-washington-event/2016/02/06/695d4094-cd0a-11e5–88ff-e2d1b4289c2f_story.html?tid=a_inl.

4. Sir Ken Robinson, "RSAnimate, Changing Education Paradigms" (June 16, 2008), https://www.thersa.org/discover/videos/rsa-animate/2010/10/rsa-animate—changing-paradigms.

5. M. Rex Miller, *The Millennium Matrix: Reclaiming the Past, Reframing the Future of the Church* (San Francisco: Jossey-Bass, 2004).

6. "Iatrogenesis," *Wikipedia*, Wikimedia Foundation. Web (accessed April 3, 2016). https://en.wikipedia.org/wiki/Iatrogenesis.

7. Michael Summer, "It's a Miracle Michael Brown Even Graduated from This Beleaguered School," *Daily Kos* (August 14, 2014).

8. Abby Phillip, William Wan, and Robert Samuels. "Tyrone Harris Jr. 'Was Pulling It Together. And Then, This Happened.'" *Washington Post* (August 10, 2015).

9. Rebecca Rivas, "Dr. Joseph Davis Appointed as Superintendent of Ferguson-Florissant School District," *St. Louis American* (February 11, 2015), www.stlamerican.com/news/local_news/article_71e0c6bc-b250–11e4-a14d-6f0817ba1cc2.html.

10. Tough, Paul. 2012 *How Children Succeed: Grit, Curiosity, and the Hidden Power of Character*. New York: Houghton Mifflin Harcourt Publishing Company.

11. "Benito's Story: One Goal Graduation Gala 2015" (April 28, 2015), www.youtube.com/watch?v=obA7JhODwRo (accessed Apr. 3, 2016).

12. "Jeff Nelson—OneGoal," *Vimeo* (November 13, 2013).

13. Matthew 25:36–40, from the *Holy Bible*, New Living Translation, copyright © 1996, 2004, 2007. Used by permission of Tyndale House Publishers, Inc., Carol Stream, Illinois, 60188. All Rights Reserved.

14. Renee Glover, "The Road to Restoring Human Dignity," *Lessons Learned; AHA Blog* (February 9, 2010), http://ahalessonslearned.blogspot.com/2010_02_01_archive.html.

Chapter 11. The Healing Power of Social Emotional Literacy

1. Poem written by Norman Bouffard and Will Richey.

2. TEDxTalks. "DaVerse Lounge at TEDxSMU 2013." *YouTube* (November 1, 2013). https://www.youtube.com/watch?v=_XUDCZfxGk0.

3. "K–12 Facts." *The Center for Education Reform* (February 2016).

4. Brandon Busteed, "The School Cliff: Student Engagement Drops with Each School Year," *Gallup.com*) (January 7, 2013).

5. Louis J. Cozolino, *Attachment-Based Teaching: Creating a Tribal Classroom*. The Norton Series on the Social Neuroscience of Education (New York: Norton, 2014).

6. Himmele, Pérsida, and William Himmele. *Total Participation Techniques: Making Every Student an Active Learner*. Alexandria: ASCD, 2011. Print.

7. See Dr. Frickey's website for more details: www.studentengagement.net.

8. Glennon Doyle Melton, "Share This with All Schools, Please," momastery.com/blog/2014/01/30/share-schools (accessed May 4, 2016).

9. Cozolino, *Attachment-Based Teaching*.

Chapter 13. How Technology Is Supposed to Work

1. Personal interview with Dr. Eric Hamilton. Pepperdine University. August 21, 2015. Permission was granted.
2. Ken Robinson and Lou Aronica, *The Element: How Finding Your Passion Changes Everything* (New York: Viking, 2009).
3. Kenneth Jackson, "1920s Machines—Tractors." *1920s Machines—Tractors*. Web (accessed May 19, 2016). http://www.livinghistoryfarm.org/farminginthe20s/machines_08.htm.
4. Issie Lapowski, "What Schools Must Learn from LA's IPad Debacle," *Wired.com* (May 8, 2015).
5. Personal interview with Shannon Buerk. Corpus Christi, TX. July 13, 2015. Shannon Buerk is part of the K–12 team and a friend. Permission was granted.
6. Request a copy of the STEM Continuum at http://engage2learn.org.
7. Natalie Denmeade, *Gamification with Moodle: Use Game Elements in Moodle Courses to Build Learner Resilience and Motivation* (Birmingham: Packt Limited, 2015).
8. Personal interview with Jaime Casap. ISTE Conference, Philadelphia, PA. June 29, 2015. Permission was granted.

Chapter 14. Designing a Place That Inspires and Equips

1. American Society of Civil Engineers.
2. Aline Peterson, "Infographic: 2016 State of Our Schools: America's K–12 Facilities," *Center for Green Schools* (March 23, 2016).
3. Phillip Elliott, "Report: Half Trillion Needed to Update U.S. Schools," *Lubbock Online* (March 11, 2013).
4. Joseph Cappriglione, "Whatever Happened to Mark Zuckerberg's $100 Million Gift to Newark's Schools?" *WNYC* (July 16, 2014).
5. Julia James, "High School Students Sit for Too Long, New Health Research Suggests," Culture & Features, Peninsula Press Archive (April 10, 2011).

Chapter 15. The Power of Positive

1. CoreClarity is a tool and process to enhance the results of the Clifton Strengthsfinder assessment. https://www.gallupstrengthscenter.com/Purchase/en-US/Index.
2. Mihaly Csikszentmihalyi, *Flow: The Psychology of Optimal Experience* (New York: Harper & Row, 1990).

3. "What Is Positive Psychology?" (n.p., n.d.), Web (accessed April 29, 2016).

4. Malte Jung, Jan Chong, and Larry Leifer, "Group Hedonic Balance and Pair Programming Performance: Affective Interaction Dynamics as Indicators of Performance" (2012). *Proceedings of the SIGCHI Conference on Human Factors in Computing Systems*, 829–838

5. Raluca Petrican, Morris Moscovitch, and Cheryl Grady, "Proficiency in Positive vs. Negative Emotion Identification and Subjective Well-being among Long-term Married Elderly Couples," *Frontiers in Psychology* (Frontiers Media S.A., April 2014).

6. Louis J. Cozolino, *Attachment-Based Teaching: Creating a Tribal Classroom*, The Norton Series on the Social Neuroscience of Education (New York: Norton, 2014).

7. Gallup, Inc., "Lack of Teacher Engagement Linked to 2.3 Million Missed Workdays" (January 9, 2015), www.gallup.com/poll/180455/lack-teacher-engagement-linked-million-missed-workdays.aspx.

8. Cozolino, *Attachment-Based Teaching*.

9. www.gallup.com/opinion/gallup/170525/school-cliff-student-engagement-drops-school-year.aspx.

Chapter 16. Leading Change at Your School

1. "The Atlanta Public Schools Cheating Scandal," Georgia Public Policy, April 16, 2015, www.georgiapolicy.org/2015/04/the-atlanta-public-schools-cheating-scandal.

2. John Hudson, "An Urban Myth That Should Be True," *The Atlantic* (July 2, 2012).

3. The Institute for Coalition Building developed *The Stakeholder Engagement Process*. http://pinmembers.com/wp-content/uploads/2016/06/RegionalTalentSystem.pdf.

4. Texas Association of School Administrators, *Creating a New Vision for Public Education in Texas* (Austin: Texas Association of School Administrators, May 2008).

5. From the Institute of Coalition Building *Stakeholder Engagement Process*. http://pinmembers.com/wp-content/uploads/2016/06/RegionalTalentSystem.pdf.

6. Michael Wesch, "From Knowledgeable to Knowledge-Able." TEDxTalks (October 12, 2010). Web (accessed June 12, 2016). https://www.youtube.com/watch?v=LeaAHv4UTI8.

7. Michael Wesch, "Digital Ethnography" (Biola University, 2013).

Chapter 17. Humanity High

1. Rebecca Gordon, "Green Architecture: What Makes a Structure a 'Living Building'?" *Scientific American* (December 15, 2009).

2. The Carnegie Unit is 120 hours of class or contact time with an instructor over the course of a year at the secondary (American high school) level. Strictly speaking, this

breaks down into a single one-hour meeting, on each of five days per week, for a total of 24 weeks per year. Wikipedia. https://en.wikipedia.org/wiki/Carnegie _Unit_and_Student_Hour.

3. Clay Shirky paraphrased the work of Jacques Barzun at The Future of Higher Education in a Digital Age summit, New York University, December 2015.

REFERENCES

Adler, Mortimer Jerome, and Charles Lincoln Doren. 1972. *How to Read a Book*, New York: Touchstone, rev. ed.

Adler, Mortimer Jerome. 1982. *The Paideia Proposal: An Educational Manifesto*. New York: Macmillan.

Adler, Mortimer Jerome. 1985. *Ten Philosophical Mistakes*. New York: Macmillan.

Ahuja, Alka, Joanna Martin, Kate Langley, and Anita Thapar. 2013. Intellectual Disability in Children with Attention Deficit Hyperactivity Disorder." *The Journal of Pediatrics 163*(no. 3): 890–895.

Alberts, David S., and Richard E. Hayes. 2003. *Power to the Edge: Command, Control in the Information Age*. Washington, DC: CCRP Publication Series.

Aldrich, Clark. 2011. *Unschooling Rules: 55 Ways to Unlearn What We Know about Schools and Rediscover Education*, 2nd ed. Austin, TX: Greenleaf Book Group.

Aldridge, Clark. 2011. Unschooling Rules: If You Send Your Children to School, You Are Inhibiting Schools Reform. (February 22). Web. http://unschoolingrules. blogspot.com/2010/12/if-you-send-your-children-to-school-you.html.

Annie E. Casey Foundation. 2010. "Early Warning! Why Reading by the End of Third-Grade Matters (January 1, 2010). Web. http://www.aecf.org/resources/early-warning-why-reading-by-the-end-of-third-grade-matters/ (accessed Apr. 2, 2016).

Atlanta Public Schools Cheating Scandal. n.d. *Wikipedia*. Web (accessed April 30, 2016).

Aviv, Rachel. 2016. Wrong answer. *The New Yorker* (July 14).

"Benito's Story." OneGoal Graduation Gala 2015. *YouTube* (April 28). www.youtube .com/channel/UCXmcvQh4hDk2dUcF6tus4bw (accessed April 3, 2016).

Berry, Barnett, and Ann Byrd. 2013. *Teacherpreneurs: Innovative Teachers Who Lead but Don't Leave*. San Francisco: Jossey-Bass.

Block, Peter. 2008. *Community: The Structure of Belonging*. San Francisco: Berrett-Koehler.

Blume, Howard. 2015. L.A. School District Demands iPad Refund from Apple. *Los Angeles Times* (April 16).

Brooks, David. 2015. *The Road to Character*. New York: Random House.

Brooks, David. 2010. Children of the '70s. *The New York Times* (May 17). http://www.nytimes.com/2010/05/18/opinion/18brooks.html

Brown, Tim, and Barry Tz. 2009. *Change by Design: How Design Thinking Transforms Organizations and Inspires Innovation.* New York: Harper Businesss.

Busteed, Brandon. 2013. The School Cliff: Student Engagement Drops With Each School Year. Gallup.com (January 7).

Busteed, Brandon. 2014. Make a Difference: Show Students You Care. *Education Week* (September 30). http://www.edweek.org/ew/articles/2014/10/01/06busteed.h34.html.

Capriglione, Joseph. 2014. Whatever Happened to Mark Zuckerberg's $100 Million Gift to Newark's Schools?" *WNYC* (July 16).

Cardoza, Matt. 2009. GADOE Georgia Department of Education—Communications. *GADOE Georgia Department of Education—Communications* (February 20).

Carter, Carol J. 2013. Why Aren't Low-Income Students Succeeding in School? *The Huffington Post* (May 19).

Casap, Jaime. 2014. Jaime Casap's 2015 Personal Statement: Beating the Low Expectation Syndrome. EdSurge (December 17).

Casap, Jaime. 2015. Education Evangelist. *Education Evangelist* (July 23).

"Child Population by Gender/Kids Count Data Center. 2015. National Kids Count (July). Web http://datacenter.kidscount.org/data/tables/102-child-population-by-gender?loc=1&loct=1#detailed/1/any/false/869,36,868,867,133/14,15,65/421,422.

Christensen, Clayton M., and Michael B. Horn. 2008. *Disrupting Class: How Disruptive Innovation Will Change the Way the World Learns.* New York: McGraw-Hill.

"A City in Central Florida Is Subsidizing Uberrrdrr." 2016. *Marketplace—NPR* (March 25).

College Graduation Rates. 2015. *National Center for Education Statistics.* Web (accessed February 13, 2016). https://nces.ed.gov/fastfacts/display.asp?id=40.

Connelly, Christopher. 2016. Turns Out Monkey Bars and Kickball Might Be Good for the Brain. NPR (January 3).

Cook, William J. 2005. *Unencorporating Education: Learning and Teaching for a Free Society.* Montgomery, AL: Cambridge Institute.

Corliss, Julie. 2015. Too Much Sitting Linked to Heart Disease, Diabetes, Premature Death. *Harvard Health Blog RSS* (January 22). http://www.health.harvard.edu/blog/much-sitting-linked-heart-disease-diabetes-premature-death-201501227618.

Couts, Andrew. 2011. Mac vs PC: User Differences Fit Stereotypes, Study Shows. *Digital Trends* (April 22).

Cozolino, Louis J. 2014. *Attachment-Based teaching: Creating a tribal classroom.* New York: Norton.

Crabb, Larry. 1997. *Connecting: Healing for Ourselves and Our Relationships: A Radical New Vision.* Nashville: Word Publishing.

Crawford, Matthew B. 2009. *Shop Class as Soulcraft: An Inquiry into the Value of Work.* New York: Penguin.

Csikszentmihalyi, Mihaly. 1990. *Flow: The Psychology of Optimal Experience.* New York: Harper & Row.

Darwin, Charles and R. D. Keynes. 1988. *Charles Darwin's Beagle Diary.* Cambridge, UK: Cambridge University Press.

Denmeade, Natalie. 2015. *Gamification with Moodle: Use Game Elements in Moodle Courses to Build Learner Resilience and Motivation.* Birmingham, UK: Packt Limited.

Deutschman, Alan. 2007. *Change or Die: The Three Keys to Change at Work and in Life.* New York: Regan.

Digital divide. Wikimedia Foundation. Web (accessed Mar. 29, 2016). http://smart.com .ph/About/newsroom/press-releases/2014/12/11/smart-wikimedia-partnership-helps-bridge-the-digital-divide.

Doshi, Neel, and Lindsay McGregor. 2015. *Primed to Perform: How to Build the Highest Performing Cultures through the Science of Total Motivation.* New York: HarperCollns.

Dweck, Carol S. 2006. *Mindset: The New Psychology of Success.* New York: Random House.

Eilperin, Juliet. 2015. Here's How the First President of the Social Media Age Has Chosen to Connect with Americans." *Washington Post.*

Elliott, Phillip. 2013. Report: Half Trillion Needed to Update U.S. Schools. *Lubbock Online* (March 11).

Ellul, Jacques. 1964. *The Technological Society.* New York: Knopf.

"Ensuring School Success: A Tale of Two Studies/Nieer.org." *Ensuring School Success: A Tale of Two Studies/Nieer.org.* Web (accessed April 2, 2016).

"Epiphany." *Dictionary.com.* Web (accessed April 21, 2014). http://www.dictionary .com/browse/epiphany.

Freeman, R. Edward. 1984. *Strategic Management: A Stakeholder Approach.* Boston: Pitman.

Frei, Frances, and Anne Morriss. 2012. *Uncommon Service: How to Win by Putting Customers at the Core of Your Business.* Boston: Harvard Business Review.

Freire, Paulo. 2000. *Pedagogy of the Oppressed.* 30th Anniversary ed. New York: Continuum.

Frequently used acronyms in education. *GreatKids.* Web (accessed April 2, 2016). http:// www.greatschools.org/gk/articles/acronyms-in-education.

Friedman, Edwin H. and Margaret M. Treadwell. 2007. *A Failure of Nerve: Leadership in the Age of the Quick Fix* (rev. ed.). New York: Seabury.

Friedman, Milton, and Rose D. Friedman. 1980. *Free to Choose: A Personal Statement.* New York: Harcourt Brace Jovanovich.

Gardner, Howard. 1983. *Frames of Mind: The Theory of Multiple Intelligences.* New York: Basic.

Gardner, Howard. 1991. *The Unschooled Mind: How Children Think and How Schools Should Teach.* New York: Basic Books.

Golden age of television. *Wikipedia*. Web (accessed March 26, 2016). https://en .wikipedia.org/wiki/Golden_Age_of_Television.

Gonzalez, Jennifer, and Mark Barnes. 2015. *Hacking Education: 10 Quick Fixes for Every School*. Seattle: Amazon Digital Services.

Gray, Dave, and Thomas Vander Wal. 2012. *The Connected Company*. Sebastopol, CA; O'Reilly Media.

Hagel, John, and John Seely Brown. 2014. *Shift Happens: How the World Is Changing, and What You Need to Do about It*. Houston, TX: Idea Bite Press.

Hagel, John, and John Seely Brown. 2010. *The Power of Pull: How Small Moves, Smartly Made, Can Set Big Things in Motion*. New York: Basic Books.

Hammond, Linda. 2010. *The Flat World and Education: How America's Commitment to Equity Will Determine Our Future*. New York: Teachers College.

Hart, Betty and Risley, Todd R. 2011. "The Thirty Million Word Gap." *The Thirty Million Word Gap*. Web. April 2, 2016. http://www.aft.org/sites/default/files/ periodicals/TheEarlyCatastrophe.pdf.

Heath, Chip, and Dan Heath. 2010. *Switch: How to Change Things When Change Is Hard*. New York: Broadway.

Hechinger Report. 2016. "Study: Schools Exacerbate Growing Rich-Poor Achievement Gap." *US News* (October 19).

Heffernan, Margaret. 2015. *Beyond Measure: The Big Impact of Small Changes*. New York: TEDBooks (Simon & Schuster).

Herman, Arthur. 2001. *How the Scots Invented the Modern World: The True Story of How Western Europe's Poorest Nation Created Our World and Everything in It*. New York: Crown.

Herman, Juliana, Sasha Post, and Scott O'Halloran. 2013. The United States Is Far Behind Other Countries on Pre-K. *Center for American Progress*. (May 2).

History.com Staff. 2010. "The Kennedy-Nixon Debates." History.com. Web (April 24, 2016). http://www.history.com/topics/us-presidents/kennedy-nixon-debates.

History of Television *Facts-Stats*. Web (accessed April 24, 2016). http://www.tvhistory .tv/facts-stats.htm.

Hoffer, Eric. 1951. *The True Believer: Thoughts on the Nature of Mass Movements*. New York: Harper and Row.

Hokanson, Brad. 2014. *Design in Educational Technology: Design Thinking, Design Process, and the Design Studio*. New York: Springer International Publishing.

Horn, Michael B. and Heather Staker. 2015. *Blended: Using Disruptive Innovation to Improve Schools*. San Francisco, CA: Jossey-Bass.

Houston, Jean. 2012. *The Wizard of Us: Transformational Lessons from Oz*. New York: Atria Books.

Hudson, John. 2012. "An Urban Myth That Should Be True." *The Atlantic* (July 2).

IBM. 2014. *Leading through Connections Insights from the Global Chief Executive Officer Study*. http://www-935.ibm.com/services/us/en/c-suite/ceostudy2012.

Illich, Ivan. 1971. *Deschooling Society*. New York: Harper & Row.

Insel, Thomas. 2014. Director's Blog: Are Children Overmedicated? NIMH RSS (June 6).

Iatrogenesis. *Wikipedia*. Web (accessed Apr. 3, 2016). https://en.wikipedia.org/wiki/Iatrogenesis.

Jackson, Kenneth. 2016. 1920s machines—tractors. *1920s Machines—Tractors*. Web (May 19). http://www.livinghistoryfarm.org/farminginthe20s/machines_08.htm.

Jacobe, Dennis. 2002. "Warning: Corporate Scandals May Demoralize Employees." (October 10). Web. http://www.gallup.com/businessjournal/826/warning-corporate-scandals-may-demoralize-employees.aspx.

Jacobson, Michael J. and Peter Reimann. 2010. *Designs for Learning Environments of the Future: International Perspectives from the Learning Sciences*. New York: Springer.

James, Julia. 2011. "High School Students Sit for Too Long, New Health Research Suggests." *Peninsula Press Archive* (2010–Sept.). (April 10).

Jeff Nelson—OneGoal. 2013. *Vimeo* (November 13). https://vimeo.com/141925775.

Johansen, Robert. 2012. *Leaders Make the Future: Ten New Leadership Skills for an Uncertain World*. San Francisco: Berrett-Koehler.

Jung, Malte, Jan Chong, and Larry Leifer. 2012. "Group Hedonic Balance and Pair Programming Performance: Affective Interaction Dynamics as Indicators of Performance." *Proceedings of the SIGCHI Conference on Human Factors in Computing Systems*, 829–838. Web (Apr. 29, 2016).

Kamenetz, Anya. 2010. *DIY U: Edupunks, Edupreneurs, and the Coming Transformation of Higher Education*. White River Junction, VT: Chelsea Green.

Kaplan, Fred M. 2013. *The Insurgents: David Petraeus and the Plot to Change the American Way of War*. New York: Simon & Schuster.

"Keeping Kids in School Preventing Dropouts." April 5, 2007. www.centerforpubliceducation.org.

Kim, W. Chan, and Renée Mauborgne. 2005. *Blue Ocean Strategy: How to Create Uncontested Market Space and Make the Competition Irrelevant*. Boston: Harvard Business School.

Kohler, Brittney. 2016. "State/2013 Report Card for America's Infrastructure." *2013 Report Card for Americas Infrastructure*. (March 29).

Kwoh, Leslie. 2013. "When the CEO Burns Out." Wall Street Journal (May 7).

Lapowski, Issie. 2016. "What Schools Must Learn From LA's iPad Debacle." Wired.com (May 8).

Lasch, Christopher. 1977. *Haven in a Heartless World: The Family Besieged*. New York: Basic Books.

Lasch, Christopher. 1978. *The Culture of Narcissism: American Life in an Age of Diminishing Expectations*. New York: Norton.

Lau, Hillary. 2014. "Coppell Opens First 'Net-Zero' Elementary School in the U.S." FrontBurner (August 27).

Leaf, Caroline. 2013. *Switch On Your Brain: The Key to Peak Happiness, Thinking, and Health*. Grand Rapids, MI: Baker Books.

Lengel, James G. 2013. *Education 3.0: Seven Steps to Better Schools*. New York: Teachers College.

Lichtman, Grant. 2014. *EdJourney: A Roadmap to the Future of Education*. San Francisco, CA: Jossey-Bass.

Mathews, Jay. 2009. *Work Hard. Be Nice.: How Two Inspired Teachers Created the Most Promising Schools in America*. Chapel Hill, NC: Algonquin of Chapel Hill.

McLuhan, Marshall. 1964. *Understanding Media: The Extensions of Man*. New York: Signet Books.

Medina, Jennifer. 2015. "Laurene Powell Jobs Commits $50 Million to Create New High Schools." *New York Times* (September 14).

Melton, Glennon Doyle. 2013. *Carry On, Warrior: Thoughts on Life Unarmed*. New York: Scribner.

Metzler, Mark. 2015. "Carstarphen: APS Making Progress." (September 28). Web (accessed May 26, 2016).

Miller, M. Rex. 2009. *The Commercial Real Estate Revolution: Nine Transforming Keys to Lowering Costs, Cutting Waste, and Driving Change in a Broken Industry*. Hoboken, NJ: John Wiley & Sons.

Miller, M. Rex. 2004. *The Millennium Matrix: Reclaiming the Past, Reframing the Future of the Church*. San Francisco: Jossey-Bass.

Miller, Rex, Mabel Casey, and Mark Konchar. 2014. *Change Your Space, Change Your Culture: How Engaging Workspaces Lead to Transformation and Growth*. Hoboken, NJ: John Wiley & Sons.

"A Nation at Risk: The Imperative for Educational Reform." 1983. *US Department of Education*, National Commission on Excellence in Education (April).

New York School Rankings. *SchoolDigger*. Web (February 29, 2016). http://www.schooldigger.com/go/NY/schoolrank.aspx.

Nisbet, Robert A. 1969. *The Quest for Community*. London: Oxford University Press.

Nisen, Max. 2014. "Why Google Doesn't Care about Hiring Top College Graduates." *Quartz* (February 24).

Ong, Walter J. 1967. *The Presence of the Word: Some Prolegomena for Cultural and Religious History*. New Haven: Yale University Press.

Owp/P, Architects, Furniture VS, and Bruce Mau Design. 2009. *The Third Teacher: 79 Ways You Can Transform Your Teaching and Learning*. New York: Abrams.

Pappano, Laura. 2015. "First-Generation Students Unite." *New York Times*. (April 11).

Patterson, Tony. 2009. "Hell and High Water: The Fastnet Disaster." *The Independent*. Web (July 17).

Perkins, David N. 2014. *Future Wise: Educating Our Children for a Changing World*. San Francisco, CA: Jossey-Bass.

Perry, Mike. 2014. "Fortune 500 Firms in 1955 vs. 2014; 88% Are Gone, and We're All Better Off Because of That Dynamic 'Creative Destruction.'" *AEI* (August 18).

Peterson, Aline. 2016. "Infographic: 2016 State of Our Schools: America's K–12 Facilities. *Center for Green Schools* (March 23).

Petrican, Raluca, Morris Moscovitch, and Cheryl Grady. 2014. "Proficiency in Positive vs. Negative Emotion Identification and Subjective Well-being among Long-term Married Elderly Couples." *Frontiers in Psychology* (Apr. 28).

Phillip, Abby, William Wan, and Robert Samuels. 2015. "Tyrone Harris Jr. 'Was Pulling It Together. And Then, This Happened.'" *Washington Post* (August 10).

Pink, Daniel H. 2006. *A Whole New Mind: Why Right-brainers Will Rule the Future*. New York: Riverhead.

Pink, Daniel H. 2009. *Drive: The Surprising Truth about What Motivates Us*. New York: Riverhead.

Postman, Neil. 1985. *Amusing Ourselves to Death: Public Discourse in the Age of Show Business*. New York: Viking.

Presidential approval ratings—Gallup historical statistics and trends. *Gallup.com*. Web (April 24, 2016). http://www.gallup.com/poll/116677/presidential-approval-ratings-gallup-historical-statistics-trends.aspx.

"Program for International Student Assessment (PISA)—Overview." 2014. National Center for Education Statistics (July. Web.

Putnam, Robert D. 2016. *Our Kids: The American Dream in Crisis*. New York: Simon & Schuster.

Quinn, Robert E. 2015. *The Positive Organization: Breaking Free from Conventional Cultures, Constraints, and Beliefs*. Oakland, CA: Berrett-Koehler Publishers, Inc.

Rath, Tom, and Donald O. Clifton. 2004. *How Full Is Your Bucket?: Positive Strategies for Work and Life*. New York: Gallup.

Rath, Tom. 2007. *Strengthsfinder 2.0* New York: Gallup.

Ravitch, Diane. 2010. *The Death and Life of the Great American School System: How Testing and Choice Are Undermining Education*. New York: Basic Books.

Ravitch, Dianne. 2015. "The Educational Industrial Complex." Diane *Ravitchs Blog* (October 24). Web. https://dianeravitch.net/2015/10/24/the-educational-industrial-complex.

Reardon, Sean. 2011. "The Widening Academic Achievement Gap Between the Rich and the Poor: New Evidence and Possible Explanations." Web (April 2, 2016). http://cepa.stanford.edu/content/widening-academic-achievement-gap-between-rich-and-poor-new-evidence-and-possible.

Ripley, Amanda. 2013. *The Smartest Kids in the World: And How They Got That Way*. New York: Simon & Schuster.

Robinson, Ken, and Lou Aronica. 2015. *Creative Schools: The Grassroots Revolution That's Transforming Education*. New York: Penguin Books.

Robinson, Ken. 2006. "Do Schools Kill Creativity?" TED (June). https://www.ted
.com/talks/ken_robinson_says_schools_kill_creativity/transcript?language=en.

Robinson, Ken, and Lou Aronica. 2009. *The Element: How Finding Your Passion Changes Everything*. New York: Viking.

Robinson, Ken. 2011. *Out of Our Minds: Learning to Be Creative*, rev. ed. Oxford, UK: Capstone.

Rodriguez, Daniel. 1955. "'All In' Campaign Aims To Get More Latino Students in AP Classes." *NBC News*. (July 7). http://www.nbcnews.com/news/latino/all-campaign-aims-get-more-latino-students-ap-classes-n388101.

Russakoff, Dale. 2015. *The Prize: Who's in Charge of America's Schools?* New York: Houghton Mifflin Harcourt Publishing Company.

Sax, Leonard. 2007. *Boys Adrift: The Five Factors Driving the Growing Epidemic of Unmotivated Boys and Underachieving Young Men*. New York: Basic Books.

Schwartz, David B. 1997. *Who Cares? Rediscovering Community*. Boulder: Westview.

Seligman, Martin E. P. 2006. *Learned Optimism: How to Change Your Mind and Your Life*. New York: Vintage.

Seligman, Martin E. P. 2011. *Flourish: A Visionary New Understanding of Happiness and Well-being*. New York: Free Press.

Shaw, Jonathan. 2012. "A Radical Fix for the Republic." *Harvard Magazine* (July–August).

Shirky, Clay. 2008. *Here Comes Everybody: The Power of Organizing without Organizations*. New York: Penguin.

Shirky, Clay. 2010. *Cognitive Surplus: Creativity and Generosity in a Connected Age*. New York: Penguin.

Shirky, Clay. 2011. "Tag Archives: Clay Shirky." *Social Capital Blog* (January 26).

Shostak, Arthur. 2008. *Anticipate the School You Want: Futurizing K–12 Education*. New York: R&L Education.

Spinelli, Stephen, and Heather McGowan. 2014. *Disrupt Together: How Teams Consistently Innovate*. Upper Saddle River, NJ: Pearson Education, Inc.

Strauss, Valerie. 2016. "An Astonishing Admission from a Controversial School Reformer." *Washington Post* (February 7).

Strickling, Lawrence E. and Mark Doms. 2013. *Exploring the Digital Nation: America's Emerging Online Experience*. Washington, DC: US Department of Commerce.

Summer, Michael. 2014. "It's a Miracle Michael Brown Even Graduated from This Beleaguered School." *Daily Kos* (August 14).

"The Superintendent Who Turned around a School District." NPR (January 3, 2016).

SXSWedu. 2015. "Transforming Schools Using Brain Science." *Vimeo* (March).

Szalavitz, Maia. 2011. "What Does a 400% Increase in Antidepressant Use Really Mean?" *Time* (October 20).

Tapscott, Don. 1998. *Growing up Digital: The Rise of the Net Generation*. New York: McGraw-Hill.

TEDxTalks. 2013. "DaVerse Lounge at TEDxSMU." *YouTube* (November). Web (accessed June 8, 2016.) https://www.youtube.com/watch?v=_XUDCZfxGk0.

Tett, Gillian. 2015. *The Silo Effect: The Peril of Expertise and the Promise of Breaking down Barriers*. New York: Simon & Schuster.

Texas Association of School Administrators 2008. *Creating a New Vision for Public Education in Texas*. Austin: Texas Association of School Administrators.

Thomas, Douglas, and John Seely Brown. 2011. *A New Culture of Learning: Cultivating the Imagination for a World of Constant Change*. Lexington, KY: CreateSpace.

Toffler, Alvin. 1970. *Future Shock*. New York: Random House.

Toppo, Greg. 2015. *The Game Believes in You: How Digital Play Can Make Our Kids Smarter*. New York: St. Martin's Press.

"Top 10 Uses Of Smartphone's—Top10-Now.com." 2015. Top10Nowcom. Web.

Tough, Paul. 2012. *How Children Succeed: Grit, Curiosity, and the Hidden Power of Character*. New York: Houghton Mifflin Harcourt Publishing Company.

Total and current expenditures per pupil in public elementary and secondary schools: Selected years, 1919–20 through 2009–10. *National Center for Education Statistics*. Web (accessed March 29, 2016). https://nces.ed.gov/programs/digest/d12/tables/dt12_213.asp.

Transformation Theory. *Wikipedia*. Web (accessed June 5, 2016). https://en.wikipedia.org/wiki/Transformation_theory.

Urban Debate League *Wikipedia*. Web (accessed Apr. 28, 2016). https://en.wikipedia.org/wiki/Urban_debate_league.

Wagner, Tony, and Ted Dintersmith. 2015. *Most Likely to Succeed: Preparing Our Kids for the Innovation Era*. New York: Scribner.

Wagner, Tony. 2008. *The Global Achievement Gap Why Even Our Best Schools Don't Teach the New Survival Skills Our Children Need—and What We Can Do about It*. New York: Basic Books.

Weber, Karl. 2010. *Waiting for "Superman": How We Can Save America's Failing Public Schools*. New York: PublicAffairs.

"What Is Positive Psychology?" Web (accessed April 29, 2016). http://www.pursuit-of-happiness.org/science-of-happiness/?gclid=CPr9zvLClM4CFdgVgQodzaUNuQ.

Whittaker, Richard. 2013. "Carstarphen Report Card: B for Bland: AISD Head Receives Lukewarm Review." (December 20). http://www.austinchronicle.com/news/2013–12–20/carstarphen-report-card-b-for-bland.

"Why Kids Drop Out of School—EduGuide." 2016. Web (May 21, 2016). http://www.eduguide.org/article/why-kids-drop-out-of-school.

Whyte, William Foote, and Kathleen King Whyte. 1991. *Making Mondragon: The Growth and Dynamics of the Worker Cooperative Complex*, 2nd ed. Ithaca, NY: Cornell University Press.

Willingham, Daniel T. 2009. *Why Don't Students Like School? A Cognitive Scientist Answers Questions about How the Mind Works and What It Means for the Classroom.* San Francisco: Jossey-Bass.

Wyner, Joshua S., John M. Bridgeland, and John J. DiIulio, Jr. 2007. "Achievement Trap: How America Is Failing Millions of High-Achieving Students from Lower-Income Families." Lansdowne, VA: Jack Kent Cooke Foundation. September 1.

Zhao, Yong. 2012. *World Class Learners: Educating Creative and Entrepreneurial Students.* Thousand Oaks, CA: Corwin.

CORE LEADERS

The name of each core leader is followed by contact information and his or her Clifton Strengthsfinder assessment results.

Dan Boggio
PBK Architects, Inc.
President & CEO
dan.boggio@pbk.com
1. Achiever
2. Competition
3. Ideation
4. Individualization
5. Includer

Brian Cahill
Balfour Beatty Construction
President, California Division
bcahill@balfourbeattyus.com
1. Strategic
2. Context
3. Communication
4. Activator
5. Responsibility

John Crawford
MeTEOR Education
President & COO
JCrawford@contrax.com
1. Belief

2. Self-Assurance
3. Strategic
4. Focus
5. Achiever

Pete Dugas
TSAV
President
petedugas@tsav.com
1. Individualization
2. Strategic
3. Achiever
4. Activator
5. Arranger

Kristen Hamer
MooreCo, Inc.
VP of Business Development
KHamer@moorecoinc.com
1. Individualization
2. Command
3. Activator
4. Learner
5. Achiever

Mark Hubbard
Paragon Furniture/Paragon, Inc.
Owner
mhubbard@paragoninc.com
1. Achiever
2. Strategic
3. Learner
4. Developer
5. Activator

Ricky Kassanoff
Paragon Furniture/Paragon, Inc.
CEO
Rkassanoff@paragoninc.com
1. Empathy
2. Relator
3. Adaptability
4. Developer
5. Maximizer

Bill Latham
MeTEOR Education
CEO
BLatham@contrax.com
1. Strategic
2. Ideation
3. Command
4. Communication
5. Belief

Greg Moore
MooreCo, Inc.
CEO
gmoore@moorecoinc.com
1. Strategic
2. Individualization
3. Competition
4. Ideation
5. Adaptability

Chris Petrick
Bretford
CEO
cpetrick@bretford.com
1. Activator
2. Connectedness
3. Arranger
4. Positivity
5. Individualization

Summit Leaders

The name of each summit leader is followed by contact information and his or her Clifton Strengthsfinder assessment results.

Dan Beerens
Dan Beerens Educational Consulting, Inc.
Owner
danbeerens@gmail.com
1. Connectedness
2. Learner
3. Intellection
4. Ideation
5. Strategic

Shannon Buerk
Engage2Learn
CEO
shannon@engage2learn.org
1. Achiever
2. Learner
3. Ideation
4. Belief
5. Individualization

Page Dettmann
MeTEOR Education
Executive Vice President of
    Educational Design
pdettmann@contrax.com
1. Achiever
2. Strategic
3. Learner
4. Ideation
5. Futuristic

Lynn Frickey
Scale of Student Engagement/
    Disengagement
Researcher, Developer, Educator
lfrickey@comcast.net
1. Maximizer
2. Ideation
3. Relator
4. Learner
5. Activator

Eric Hamilton
Pepperdine University
Professor of Education with
    Appointment in Mathematics
Eric.Hamilton@pepperdine.edu
1. Strategic
2. Includer
3. Activator
4. Ideation
5. Adaptability

Jack Hess
Institute for Coalition Building
Executive Director
jhess@coalitionbuilding.org

1. Learner
2. Achiever
3. Futuristic
4. Strategic
5. Maximizer

Stan Rounds
Las Cruces Public Schools
Superintendent
srounds@lcps.k12.nm.us
1. Achiever
2. Futuristic
3. Strategic
4. Activator
5. Input

Nathan Siebenga
Hamilton District Christian
    High
Principal
nsiebenga@hdch.org
1. Strategic
2. Input
3. Futuristic
4. Deliberative
5. Individualization

David Vroonland
Mesquite Independent School
    District
Superintendent
dvroonland@frenship.us
1. Strategic
2. Futuristic
3. Learner
4. Self-Assurance
5. Activator

Ellen Wood
Teaching Trust
Co-Founder & Fundraising
ewood@teachingtrust.org
1. Input
2. Learner
3. Intellection
4. Responsibility
5. Achiever

Interviews and Site Visits

Amandula Anderson
UNEC
Executive Director
Indianapolis, Indiana

Linda Anderson
Birdville Career and Technology
    Center
Principal
North Richland Hills, Texas

David Anthony
Raise Your Hand Texas
President
Austin, Texas

Joel Barker
Infinity Limited, Inc.
Futurist
Phoenix, Arizona

Barbara Barnes
It's the Kids
Author/Principal
San Diego, California

Denise Benavides
Schools of Talent
Independent Education Consultant
Del Norte, California

Jaime Casap
Google, Inc.
Global Education Evangelist
Phoenix, Arizona

Tom Cousin's
Cousins Properties
Founder
Atlanta, Georgia

Lou Cozolino
Pepperdine University
Professor of Education and
    Psychology
Malibu, California

Mike Feinberg
Kipp Academy
Cofounder
Houston, Texas

Renee Glover
Former CEO of the Atlanta
    Housing Authority

Eric Hamilton
Pepperdine University
Professor of Education with
    Appointment in Mathematics
Malibu, California

Michael Horn
Clayton Christensen Institute
Executive Director
Lexington, Massachusetts

Amy Kelton
Shelton School
Assistant Head of School
Dallas, Texas

Michelle Kinder
Momentous Institute
Executive Director
Oak Cliff, Texas

Leo Linbeck
Linbeck Group, LLC
Chairman of the Board
Houston, Texas

Natasha Morse
Da Vinci Schools
Real World Learning Director
El Segundo, California

Carolyn Naughton
Purpose Built Communities
Vice President
Atlanta Georgia

Rosemary Perlmeter
Teaching Trust
Cofounder
Dallas, Texas

Suzanne Stell
Shelton School
Executive Director
Dallas, Texas

Jeff Turner
Texas Association of Suburban/
    MidUrban Schools
Educational Consultant
Coppell, Texas

Shoshana Vernick
Sterling Partners
Managing Director
Chicago, Texas

Allison Vinson
Birdville Independent School
    District
Career and Technology Education
    Coordinator
North Richland Hills, Texas

Stephen Waddell
Lewisville Independent School
    District
Retired Superintendent
Lewisville, Texas

Tony Wagner
Harvard University
Expert in Residence at Harvard
    University Innovation Lab
Boston, Massachusetts

Matthew Wunder
DaVinci Schools
CEO
El Segundo, California

Subject Matter Experts and Summit Participants

Kurt André
TAG Consulting
Senior Partner

Peter Balyta
Texas Instruments, Inc.
President, Education
    Technology

Eric Batten
Texas Instruments, Inc.
Grant Partnership Consultant

Peter Bishop
Teach the Future
Executive Director

Alicia Fisher
MeTEOR Education
Lead Education Interior
    Designer

Joe Hollenbach
Madison Southern High School
Social Studies Teacher/Boys
    Soccer Head Coach

Dennis Johnston, PhD
AVID Center
Vice President, Quality Initiatives,
    Research & Outreach

Katie King
KnowledgeWorks
Graduate Intern

Lisa Miller
Go MindShift
Home School Educator

Peg Sullivan
Library Resource Group
Principal

Joe Tankersley
Unique Visions, Inc.
Principal Consultant & Futurist

Amy Yurko
Brain Spaces
Architect

ACKNOWLEDGMENTS

As a writer I prefer to stand on a distant hill so that I can see the whole forest. I enjoy connecting the dots in order to find the big ideas. This project, however, took me off the hill and deep into the woods, both intellectually and emotionally. That's why I feel very fortunate that our K–12 cohort of more than 70 educators, students, experts, parents, and leaders accompanied me into those dark woods.

Richard Narramore, Wiley's senior editor, channeled our diverse energies and perspectives into the focus required to produce a coherent book. He also saw the need for a manifesto and map for those ready to launch their own local learning revolution.

Our K–12 MindShift began with Bill Latham, John Crawford, and Brian Cahill. I thank Bill and Brian for their willingness to coauthor this book. We could not have attracted the caliber of educators and thought leaders without their conviction and reputations.

I thank Dan Boggio for his visionary leadership. Dan's deep understanding of the battle helped us craft our questions and stories for others in, or just arriving to, the frontlines.

Chris Petrick, Ricky Kassanoff, Greg Moore, and Mark Hubbard deserve and will always have my deep gratitude. I appreciate the way these manufacturers supported our process and did so without ever—not once—asking to take the stage in order to promote their products or business.

Shannon Buerk, Jack Hess, Page Dettmann, Lynn Frickey, and Pete Dugas provided anchors that grounded us in the process of change, community engagement, and representing the kids most at risk. I thank each of them.

Our superintendents certainly modeled the role of change leadership. We are all indebted to Stan Rounds, David Vroonland, and Jeff Turner. David, I am forever grateful for "the collaborative hum."

Our subject experts not only brought depth to our conversations but also confronted us when we wanted to move on. So I thank Eric Hamilton, Amy Yurko, Dan Beerens, Jaime Casap, Dennis Johnston, Ellen Wood, Katie King, Peter Bishop, and Kurt Andre for standing firm for what they know and we needed to know.

I thank other key summit participants for their fine work—Candis Parker, Arol Wolford, Tom Wimmer, Cindy Weinschreider, Chelsea Poulin, Alicia Fischer, Eric Batten, Joe Tankersley, Jordon Lockhart, Patrick Horne, and David Kinley.

We appreciate all of the teachers, principals, and administrators who helped us in so many ways: Joe Hollenbach, Nathan Siebenga, Michelle Kinder, LeAnne Kelley, Neil May, Linda Anderson, Martha Phillips, Allison Vinson, Suzanne Stell, Amy Kelton, Donyall Dickey, Angela Smith, Emily Massey, Paul Brown, and others whom I fear I've forgotten.

You will read about many others who directly contributed to our journey, including Tony Wagner, Joel Barker, Barbara Barnes, Michael Horn, Ken Robinson, Mike Feinberg, Larry Rosenstock, and Lou Cozolino. These leaders all gave us more than was necessary or expected; I am profoundly grateful for their help.

Michael Lagocki and Ed Chinn were instrumental partners in this project. Michael was the lead designer and facilitator for our summit event. He also captured our sessions as a live scribe and produced our comic. After Ed edited my previous book, I chose to include him in all of our summits. Doing so greatly helped the process.

I also thank my wife, Lisa; she participated in the summits as a mom, educator, and partner. She was the first one to read the draft of a chapter. If she said, "That's nice," I knew I had to start over. If she said, "Wow . . ." I knew I had something. And, of course, I could not done this without a partner who made room for me to disappear for several writing retreats and to be somewhere else, even when I was home.

I also thank my children. I appreciate Nathan for traveling with me and taking part in the summits; he added a strong millennial voice to our deliberations.

And, I thank my son Tyler who let me interrogate his high school friends. I also thank Michelle for adding compelling and essential insight about her experience with the Machine. Sadly, most of that had been invisible to me.

I thank everyone I met while traveling. If I mentioned our K–12 project, everyone had a story about his or her encounter with the Education Machine as student or teacher or parent. It was a universal icebreaker. *Everyone* has a story about a school or a teacher.

I even thank everyone who shared their (sometimes loud) opinions about how to "fix" our schools. I'm glad we had that little talk.

Finally, I have learned that we all reap what we sow. If we invest in our kids, our nation will have a hope-filled future.

INDEX